The Magician
of Sunset Boulevard

The Improbable Life of
Paul Kohner, Hollywood Agent

by Frederick Kohner

By the same author:

Kiki of Montparnasse

Cher Papa

Gidget

English Language Copyright © 1977 by Frederick Kohner

First English language edition by Morgan Press, Palos Verdes, Ca., USA

ISBN 0-89430-004-0
Library of Congress Catalog Number: 78-175270

Copyright © 1974 by Droemersche Verlagsanstalt Th.Knaur Nachf., Munich/Zurich
First published in German by Droemer Knaur

Morgan Press
Palos Verdes, CA, USA

Manufactured in the United States of America

For Walter and Hanna
and in loving memory of
the Kino-Kohner

"Who cares about the moods or problems of a stranger, however glamorous he is? But when a brother speaks, all he says is vital. His troubles, confusions and adventures are our own. It is not a blood tie that makes him important and meaningful to us; it is the fact that we know him well."

— Ben Hecht
(*A Child of the Century*)

Contents

Introduction

By Charles Champlin

Paul Kohner is a tall and courtly gentleman who would be perfectly cast as the wise and steadying prime minister of a whimsical monarchy currently being ruled by impetuous children.

His Old World dignity and charm seem as distant from the denim flash of present Hollywood as Bohemia is from the LaBrea Tar Pits, or as the fictional movie agent, cigar-chewing and profane, is from his own reality.

He has been eye-witness to and participant in more than half of the total history of the movies in America—longer than some of his present clients and customers have lived—and he continues to be a fierce and enthusiastic battler in the Hollywood wars.

Out of a unique life story, as chronicled in this understandibly knowledgeable and affectionate biography by his brother Frederick, Paul Kohner has become a unique figure in the motion picture industry. He is the most profoundly and effectively international of talent agents in a time when the making of movies is more truly international than it has ever been. Not the least of his credits is that he has significantly widened the audience in the United States for the matchless talents of Ingmar Bergman, an achievement for which we all have reason to be grateful.

His offices on Sunset Boulevard are a splendid cosmopolitan chaos, and his representation of many of the most distinguished European film artists is at least reasonably well known. What I had not known of until I read about them in this book were his unheralded, unstinting and often ingenious assistances to dozens of actors, actresses and other film people forced to flee Europe immediately before and during World War II. The

Kohners treat it lightly and modestly enough, but you sense there are the makings of another whole book lurking just below the anecdotes.

Paul Kohner's story is interesting and indeed fascinating. For me it has a double interest and importance as a further record of the extraordinary evolution of Hollywood, from the feisty and formative Twenties to the golden and triumphant days of the major studios in the Thirties and early Forties, into the uncertainties and readjustments of the Fifties and Sixties and Seventies, when the arrival of television changed forever the nature of the industry, and of the product. The Kohner career remarkably reflects a time of continuing change.

But what times. This book reminds us that even on the accelerating and telescoping time-scale of our world, the movies are still relatively young. For anyone who follows and cares about the movies it is beguiling to think of Paul Kohner as having dealt, let's say, with both "Uncle" Carl Laemmle, the founder of Universal, and Dino di Laurentiis, with both Irving Thalberg and Maria Schneider. It boggles the mind ever so slightly to read of the days when Paul and a young friend named William Wyler, both fresh off the boat, were both dreaming up publicity ideas for Universal in New York and angling to get where the real action was, out west in Hollywood.

They both made it, of course, and unforgettably, Wyler to become one of the world's most honored filmmakers. Kohner's own early adventures as a producer yield a vivid portrait of Hollywood in the making and on the make, a boom town full of people who were sometimes imaginative and talented and sometimes only ruthlessly ambitious. It was then, as it still is, a place that could be unbelievably rewarding and unthinkably cruel, a town that lived by making dreams but could shatter tham as well, creating and destroying hopes and careers by what seem the most fickle of chances.

Life in the cinema has in fact always had a way of producing cinematic lives. One of the most affecting passages in the book is as Paul remembers driving back from a holiday in the mountains to begin producing the project of his dreams, made possibly by the endorsement of Irving Thalberg. Then on the car radio, a news flash on the swift and unexpected death of Thalberg, and the death (it seemed certain and proved to be) of the dream, too. It is a moment worthy of a movie.

History can always be seen as a series of accidents, and when we are lucky, our accidents are lucky. It is fortunate, for example, that the movies were born without sound, because silence forced them to develop a visual language. (As it is, Alfred Hitchcock was speaking sarcastically not long ago about the photographs of people *talking* that the *motion* pictures have become.) But silence also let the movies be international from the beginning. The movies and the men who made them crossed back and forth over the boundaries of the world with nearly the ease and fluency of men who make music, because film like music was a universal language. Hollywood was an international settlement early.

And so some happy accidents wove together. Kohner's father, quickly alert to the possibilities of the new medium, publishes a pioneer film trade paper in what is now Czechoslovakia. Carl Laemmle, a German emigre who has found fame and fortune in the movies in America, comes home on a triumphal visit. The youthful Paul Kohner, flourishing a newly printed business card, interviews him cleverly for the family paper, wins his admiration and the promise of a job in New York. And so commences the trek that peaks magically on the Sunset Strip. It is a wonderful story, which is being lived as well as remembered.

It is as if a whole life had been designed as preparation for the particular challenge and opportunity of the Hollywood Seventies. The decline of the major studios and a shifting of the nature of executive expertise at the majors (from picture-making to deal-making) have given the talent agents and agencies a kind of creative influence and power they have never had before. It is a power sometimes executed balefully, in the least imaginative of package deals, but it is a power that can be used felicitously as well by those who, like Paul Kohner, are able to respond to the movies in both of their guises, as art and commerce, reconciling them optimistically into the single art of the possible.

Whether Paul is a magician I leave to the assessment of his clients. But that his love of art, and the art of the movies most especially, is deep and abiding I know beyond doubt. His love of the movies is what makes him so able and imaginative an agent, and so successful at finding American distribution for some uncommonly fine European films. He is a master at proposing the unlikely but then inevitable casting, the matching-up of director and story that had occurred to no one else, the potential of the property that had been overlooked.

It is, at that, a kind of magic.

Book I:
The Apprentice

1

Deal

O N A BLUE, drafty day in midwinter a few years ago, my brother Paul—a Hollywood agent—stepped out of an elevator on the fifteenth floor of a steel-and-glass skyscraper in Century City. He walked down the empty and impersonal corridor, a portly but dapper man with a still-youthful stride to his sixty-some years.

He looked at his watch. Eleven. He had left his Bel Air home early to enjoy a leisurely shave and trim at Harry Drucker's hairstyling salon in Beverly Hills. But it didn't take as long as he had figured. He was right on time, which made him feel a bit nervous. He wasn't known for punctuality.

Before entering the offices of ABC Pictures, he glanced at his reflection in the full-length hallway mirror. He was wearing a soft, grey, well-tailored Tartaglia suit, a Sulka shirt, a John Weitz tie. Yes, there was a polished, prosperous and positive air about him. He approved of what he saw, and proceeded inside.

The receptionist smiled up at him. "Go right in, Mr. Kohner. They're waiting."

He smiled back at her—she was a pretty girl—and then briskly entered the office of Marty Baum, the head of the motion-picture division of the American Broadcasting Company.

In the big office, the size of a squash court, there were no hints of show business. Just an abundance of black ashtrays. And a widescreen view of the city of Los Angeles.

Paul shook hands with Baum, who had once been an agent too. Baum in turn introduced Paul Kohner to the network's top brass. After the usual exchange of amenities, Baum came right to the point.

"We've mulled over the Bergman proposal, Paul—and are prepared to go ahead."

"I'm very pleased to hear it," Paul said.

"But first we want to see the script he plans to film." When Baum looked at Paul now, he seemed uneasy—as if he had expected to see the story tucked under the agent's arm.

"There is no script," Paul said.

"I don't quite understand—" Baum looked almost embarrassed. "I told the boys—"

Paul smiled engagingly but stood his ground. "Sorry, Marty." He shrugged.

"But there must be a story," Leonard Goldenson asserted. He was smooth, alert. The president of the entire ABC operation.

"There is one, of course. However, it's not on paper."

The men exchanged glances. This was most unusual.

"Does Bergman expect us to hand over a check for one million just on good faith?"

"Naturally not. He has the plot all worked out. And he'll be glad to tell you the story."

"When can he come here?"

"I'm afraid he can't. He doesn't like to fly. But he's going to be in London next month, directing a play. He told me he could meet you gentlemen there. In fact, he insists on meeting *all* of you."

Normally, negotiations would end right at this point. But this was hardly a normal situation.

Ingmar Bergman, an indisputable genius of the modern cinema, had written, directed and produced more than thirty films in the Swedish language. All had been released in America with English subtitles. Masterpieces like *Wild Strawberries, The Silence, Persona, The Seventh Seal, Shame*. Each a unique work of art dealing with the ultimate questions of life and death; each a "moneymaker" too, though modestly so. Now for the first time Bergman had consented to make a film in the English language. And ABC was the first company Paul had approached with the project.

He waited calmly, confidently. He felt certain he had ABC in the bag. *Almost* certain. You never knew until the contract got signed.

"We'll have to think this over," Goldenson said carefully and looked at Baum.

"Definitely, Lenny," Baum said. "We'll be in touch with you, Paul."

Paul got up.

"And tell Mr. Bergman he'll hear from us," Baum added.

"It will have to be soon. You know I gave you first call."

"Very soon," Goldenson said—rather quickly.

"He's quite excited about doing this film," Paul said, now in motion. "I assured him he'd be happy to be associated with ABC."

"And we'll be happy if he would make a picture for us," Goldenson said. "Provided the story—"

"Of course I understand," Paul said. "And Mr. Bergman understands.

That's why he wanted to meet all of you. So there would be a mutual accord of intentions." Paul was walking toward the door.

"How is Bergman's English?" Goldenson asked.

"Excellent."

"Can he write scripts in English?"

"This one he will."

"Then no translation. Good."

In the deserted corridor Paul stopped again at the mirror. He grinned like a man who has just had a gusher erupt in his backyard. Probably by the time he got to his office he would have the confirmation from ABC.

He drove northward through Beverly Hills to his building on Sunset Boulevard, just at the western edge of "The Strip."

His perennial secretary, Miss Irene Heymann, was waiting expectantly with a telephone message sheet two pages long. And Paul's business day had scarcely begun.

"Okay," Paul said. "Let's start with the calls."

At this moment one of the four desk phones began ringing. Miss Heymann lifted the receiver. "I don't think he's come in yet," she said routinely. "Let me see—" She held her hand over the mouthpiece and told her boss that Marty Baum was on the other end of the line.

Paul smiled broadly and nodded.

"He just walked in," Miss Heymann said. "Hold on, Mr. Baum."

Paul waited a few seconds, savoring the interval. Then he took up the receiver. "Hello, Marty."

Baum told him what he had expected to hear. The ABC executives would go to London and listen to Bergman tell his story.

"Absolutely delighted, Marty. I'll call Bergman right away."

Ingmar Bergman was one of Paul's top clients. He was also his friend. Thus he felt doubly happy over the success.

Yet Paul's deal wasn't as easy to do as it sounds. Every master magician's act has taken years of training, preparation and performances. Before this he had invested years of pursuing Bergman, whose work he ardently admired, as a prospective client. Until now the Swedish filmmaker had never needed or used an agent in America to arrange financing for his productions.

Furthermore, behind this deal were five decades of Paul's own lifework connected with the movie industry—which gave him the skills, contacts, self-confidence and reputation essential in handling such high-level matters. Not only did he possess superb finesse in acquiring talented creative people as clients and then knowing ways to keep them contented, but also he was generally liked, respected and trusted by the people in power positions who paid for the talent that made the movies.

This contract for Bergman was not as big as some Paul negotiated before or afterwards. But he had succeeded at long last in putting Bergman together with an American production company.

In addition there would be the handsome commission for himself and his agency.

And ten percent of a million—at any time—was tantamount to having struck gold.

A Man Out There in the Blue

PAUL STRUCK GOLD almost from the moment he hung out his shingle on Sunset Boulevard. Sometimes it came in the form of small but solid nuggets, at other times in whole veins. And now and then he practiced the art of alchemy, transforming some baser metal into a precious, glittering, coveted substance.

His sign still hangs there. Paul Kohner isn't the only independent talent agent around Hollywood who runs a profitable business. But I haven't come across another one yet who has kept an agency going for so long without ever declaring bankruptcy. By now, of course, a number of his peers have earned perpetual resting places in the town's better cemeteries, and only the people in the "trade" are occasionally reminded of their past existence—via a little black-bordered anniversary notice in *Variety.* Then there are those who have retired in comfort to Palm Springs, or can still be found sitting on park benches or playing in pool rooms or watching the tickertape at stock brokerages.

Being busy keeps Paul alive and well and makes for a thriving business. If you walked into 9169 Sunset Boulevard, you'd probably find him—unless he happened to be abroad—frantically juggling at least several telephone receivers. The telephone is his major lifeline to the rest of the world. Through it he transacts much of his important daily work, as well as communicates easily with friends and family. To be sure, he may have business conferences over brunch or dinner, important meetings at movie studios, complicated consultations with clients and lawyers at their place or his. But by and large with the telephone's assistance Paul can handle almost any matter by talking through a wire. And that means making or taking anywhere from fifty to a hundred calls each day.

There's one more item that's absolutely essential to Paul's business.

Irene Heymann, his secretary. Operating in four languages and on four telephones, she looks like a many-tentacled superrobot in full action. But she's very much of a human being. She has been with Paul for years—not all of them easy. She is a lady of fierce loyalty—and fierce temper. Surrounded by piles of correspondence, manuscripts, contracts, photos and buzzer systems, she rarely leaves her swivel chair. Devoted to duty, sometimes she doesn't go home till midnight. How she manages to keep track of all the details and fine nuances of Paul's business I cannot fathom. But I do know that she is quite indispensable. Hers may be the most remarkable talent around the agency. Yet it's not for sale.

Once in a while I encounter someone who doesn't know what a talent agent is and does. This lack of contact or information surprises me. But then I've spent much of my life around my brother Paul, at the sidelines of his enterprise. And as a writer I've always had to have an agent. Of course I'm aware that the town of Hollywood—more a state of mind than an actual place—might never have been created without agents of one kind or another. And wouldn't exist nowadays at all without them, for almost every bit of business with films starts and gets finalized through agents' contacts and contracts.

There was the time I met a cute German girl waiting for Paul at his office. He had noticed her at a party and given her his card. "I'm an agent, " he told her. "Come and see me."

"What kind of agent is he?" she asked me now with wide-eyed innocence.

This lovely Lorelei, was new to Hollywood and had never read a fan magazine or a gossip columnist. So perhaps her naïveté was understandable. Luckily for her, she had come to a safe place.

Since my brother hadn't arrived yet, I took the time to enlighten her. Paul was a Hollywood agent, I told her. A middleman whenever and wherever there is buying and selling of creative abilities in filmmaking. A salesman—with talent as the commodity. Artists looking for employment in the motion picture industry come to him. Actors, actresses, directors, writers, composers. Or he seeks them. And a contract is signed by them both, which obligates the agent to provide suitable employment opportunities within a specified period of time—usually three months—or else the client is free to terminate his services, on written notification, and go elsewhere. The client, in turn, is legally bound to share ten percent of his motion picture earnings with his agent. For his agent makes the rounds of the studios, peruses the trade papers and generally keeps his ear to the ground in scouting out prospective jobs for his clientele. He usually works hard enough for his ten-percent share.

The young woman's face brightened as I explained Paul's role. Ah yes, she was beginning to understand. He is something like an impresario.

Correct, I said. Only in Hollywood he is just called an agent. And agents here are as common as palm trees. Everybody who is anybody in show business or aspires to be somebody or claims to be someone has an agent. Not only actors, directors, writers—but even trained birds or chimpanzees. To be in Hollywood without an agent is being nowhere.

"How many agents are there in Hollywood?" she asked.

"A few hundred. Huge corporations that have offices all over the world keep a large staff here. Smaller outfits may have up to thirty subagents. And then there are the really small ones. Exclusive ones."

"Like your brother's?"

"Like my brother's."

"Are there many agencies like his?"

"There were once. But most of the small ones got swallowed up by the big ones. It's like every other business. Big fish eat little fish. Supermarkets push out neighborhood grocers. Goliath kills David."

"Then your brother must be something special to have survived. How did he do it?"

"It would take a book to tell."

And just then Paul came through the door, spotted the girl, smiled, waved at me and ushered her into his private office. First things first.

It was a summer day. The sun streamed through the glass doors facing the street. I sat for a while in the foyer, where it was pleasantly quiet and air-conditioned, and thought about the girl's last question and about my response. If I ever wrote a book about Paul and his career as an agent, how would I really answer it? Just how *had* he done it? And not only survived, but prospered?

Certainly a good deal of luck was involved in his survival, but that still wouldn't explain it. I thought of Paul's kaleidoscopic personality, which combines charismatic charm and arrogance, sensitivity and toughness, generosity and shrewdness, ease and tension, the natural and the posed.

And I thought too of the old Spanish saying: "With the mighty and the rich—always a little patience." He surely had adhered to it in his dealings with powerful moguls and the well-endowed but mercurial artist-clients. How else could he have made his way through the Hollywood jungle? How otherwise could he embrace people who only yesterday had betrayed him?

("In this business," he once told me, "you cannot be an elephant. You must forget. When clients vilify you and leave you, just remember they may be back tomorrow. So wish them luck. Remaining angry for long is like harboring a disease. Success and failure both must be like meals—consumed and then forgotten.")

I got up and went outside. The air was hot and full of fumes. Cars raced up and down the boulevard. Paul's office seemed like an oasis or retreat miraculously in the midst of big-city traffic and noise. No wonder he remained there. And no wonder clients liked to come there too, experiencing a special and personable atmosphere impossible to find in the nearby cold, anonymous high-rise buildings where most of the other agencies had their premises.

I looked up now at the handsome two-storey building, then at the sign with its black letters proclaiming PAUL KOHNER, INC. This had been my brother's business base, his home away from home, since the mid-Thirties. Here, full of enthusiasm for his new métier, he had made his start as an agent. Here he prospered in the lush Forties, fought in the barren Fifties, survived the murderous Sixties. And here he now marches forward through the mixed-up Seventies—cassettes and all. Still wheeling and dealing, still chockful of plans, schemes and projects, his ear still glued to the telephone with wires whirring all over the globe, and still riding at the top of the ferris wheel. Like Arthur Miller's salesman Willy Loman, he's the man way out there in the blue, with a shine and a smile—and people all over are still smiling back at him.

But supposing I did try to tell the story of Paul's life. Perhaps I could only offer fragments in the form of a synopsis of his seven busy decades of living and working. And wouldn't it often be misleading? For in career biographies the spotlight usually falls on the dramatic high points, the dismal low points or the entertaining anecdotes and interesting peripheral characters. One might tend to neglect the real people affecting the subject's thoughts and emotions and actions. And how to select what to say without overloading the tale with details and dates? It seemed to me that I might be able to construct a simple and fairly faithful account of my brother's career. And yet I knew, given the wealth of material, I or somebody else could write another accurate life history without repeating a single episode.

Anyway, I told myself, how could I even start out to tell about Paul? And where would I begin?

Then I suddenly recalled an evening not long before, when we were walking down Stone Canyon Road in Bel Air. It was one of our rare moments alone together—reflecting about the past, meditating about the future. Paul's seventieth birthday loomed ahead, and like any other man approaching old age he was obviously searching for the secrets, the meanings, of his long life.

"Tell me," I asked. "Was it worthwhile?"

He stopped, startled. "What do you mean?"

"When you look back, do you think it was okay? Did you get what you wanted out of it all?"

The expression on his face seemed to say: Don't you know? After all, we had been through a lifetime together.

But I really didn't know. Few people really knew Paul intimately. Of our many years of brotherhood, lived mostly in close proximity, I could recall hundreds of things he did—but little of what he actually felt. For he seldom told me.

Now he did.

"Of course," he said. "Of course it was worthwhile. After all, I did what I knew how to do best. I did what Papa did best. I sold."

Big Brother

HE DID, HOWEVER, more than selling. He promoted. Created. Just as other men create industries or works of art, all his life he created opportunities for himself, his family, his friends.

One incident is sharply etched in my mind, for it laid the groundwork of our relationship. How baffling is the human brain in its ability to retain an event of seemingly no significance while discarding others it has simply chosen to forget!

I was about five then, my brother eight. Our parents took us to a German sea resort. Swinemünde. Not everyone could take his family to such a faraway, exotic place. Only a man of substance might—like our father, who operated a small factory in the old spa of Teplitz-Schoenau in Bohemia. The "Publicity Kohner" he was called then. In his factory he had a printing plant, produced publicity items, gadgets, calendars, novelties. Later on he would open the first movie house in our town and publish the first film trade paper in Czechoslovakia.

To Swinemünde on the eastern seaboard of Germany we went one beautiful summer morning. Living in a landlocked country, we children had never before seen the sea. First there had been the crossing of the border, the long train ride through a foreign landscape at night. Then, upon opening one's eyes, the first sight of the sea. Blue water. Bright light. And, right after arrival, rushing to the white sand. Coral and shells along the beach. Enormous shells, pressed against our ears, reproducing the churning of the waves. All around us the swirl of German boys and girls. Children and their nannies. White, starched uniforms. Our father in a striped black and white bathing suit. Our mother with a flower-garden hat, a dainty red umbrella.

Most of the day we played around the cabana while other children were building sand fortresses. And shooting at us—foreigners from Bohemia. As was de rigueur, our mother sat fully dressed in the cabana, pale and uncomfortable. Not a speck of flesh revealed to the summer sun.

One afternoon a white German battleship appeared offshore. The *S.S. Bismarck*. Shouts: "The Kaiser! THE KAISER!" Suddenly hundreds of binoculars trained at the ship. I was handed a pair. I saw him, The Kaiser, in white uniform, looking martial.

Then on Sunday afternoon a children's festival arranged by the hotel. Fun and games. A husky German, blond, tanned, explaining the contests.

Running with an egg on a soup spoon and reaching the finish line without dropping it. A sausage dangling from a rod; the rod is raised, lowered; one had to snap like a dog to get one's teeth into the sausage. Blindfolded eyes: pinning the tail on the donkey.

My brother won every single contest. Gold and silver medals sprouted on his sailor's jacket. Full of pride and envy, I thought: Why not me? Just *one* little medal.

My brother's eyes were fixed on me.

Now the sack hopping. A brown, rough-woven potato sack open at one end. You had to step into the sack, fasten it around the waist. Then at a given signal, run. The first to cross the line got the prize. A golden star.

Paul helped me tie the strings around my waist. Suddenly he was close to my ear, whispering: "I'm going to cut the bottom of the sack. Fake a couple of tumbles. You can win your own star." He dropped down on his knees to adjust the hem-line of the sack. And astoundingly, out of his pocket and into his hand appeared a small pair of scissors. No one noticed when he cut through the sack.

The starting signal. I ran. Tumbled. Got up and ran—ran and tumbled—ran some more. I was the first to finish.

The face of my brother. Jubilant. We wandered off. "I wanted you to win too," he said.

There is still a photo—sepia, slightly faded—recording that day. My big brother Paul on a sailboat, his chest decorated with paper stars. Me, leaning awkwardly against him, a diffident smile, the lovely golden star gleaming on my sailor's jacket.

Teplitz

FROM THEN ON, whenever I got myself into a jam or wanted something badly, there was my big brother at my side always producing—figuratively—another pair of scissors to help me out.

"Paul is a magician," our father said. He conjured up bread for us out of nowhere during the starving days of World War I. With some swift legerdemain he got me into the *kino* (as the movie house was called)—the kino we were forbidden to enter. And later Paul even juggled his own coming to America.

We were born in an enchanted place, right in the heart of Europe. Still enchanting today, even after the ravages of war and the destructive incursion perpetrated by the new Marxists. The old spa of Teplitz lies at the foot of the undulating ore mountains known as the Sudeten. The springs were discovered by the Romans on their march northwards, and Caesar's generals reputedly traveled all the way from Rome to immerse themselves in the hot, sulphurous waters: a healing agent for rheumatic diseases. During a summer's rest in Teplitz Richard Wagner composed his *Tannhauser.* Johann Wolfgang von Goethe took up residence there year after year and praised the spa's rejuvenating powers. And only a short distance from our house stood the baroque villa where Beethoven wrote part of his Eighth Symphony. Once Goethe and Beethoven met in the spa, it was said, and took an instant and hearty dislike to each other.

Toward the end of the nineteenth century a major ecological tragedy took place in Teplitz. The healing springs caved in, and the muddied water had to be pumped to the surface. For a while the town fathers tried to hush up the calamity, but when the truth seeped out, the crowned heads and celebrities who had flocked to Teplitz rerouted their carriages to the nearby spas of Karlsbad and Marienbad. But even in its declining days, Teplitz served as an inspiration of sorts. Ibsen used the incident of the cave-in and the frightened *buergers* for his play *An Enemy of the People.*

Growing up in such a center of "Kultur" affected my brother long before he crossed the Atlantic. We had fine schools, private instruction in French and English, music lessons and the like. The Kohners were a well-to-do bourgeois family, and the only difference perceptible between us and most of our neighbors was that they attended churches whereas we went to the local synagogue. At the time, being Jewish was rarely considered strange or undesirable.

Our town of thirty thousand inhabitants had not only a first-class legitimate theatre, an opera house and a symphony orchestra of high standing, but also a library which compared favorably with that of Prague's world-famous King Charles University.

The movie house, however, was not exactly a center of culture—except to us children.

It was a dilapidated structure in an arcade, frequented by the kind of riffraff that patronized traveling carnivals. If an average citizen slunk into this establishment, he did so with stealth and under the cover of night.

We children were strictly banned from the *kino*—even though, or because, our father owned it. But Paul, ever the prestigitator, smuggled me through a dark corridor and past red velvet curtains, straight into paradise.

My first motion picture is still vividly with me—a bloody contest between the white man and the cunning redskin. Identification was immediate. We had devoured all seventy volumes of a writer called Karl May, who lived in the nearby town of Radebeul and whose lifework consisted of glorifying a Wild West he had never seen.

What bliss on those sweet afternoons in our kino. After all the thousands upon thousands of reels of film we have watched since then, we can never rid ourselves of the spell that the heroes of our youth cast over us: Max Linder, Harry Piel, Waldemar Psylander, Luciano Albertino— and Tom Mix.

And ah!—those German sex films, camouflaged as "cultural enlightenment." How can one ever forget the prostitute beckoning a customer to enter a redlight-district house with just a slight twitch of her eyebrows? What happened inside the house was never shown. But the magic of imagination, the thrill of novelty, the drama of subtlety entranced us and stays with us still. My brother and I agree that all the hard-core pornography slobbering over the screen these days cannot match the sight of Lya de Putti's white leg wriggling its way tantalizingly through the slit of a black curtain.

But the day came when we were caught in our hiding place by the "Kino-Kohner"—as our father was dubbed now. He threw us out boldly and, at home, broke a cane on our youthful behinds.

We had lost paradise.

Laemmle from Laupheim

I SUPPOSE IT seems too simple to survey the road of a man's life and say with certainty: That's when it happened.

But with regard to my older brother, there is no doubt in my mind. Paul's amazing career began on August 15, 1921. He was eighteen years old.

World War I had come to an end. Bohemia was now part of the Republic of Czechoslovakia. We had to learn the Czech language. For us nothing else had changed. Again, as in the old monarchy, we had *Kipferln* for breakfast.

It was early in the morning. We sat around the breakfast table. My father had opened the new copy of the film trade paper *Filmschau*. He read the paper holding it with one hand, using the other to dunk his *Kipferl* into the coffee cup. His absorbing interest in the paper was understandable: he was the publisher. An enterprising man, he had branched out into the publishing field. He also ran the newly built and now respectable movie house of our hometown.

Slowly the "Kino-Kohner" turned to his oldest son. "Ever heard of a man called Laemmle?"

Paul shook his head.

"It says here he is taking the cure in Karlsbad. He is the president of Universal Pictures."

"Oh, sure. Universal. They're producing the films with Mary Pickford," Paul said.

"Maybe I should get an interview with the man," our father said, inspecting his watch. Then he announced: "I am taking the ten o'clock to Karlsbad."

The spa of Karlsbad was a three-hour train ride from Teplitz, and from our house to the train station was a ten-minute walk.

"It's a quarter to ten, Julius," my mother permitted herself to caution him.

"Get me a fresh shirt," he said, silencing my mother, who was already rushing off to get the shirt.

Local trains were usually late, and our father always counted on this. He would arrive at the station at the very last minute and jump up the steps of an already moving car.

He was not lucky that morning. Half an hour after he left, he came back—limping. Trying to leap onto the train, he had slipped and hurt his ankle.

"Why don't you send me to Karlsbad, Papa?" Paul suggested.

Our father lit his favorite brand of cigar, a Trabucco, looked over the rim of his glasses and considered the proposal. "All right," he said. "Why not? Go ahead—and be sure to get a good story."

My brother promptly proceeded to the printing plant to have a card made up which read: PAUL KOHNER, Associate Editor of the *Filmschau*. Then he donned his best suit and took the afternoon train to Karlsbad.

I would have loved to go along. Teplitz was a poor relation to the splendid Karlsbad. That town was fairyland itself—a sight to dazzle the most blasé and worldly. Day and night, life seemed to bubble forth like the gushing geyser in the glass arcade where thousands of guests, from all over the world, walked up and down, cups in hand, sipping the magical waters while an orchestra played a Strauss waltz. To balance the rigors of the "cure," visitors to the spa were offered diversions of the most pleasurable kinds—like concerts, balls, nightclubs, horse races and lovely young ladies devoted to the world's oldest profession.

At the end of Karlsbad's most frequented promenades, flanked by old chestnut trees and elegant stores, stood the Grand Hotel Pupp. Its guests were maharajahs, oil tycoons and just ordinary millionaires. At the Pupp Laemmle of the Movies had taken up residence.

On the morning after his arrival, Paul presented himself at the hotel desk and sent his calling card to the film man's suite. Then he paced the lobby, rehearsing an imaginary dialogue in his stilted school English.

An imposing-looking man made his appearance. It was Laemmle's secretary, Harry Zehner. Amused yet condescending, he addressed this youthful "Associate Editor."

"You wished to see Mr. Laemmle?"

"That is right."

"For what purpose?"

"An interview for our paper."

"I'm sorry to disappoint you," Zehner said, "but Mr. Laemmle has come to Karlsbad to take the cure and to rest and will not give any interviews."

Then, giving a brilliant smile that displayed his set of perfect teeth, he handed back the Associate Editor's card—and left him standing alone in the middle of the plush Persian carpet.

It was a critical moment in Paul's life. His mission had failed. He would have to return home without the interview—humiliated. How could he face our father? He felt like crying.

But instead he went over to the hotel desk and wrote on the back of the rejected calling card: "If I have taken three hours to come here, surely you can spare three minutes to see me."

And back went the card to Laemmle.

A short while later the desk phone rang. Paul was asked to come up.

Carl Laemmle was a short, pudgy, kind-looking man. Only the sharp, cautious eyes behind thick glasses explained his powerful position.

"Aren't you a bit young for an editor?" he asked.

"Joseph Pulitzer was a reporter at sixteen," Paul replied.

"Really?" Laemmle said, impressed. "Tell me something about your paper."

Paul did. He told him how his father had founded the first film trade paper in Czechoslovakia right after the war. Told him about the circulation. Told him that the readers would be keenly interested in an interview with one of the world's great film producers.

That Carl Laemmle liked. "All right, young man, I'm at your disposal."

They both settled down to a long talk. Paul had his questions well prepared. They came in rapid succession—in German. Laemmle, he discovered, had been born in Laupheim, a small hamlet in Wuerttemberg, and he enjoyed talking in his native tongue.

Laemmle's answers were careful and economical. He seemed surprised that the youthful journalist took no notes.

"I'll keep it all in my head," Paul announced loftily—without giving the slightest indication that he had never before conducted an interview.

In a while the roles changed. Laemmle began to ask the questions. He was interested in the new Czech democracy—as it related, of course, to the movies. How many movie houses were there in the country? Which films were the most popular? Who were the favorite American stars? Which Universal films had Paul seen?

Paul's answers may not have been exact. But offered with an air of assurance, they impressed Laemmle. When Zehner entered to remind him that it was time to go to the bathhouse, Laemmle asked Paul to accompany him.

While the diminutive film mogul and the son of the "Kino-Kohner" walked together along the "Old Meadow"—as the big promenade was called—Laemmle probably noticed that many a girl's head turned as they passed.

"I want you to meet my children," he said. "Junior and my daughter Rosabelle. She's about your age."

"I would be delighted," Paul said.

Rosabelle might also be delighted, Laemmle must have thought, looking up with a fatherly twinkle at the young man who towered above him.

In his young manhood Paul had unusual allure. There is no better word for it. He was personable, handsome. His countenance that of a poet, his manner courtly. The frontispiece prince in a fairytale book, he could set a whole galaxy of pretty girls in a flutter by merely entering a room. And he was extravagantly attentive: he sent long-stemmed roses not only to his girl friends but also to their mothers, when invited to their houses. Extravagance remained his trademark, for all his life he has showered favors on the worthy and unworthy alike.

Paul's undeniable charisma also attracted the little man from Laupheim—and something else too. Laemmle of the Movies had two passions in life: film and pinochle.

Film was also Paul's favorite interest.

Pinochle? He would soon find out about that.

An Offer

CARL LAEMMLE HAD an aversion to solitude. Providing a daily quota of interesting guests during his stay at Karlsbad taxed the ingenuity of his entourage. To be sure, his far-flung family converged from all parts of Germany and Switzerland. The Laemmle clan eagerly accepted "Uncle Carl's" invitation to join him when he was in Karlsbad. Brothers, aunts, cousins attended his levee. They crowded around the breakfast, lunch and dinner table, entertaining their wealthy uncle with tales of his native Laupheim—and tales of their own situations. There was always a widowed aunt who had fallen on bad times. A genius nephew who wanted to start a career in America. A cousin twice removed who had written a movie script. The daughter of a deceased brother who was permitted to brew her special matzo ball soup in the Hotel Pupp's kitchen.

They were generally simple people, but some of them were quite shrewd too. The time, one must remember, was 1921. The Germans had lost the war. Laemmle's family had been in the midst of it. Some lived in the Alsace, which had been alternately occupied by the French and the Germans. Uncle Carl was one of the few family members who had emigrated to America before the century began, and there he had risen to unimaginable riches. He owned his own city, did he not, complete with mayor, fire station and police force?

By all standards Laemmle was a kind and generous man. But he was also keenly aware of the nepotistic aspirations of those surrounding him in Karlsbad—and everywhere else, for that matter. In Paul, that morning, he probably felt he had discovered a very knowledgeable young fellow who seemed to want nothing from him but an interview for a paper. Maybe he also was thinking of his daughter Rosabelle, who was on her first trip to the Continent.

They arrived at the bathhouse. Laemmle stepped into the huge tiled bathtub. Soaking his small frame in the curative waters, he encouraged Paul to talk. Later on, pummeled and kneaded by a masseur, he listened to the young reporter unpack a trove of valuable information about film distribution in the new republic, where Universal as yet had no office.

It was noon by then. Laemmle invited Paul to join the family for lunch. Under the lovely foliage of the chestnut trees of the "Kaisergarten," Paul was introduced to the waiting clan as the young editor of an important trade paper. As an outsider, he was met by intense scrutiny. Carl Laemmle Junior—a thin, bright, good-looking boy of thirteen, the *enfant gâté* of his father—eyed Paul cautiously. Rosabelle Laemmle, an engaging teenager, turned pink.

Luncheon over, the group proceeded on its way back to the Hotel Pupp—a walk of about half an hour. Junior and Rosabelle linked arms with their widowed father, diverting his attention from this newcomer. By the time they reached the hotel entrance, Paul got the distinct feeling that he had outstayed his welcome. Taking leave, he shook hands with Laemmle Senior and Junior, then bowed deep to kiss Rosabelle's hand. She blushed. Obviously nothing like Paul had ever happened to her in her sixteen years in America.

Well, Paul had his story now. After all, that was what he had come here for. Wistfully, he watched Laemmle disappear behind the revolving door. But then the film man materialized once again. He had made a 360-degree turn.

"Do you play pinochle?"

"Naturally," Paul said quickly.

"Come up then, come up!" Laemmle seemed elated. His eyes behind the thick lenses sparkled. "That is, if you still have time to spare—"

Carl Laemmle was a zealous gambler who must have squandered a stupendous fortune during his lifetime. It is known that he sat up once for forty-eight hours playing "Faro" against continuously changing dealers in the plush casino of Caliente, south of the California border. Like all gamblers, he didn't care what he was gambling for, how long, where or for what stakes: as long as he gambled—and won. His mild demeanor belied this one wild streak. Making bets, he forsook his normally penurious ways with dollars, pesos, marks, francs, Czechoslovakian crowns.

Now, making a valiant effort to pick up pinochle as he went along, Paul lost some fifty kronen. At that time and for a young man, this was no small loss. But don't think for a moment that the president of Universal Pictures didn't accept this tidy little profit. He did.

In the meantime Zehner appeared, reminding his boss of an appointment. So it was goodbye again—and this time, it seemed, for good.

But Carl Laemmle had something on his mind. "By the way, how old are you?" he asked Paul.

"Eighteen."

"Still going to school?"

"I am enrolling at the university next month."

"What do you plan to study?"

"Business management."

"There is no better place to learn about business than America. That's where I learned it—and not at a university." He cocked his head sideways and smiled craftily at Paul. "How about it?"

"How about what?"

"Coming to America. Would you like that?"

"I'd like it fine," Paul said at once.

Laemmle seemed pleased. "Okay then. Mr. Zehner will make the arrangements for you. We're leaving in a couple of weeks."

It was that simple to him.

"Mr. Laemmle—" Paul now stammered. "My father—I don't know—I have to ask him."

"Of course. You must ask your father. Over there. Use the phone."

Our father was soaking his sprained ankle in a tub of hot water with Epsom salts. Since our mother was out on errands, I answered the telephone.

"Let me talk to Papa," my brother said. His tone of voice told me that something important and unusual had happened.

I watched our father. He had been sulking all day and the day before, ever since he hurt his leg. Not a man to hide feelings, he let us know that he was miserable.

But as our father now listened to Paul, his face underwent a sudden and remarkable change. He began to beam. Though the look was fleeting, it still lives in my memory. Like many a man who has made his way in life without schooling or help, relying solely on some inner fortitude, our father had a good father's dream: that his eldest son would surpass him, reaching a height he himself was unable to attain. That dream now seemed within the realm of fulfillment.

"He wants you to come along with him? ... When—in two weeks already? ... Why, I think this is an excellent opportunity. ... Yes, I think you should accept. This is wonderful news. ... Tell Mr. Laemmle that I have no objections, and that as soon as I can step on a train I'll come to Karlsbad to meet him. I am happy—very happy."

He cradled the receiver. He lifted his sore foot out of the tub. His face was suffused with color. And then he started to laugh.

"Your brother Paul," he said to me, laughing crazily, "is going to America."

Beware of Indians

THE FAMILY TURNED out that evening at the station to greet the returning hero. I gazed at my brother in awe. Suddenly he seemed taller and stronger. And almost a stranger. He had apprenticed himself to this mighty sorcerer who had his own city in the West of America. Where all those glittering stars lived: Pickford and Talmadge, Swanson and Tom Mix, Hoot Gibson, Harold Lloyd, Charlie Chaplin. He would meet them all. It was stirring enough to give a boy of sixteen the goosepimples.

Paul had pulled his first rabbit out of a top hat.

It's hard for people nowadays to imagine what life was like in a small town in Czechoslovakia a half-century ago. People had traveled, of course. But not long distances. My own father was perhaps the most widely traveled man in the community: Berlin, Hamburg, Paris, Amsterdam, London—once even to Africa. (We had a photo of him dressed as a Bedouin, on a dark horse, outrageously romantic.) But America?

Yes, there was a man in our town who had been there, had even lived in San Francisco. Affectedly, he still spoke his German with an accent. He had even, it seemed, gone through Indian territory. He offered Paul a host of fascinating tales of fights with the redskins.

I lived vicariously through my brother's last days at home. The preparation for his trip was hectic, for so many things had to be provided: a new wardrobe, a ship's trunk, a passport. Farewell parties were given. In the late afternoon hours when Paul appeared on the town's promenade, he was immediately surrounded by his cronies and admirers. A story had appeared in the local paper: The son of the "Kino-Kohner" had received a flattering offer of a motion-picture career in America. The date of his departure was listed. He would travel on the S.S. *Berengaria* together with the film tycoon who had hired him.

It was a miraculous time. Even now, looking back on it—remembering how the world was then, knowing who we were and what we would become—it still seems a miraculous time.

A number of phone calls came from Mr. Zehner, who gave Paul instructions about the forthcoming trip to the New World. When to arrive in port, where to get his ticket and so on. For me it was exciting and awe-inspiring to listen to my brother's business conversations—and in English at that!

Then, just a day or so before Paul's departure, our father called him to the *Herrenzimmer.* (The literal translation of this is "gentlemen's room," but it certainly wasn't anything like that. It was really an equivalent to the French *salon.*) The Herrenzimmer was the one room in every bourgeois home that was used only on special occasions. The centerpiece in ours was a magnificent Steinway piano on which we all had suffered instruction. Close by stood the inevitable vitrine. Behind the glass windows of this monstrosity were displayed the family collection of art objects, heirlooms and curios.

I, who had barely left the side of Paul, was now told to accompany my younger brother Walter, aged eight, and our "Fräulein" on a walk to the park. I did nothing of the sort. I hid in the bathroom, and as soon as Paul followed my father into the Herrenzimmer, I went behind the door and glued my ear to it.

"My boy," I heard our father say, "all this has come so suddenly that we really haven't had a chance to sit down together and talk seriously. Now I would like you to tell me truthfully—and I mean truthfully—whether this is what you wish to do. Of course, I too would have been tempted as a young man had I been offered a trip to America. But I know that 'Baked pigeons will not fly into your mouth' over there. People in America must work hard. And you don't even know what this man Laemmle has in mind for you. Maybe they'll put you to work on something you don't like. You had plans. *We* had plans for you. You are giving up your studies. You are leaving your family, your friends—going into an uncertain future in an unknown land. Now, Paul—is that what you *really* want? Or did you just feel flattered by that offer? Do you have doubts? Second thoughts? If you do, tell me. There is still time to back out. Nothing here will change. Your mother and I—"

"I want to go," my brother said.

And then the almost jubilant voice of our father: "That's all I wanted to hear."

And so the die was cast. And that wasn't all. I myself felt cast adrift—losing my brother, my champion, my confidant, my "sack-opener."

The family said goodbye to Paul at the station. Our eighty-some-year-old maternal grandmother—stiff as buckram, dressed in black, with the inevitable eagle's nest perched on her formidable black hat—took my brother aside and pressed a small black leather prayer-book into his hands. "Don't forget to go to the synagogue every Friday night," she instructed him. "Avoid bad girls! Lock your door at night! Let no one tell you he knows better. No one does. Remember your good manners! Don't drink. Don't smoke. Have courage. Walk straight! Trust in God." She planted a cold kiss on his cheek. "But most of all—beware of Indians!"

And then the train rolled into the station.

Greenhorn

EVERY WEEK A letter came.

As a rule it took about two weeks to reach us. A big event! We all sat around the table while our father read it out loud.

Paul described New York. The skyscrapers. The blaze of electric signs. The noisy, elevated streetcars. The movie palaces. The people he met. His Sunday excursions. The beautiful fall coloring of the countryside. The room in which he lived. His landlord. The view down the Hudson River.

And inside every letter was a one-dollar bill. The bill went from hand to hand. It was a rather large bill, the paper's texture far superior to our shabby Czech banknotes.

"He doesn't say much about his work," my mother ventured to say.

"He's just arrived," my father said, defensively aggressive. "They probably haven't assigned him yet."

"Assigned—to what?" she asked innocently.

I guess it was on all our minds.

"Laemmle will probably send him out West," my father said with his reckless optimism. "You don't have to worry about Paul. He'll make his way."

But he too seemed apprehensive. "You don't tell us what you are doing at work," he complained in his next letter. "Are they keeping you in New York? When will they send you to Universal City?"

Paul's answers were vague. They had not decided yet. Mr. Laemmle was out on the West Coast. In New York they were shifting him from department to department. It was "interesting" getting to know the "business." He was, after all, a "greenhorn." It would take time to find the right place to fit him in.

Evasive. Not quite lying—but almost. Already reticent about sharing his real feelings with others, especially with his family, who were counting on his swift success, Paul probably would have preferred jumping off the Statue of Liberty to divulging what had *really* happened.

It had started with the Atlantic crossing. He didn't travel with the Laemmles after all. They had decided to stay in Paris another week. He was booked tourist class. (And contrasting the surroundings and facilities there with the better offerings, he determined always in the future to go first class—or not at all.)

When Paul arrived in New York, there was no one at the pier to meet him, to tell him where to go and what to do. He collected his immense steamer trunk (fashioned in Teplitz) and took a taxi to the Hotel Astor on Broadway. Our father had a friend there, an old "Teplitzer." He was not the manager of the biggest hotel in New York, as our father had grandiosely announced—but the assistant of the assistant manager. A kind man, he gave Paul a "cheap" room, windowless, for five dollars. And he told him where to find the nearest synagogue.

Since it was Friday, Paul went to the services. He tried to talk to his neighbor in the pew, only to realize that he really couldn't speak English. The man took him home. He happened to know of a room in his apartment house, so Paul rented it. Saturday and Sunday he went sightseeing. He was alternately impressed, depressed, homesick.

On Monday he presented himself at the office of Universal Pictures on Broadway.

No one had heard about him. They had no instructions. Mr. Goldstein—a colorful, cigar-chewing New Yorker—told him to come back later, after Mr. Laemmle's return from Europe, when they'd know better what to do with him. Meanwhile, he should "get the feel of things." Enroll in an evening class for foreigners.

"Are you by any chance a nephew?" Goldstein asked guardedly.

"No," Paul said. "No relation."

Then Goldstein's eyes fastened on Paul's new "genuine American suit" tailored in Teplitz. He chuckled. "You'd better not show up here in that outfit, boy. You don't want to be spotted right away for a greenhorn."

Greenhorn! Wherever Paul went here—he was a greenhorn. He had an almost uncontrollable urge to run down to the harbor and board a boat. Any kind of boat. One day he did go down to one of the piers, where a huge liner was ready for European departure. He played with the idea of becoming a stowaway. But then the image of our grandmother, complete with her monstrous hat, made an appearance. And her stern eyes and cool voice commanded him to show courage!

So he waited. One week. The longest week he had ever lived through. On Monday he again went up to the Universal office. Carl Laemmle was there. He sat behind a huge desk in a huge room, with windows looking out on Broadway. It was the end of September. Hot.

"Well, how do you like America, Kohner?"

"It's different from what I expected," Paul answered.

"Give yourself time. You'll love it," Laemmle said reassuringly. Then he talked into the intercom. "Have Goldstein come in."

"I picked up this young fellow in Karlsbad," he explained to his office manager. "I have great faith in him. He wants to learn the business. Let's start him in shipping. We'll pay him eighteen a week."

Shipping? Not in his bleakest moments had Paul expected to be relegated to the packing department. As a boy he had helped in his father's factory wrapping calendars at Christmastime. But had he come to America for this—to pack packages?

"That's the way it is here," his landlord explained to him later. "They start you at the bottom of the ladder."

That was just another of those platitudes Paul had heard since his arrival. It can be done. Laugh and the world laughs with you. If you're so damn smart, why ain't you rich? Keep smiling.

Paul made a valiant attempt. He smiled like the rest of them, even in the dark shipping department. All the time wondering if America was really worth the effort.

9

Climbing

WITH THE FIRST paycheck Paul bought himself a suit. Paid the landlord. Sent a crisp dollar bill home.

Evenings he spent alone, surrounded by the worn and ugly furnishings in his room. Once the Murphy bed came out of the wall, he could hardly move around. On the small desk stood a photo of Emmy, the girl he had left behind in Bohemia. He wrote letters to her. America was a weird place, he said. He was lonesome. He missed her. He would save every dollar he could to come back to her. Maybe in a year.

Twice a week he went to evening class, learning American English. He improved. Bored, lonely yet still ambitious, he took Universal publicity sheets home with him and translated the texts into German. He had a list of German trade publications. He mimeographed his translations and sent them abroad. Also photos of new Universal films. And of Laemmle.

The articles were printed. In Europe there was a strong, naive interest in anything that had to do with films. Stars. Hollywood. Paul received payments for his articles. Three dollars, five dollars. One of the magazines carried Carl Laemmle's beaming face on the front page.

Proudly and with a palpitating heart, Paul ascended to Laemmle's office on the fourteenth floor. Under his arm he had proof copies of a German film trade paper. An Austrian illustrated magazine. A couple of Swiss publications. And of course his father's *Filmschau* (which by then had changed its masthead to the more flossy *Internationale Filmschau*).

Laemmle looked through the magazines. First he smiled. Then his forehead wrinkled. Then he turned purple. "Have you gone mad, Kohner?" he yelled at his new apprentice. "This will cost us a fortune."

Paul was shocked. He had toiled in his lonely evening hours to translate all that copy the publicity department was grinding out. Had sent it to Europe, paying the postage himself. Had been instrumental in getting the Universal name in a lot of papers—and even putting "Uncle Carl's" picture on a front page. But for what? To be humiliated like this?

With shaking hands, Paul extracted the few small checks from his pocket and handed them to Laemmle. "Here's what they paid me for it."

"*Paid* you for it?" Laemmle's mouth opened in utter astonishment.

Paul was equally stumped. He didn't know yet that in America one had to pay handsomely to publicize a company's product. A frontpage photo, even in those days, brought the publication a three-figure remuneration.

"You mean *we* don't have to pay for these stories?"

"Of course not."

Laemmle's expression suddenly relaxed. He had made an unusual discovery. He flipped on the intercom. "Send in Goldstein."

While they were waiting, Laemmle inquired: "And when did you translate these stories?"

"Evenings. Sundays. I took the publicity releases home."

Ah now, *that* was drive, that was ambition! The Horatio Alger story Laemmle had been stirred by as a young immigrant, reinacted.

"You know what this boy did?" he said triumphantly when Goldstein entered. "He translated our publicity into German. And not on company time, mind you." And he showed him the German papers.

Goldstein took a casual glance at the literature. "Very good, Kohner," he said sourly.

"Good? I think the boy deserves a break!" Laemmle cried. "We'll open a new department: Foreign Publicity. We'll put Kohner in charge. He'll translate stories into German and send out photos. Didn't you tell me you know French too?" He looked now at Paul with new interest.

"Not good enough to write it," Paul said. "But may I make a suggestion? Willy Wyler is working with me in shipping. He could do the French translations."

Willy was a new arrival, a son of one of Laemmle's cousins. (Despite or because of this relationship, William Wyler eventually managed to become one of the world's outstanding directors.) He had recently moved in with Paul. Now a couch was added, narrowing the *Lebensraum* further.

"You think he can do it, Kohner?"

"Definitely."

"Okay," said Laemmle. "You'll be head of the department. What's your salary?"

"Eighteen dollars."

"Make it twenty-five, Goldstein," Laemmle said. He played with the few small checks Paul had given him. "Here!" He handed them back. "You can keep these. But from now on—any money coming in belongs to Universal."

Gambler

A T HOME A picture of Paul arrived. A glossy photo—one of many that followed in quick succession. That first one must have been taken the day they painted the sign FOREIGN PUBLICITY on his door.

The room was minuscule. An American roll-away desk. A phone. A fan. Paul, pencil poised, in his genuine Teplitz-made "American" suit with its leather buttons and loud stripes. A natty collar, a knotted tie. A seemingly indestructible mop of hair. And a glint of triumph in his eyes.

The photo landed in the show window of the Teplitz sartorial salon—optimistically called OLD ENGLAND. Underneath it said: "Suit personally tailored for Mr. Paul Kohner, director of Foreign Publicity department of Universal Pictures in New York."

"See—" my father said to my mother, grandly. "Didn't I tell you? Only five months in New York, and he's already a department head."

Enclosed in every letter home now came a fresh five-dollar bill. The money was deposited in Paul's name at the venerable banking firm of Beer, Perutz & Sons.

My brother explained to us that he sent weekly publicity releases abroad. He handled the German "market" himself. Willy Wyler did the French. Soon a Spanish translator was added. And it was all his idea.

We learned of course only of the victories. Mr. Laemmle, he wrote, was so pleased with his work that he had asked him to take care of his personal German correspondence with the vast Laemmle clan.

Carl was the tenth of thirteen children. Even though his father speculated thriftily in small parcels of land, they were poor. At seventeen Carl emigrated to America, where an older brother had already put down roots.

From errand boy and then small clothier, Carl rose to become a pro-ducer—president of his own film company, a millionaire.

And if this simple country boy from Laupheim had achieved the Great American Dream, why not other Laemmles too? Thus the aim of most of the letter-writers was to follow in the footsteps of the uncle who had "made it."

Good Uncle Carl. How he loved his family. He wished he could trans-plant them all to the new land that had been so good to him. But how could he? *All* of them? All of his relatives who were looking for that precious ticket to cross the Atlantic, after which he might assume respon-sibility for their welfare?

Still—he spent hours eagerly reading every scrap of family gossip that came in letters. But he could never seem to get around to answering all his correspondence with relatives. So he turned to Paul. He could write in German. Would he be his "ghost writer"?

The choice turned out to be inspired. Paul had strong family ties himself and managed to inject into his responses the kind of homespun sentiments that Laemmle would have expressed had he been able to.

Sampling several of Paul's letters, Laemmle was delighted. From then on he signed his name without ever reading the contents. It was a matter of trust.

One winter evening—it was a Saturday—Paul was still in his small office, answering Laemmle family mail. The door opened, and Carl Laemm-le stuck his head in. In another corner of the room Willy Wyler was working away at his typewriter. Laemmle, pleased with what he saw and feeling in a generous mood, invited the two lads to come along with him to the Progress Club.

It was a most unusual occurrence. Paul's relationship with the Presi-dent of Universal was strictly formal. And anyway, Laemmle's nature did not allow him those easy exchanges between people that can ripen into friendship. He was at all times "Mr. Laemmle"—even with a true relative like Willy, who only called him "Uncle Carl" behind his back, as others did.

During Laemmle's frequent stays in New York he occupied a large but nondescript apartment on Riverside Drive. Almost always he dined out.

The Progress Club served a terrible dinner. But Laemmle went there on those special occasions when the Club turned into a gambling casino. Poker was the favored game. And Laemmle got drunk on poker the way people got drunk on bathtub gin.

Laemmle gave Paul and Willy five dollars apiece. "Here," he said. "When you've doubled your investment—stop!" Then he submerged in the whirlpool of gamblers.

The two greenhorns went into the room where a brisk crap game was going on. Cautiously, they made their bets. They won. Doubled their money. They peeked into the room where the poker players were hard at work. Uncle Carl seemed to be enjoying a winning streak. He was lost to the world. Discounting his advice, the boys went back to the crap game. Willy had quickly learned how to roll hot dice and how to court the "little Seven." The Seven came, over and over again, and money piled big in front of them. They stuffed the bills into their pockets.

In a fever, they went back to the card game room. A group of "kibitzers" had surrounded Carl Laemmle. He was losing by now. When Wyler tried to break through the circle and show his loot, the Old Man waved him away.

"Let's beat it," Paul suggested.

"One more roll!" Willy declared.

In Dostoyevskian fashion, they repaired to the crap table for the final roll. Lost. Once more. Lost.

Within half an hour they had divested themselves of the last dollar.

"We've still got our paychecks," Willy said. "Let's cash them and buy some more chips." They each got their twenty-five dollars.

At two in the morning they slunk out of the Progress Club—penniless. The club was situated on the West Side, and to get home they had to walk across Central Park. An icy wind blew through the canyons of Manhattan.

When they arrived home, it was five o'clock. They fell into their beds.

A knock at the door woke them. It was the landlord, demanding his fourteen dollars a week rent. Normally a man with a pleasant disposition, he became rapacious on pay days.

Manfully, Willy and Paul asked for a short reprieve. They had been up late. They would show up at his apartment later in the day.

A genius in his ability to improvise in a crisis, Willy made straight for his room-mate's savings bank. It was a black iron contraption that would swallow coins—nickels, dimes, quarters: money only accessible when the number twenty appeared in the window on the top. Paul had saved some eighteen dollars. Two dollars in change were needed for an open sesame.

Willy quickly dressed—and disappeared with the savings bank.

None of the small shopkeepers who opened early on Sunday trusted the greenhorn from Alsace. Or else they didn't understand his pleas to invest two dollars so he could recoup twenty and repay them on the spot.

Desperate and by now ravenously hungry, he passed Liggett's Drugstore. Sniffing the aroma of hot coffee and bacon, he went inside. He sat down and ordered breakfast: grapefruit, eggs, bacon, muffins—the bill amounting to the staggering sum of seventy-five cents. Ready to pay, he put the savings bank on the counter. The waitress, a pretty girl, happened to speak French. Trusting her countryman, she risked two dollars in small change. Twenty dollars came spurting out. Willy tipped her a lavish quarter—and returned home with seventeen dollars in silver.

The landlord was given his fourteen dollars. The fare for the rest of the week was coffee, rolls and soda crackers.

Friday. It was grey and cold. Paul suggested to Willy that they seek out the warmth of a nearby synagogue. There was always a chance of snagging a dinner invitation from one of the worshippers.

They were already on the stairway when Paul remembered the prayerbook—his grandmother's parting gift. He found it at the bottom of his suitcase. Shivering and hungry, he and Willy rushed through the snowy streets to the Beth Israel congregation.

Only a handful of elderly men were gathered for the Sabbath services. The two lads took their seats close to the heater. Aimlessly, Paul flipped the pages of the prayerbook. Something fell out, and Wyler picked it up.

"Hey—money!" he whispered.

Paul grabbed the bill. It was a Czech one-thousand crown note.

"Jesus Christ!" Willy shouted.

People craned their heads. Willy snatched the bill away and ran out of the synagogue with it. Paul caught up with him.

"How much is that in dollars?" Willy asked.

"About thirty bucks."

"Are you sure it's real money?"

Paul inspected the note, held it up against the streetlight, silently blessed his grandmother and pronounced: "It's good money."

It was after eight o'clock. All the banks and exchanges had long been closed.

Paul got an idea. "Stukitz!"

Aram Stukitz owned a restaurant on Third Avenue and 92nd Street where Willy and Paul had an occasional meal. He was a fierce man with a drooping mustache that hung down his chin in two black points. His place exuded the heady scent of goulash and stuffed peppers. Coming from neighboring Hungary, he might honor the Czechoslovakian banknote.

Mr. Stukitz took a hard look at the money, another at the starved customers—and agreed to feed them. "You can eat here tonight, tomorrow and Sunday. Monday I will go and change it and give you what you haven't eaten up by then." His bushy eyebrows quivered, and suddenly he roared: "And it better be no counterfeit—you two goddamn foreigners!"

11

"Von"

PAUL KOHNER WAS a young man in a hurry. He had traveled across the sea with the high hope of going to Hollywood. Which in the Twenties was HOLLYWOOD: a place teeming with adventurous antics of genius and flush with the trappings of success.

The former fur salesmen and owners of nickelodeons who had launched the motion picture industry at the turn of the century tirelessly promoted themselves and their studios, eventually even believing the stories concocted by their own publicity men. Paul too began to believe what he wrote about Universal and Carl Laemmle's artistry.

For six months now he had been sitting in his New York cubbyhole, reporting the glamorous goings-on in faraway Hollywood to the film fans of Europe. But it seemed he'd never get there to see it and become part of it himself. He felt restless.

Every working day now Paul's eyes beheld a gigantic electric sign-board across the way which alerted the world to the fact that Universal's Million Dollar picture *Foolish Wives* would soon open on Broadway. The figures of the forthcoming film's budget blazed out in golden Mazda bulbs. The "S" in director Eric von Stroheim's name appeared as a dollar sign.

Paul enjoyed looking at it as other men would delight in gazing at a beautiful girl's face or a lovely mountain lake. But no wonder he was rapturous about the billboard. It was his brainchild. He had received a special bonus of fifty dollars for the idea.

One morning the papers reported that Stroheim had arrived in New York, taking up residence at the Waldorf. Since boyhood Paul had admired the actor-director. Paul's head was as full of Stroheim's gestures and mannerisms as it was of literature and music.

By then Eric von Stroheim was already a part of the Hollywood mythos. There were as many legends and rumors about him as later there would be about Howard Hughes or Marilyn Monroe. Was he really a former Austrian cadet? Was he not the son of an Austrian businessman by the name of Strohbach? Could he be Jewish?

But whoever he was—Stroheim was an *enfant terrible* of the Twenties: a role which he apparently played with great relish.

Impulsively, Paul telephoned the director at his hotel suite. The secretary answered. Paul introduced himself as the head of Universal's Foreign

Publicity department. Could he come over and meet Stroheim? The secretary stayed away for a minute, and then—surprisingly—asked, "Can you come right away?"

A short time later Paul rang the bell at Stroheim's suite. There was no answer. He knocked. Still no answer. Where was the secretary? He opened the door and walked into the living room.

"Who's there?" came a commanding voice. And when Paul gave his name, "Come in, come in."

Paul proceeded into the middle of the room—and then stopped. The door to the bathroom was ajar. Von Stroheim stood in front of the mirror, shaving. He was quite naked.

"Sit down, Paul. Fix yourself a drink. I'll be right with you."

A battery of bottles stood on the low round table. There was no evidence of Prohibition in Stroheim's Waldorf suite. Paul made himself a drink and waited.

Eventually Stroheim made his entrance. He brought his heels together and executed a curt military bow. The heavy silver bracelet on his left hand rattled. It was the only thing he wore.

He sat down. Paul fastened his eyes on the sabre scar on his host's right cheek—and kept them there.

"Kohner. Sounds Austrian."

"I'm from Bohemia."

"Ah, so we're *Landsleute*," Stroheim said. And the conversation shifted from English into Viennese German.

Paul was thoroughly familiar with the director's work. He had recently seen an uncut version of *Foolish Wives*, he told Stroheim, and had some ideas about it.

"I'm most interested in hearing them," the director said as he poured himself a drink. "Excuse me a moment." He returned to the bathroom, came back with a robe and settled down again on the couch.

The uneasy feeling left Paul when at Stroheim's prodding he suggested how the picture might be improved, edited, promoted. His criticism was honest and concise, taking into account both the film's strong potentials and pitfalls. He had notions too about the musical score to accompany it, and went to the piano to improvise some of the Viennese music he thought would enhance the picture's appeal.

While he played, the door of one of the adjoining rooms opened, and an attractive girl—obviously the secretary—emerged, fully clothed, crossed the room, waved at Stroheim and was gone.

Stroheim was completely absorbed in Paul's piano performance. When Paul finished playing, he received an invitation for lunch.

Luncheon was brought up to the suite. Von Stroheim started dressing. As he dressed, he talked. If there is such a thing as "creative talking," Stroheim possessed it to the highest degree. And in his guest that day he had found not only an enthusiastic listener, but also a stimulating discussion partner. While Paul could not match him in the flow of imagery that Stroheim poured out, he was more than a match when it came to literature.

All that Stroheim seemed to have read were military manuals. On the other hand, Paul had read everything *but* military manuals. He had a thorough knowledge of the "classics"—Goethe, Schiller, Shakespeare, Dickens, Molière, but was most fascinated with contemporary books and plays. He was familiar with the works of Schnitzler and Hofmannsthal, Werfel, Feuchtwanger, Thomas and Heinrich Mann, Stefan and Arnold Zweig, Pirandello and Rilke.

Such a wealth of book knowledge greatly impressed the cadet from Vienna. Unlike the studio bosses to whom the word "intellect" was anathema, Stroheim respected education. Always in search of new stories and plots, he now confronted a storehouse of information and shrewdly began to tap it.

"I am sure you have some good ideas for me," he said.

And indeed Paul had. He told him the plot of a book by the Austrian writer Leo Perutz. *Nine to Nine* was the story of a student who, accused of stealing a precious book, is imprisoned, escapes—and then has to go through the day with handcuffs on.

Stroheim listened, electrified. Could he get an option?

Probably, Paul said. He'd look into the matter.

And how about something with a Viennese milieu? Something in the vein of *Blind Husbands?* Maybe even with a part for him to play? Paul had this too at his fingertips. There was a book he was fond of. A love story. Elderly man and young girl. Vienna. Uniforms.

"Tell me the story," Stroheim urged.

So Paul told him the plot of a book by a popular Austrian writer, Rudolf Hans Bartsch: *The Story of Hannerl and Her Lovers.* He deliberately built up the part of a minor character, an Austrian cavalry lieutenant.

"Excellent! Excellent!" Stroheim cried, jumping up. "Buy it for me, Paul."

Stroheim had obviously taken a liking to the young foreign publicity director. In Paul's presence he called Laemmle and requested Kohner as his own escort and public relations man during his stay in New York.

For days Paul accompanied the strutting von Stroheim everywhere. There were interviews. Receptions. Cocktail parties. Restaurants like the Blue Ribbon, Sardi's, Lindy's. Nightclubs. Brothels.

Two weeks after he met him, Paul escorted Stroheim to Grand Central Station. A bunch of photographers stormed the platform, asking the director to assume some Prussian attitudes. To look martial. Look like a Hun. Look like the "man you love to hate." Stroheim obligingly snapped his hand to a military salute, sneered. Flashbulbs popped.

When it was all over he asked Paul into his private railroad car.

"I talked to the Old Man," Stroheim said. "Told him you're being wasted here. You belong in Hollywood. He could use a man with your background out on the Coast."

"What did he say?" Paul asked excitedly.

"He'll think it over. But I have a feeling I'll see you there. Soon."

They shook hands.

"Thank you," said Paul.

"*Servus!*" And Eric von Stroheim clicked his heels.

Paul waited till the train cleared the platform, wondering how to shape his next act to obtain that coveted ticket to Hollywood.

Monte Carlo

AND NOW BEGAN a maddening period of waiting. Every time the phone on his desk rang, Paul hoped it would be a summons to the Front Office. But though it rarely stopped ringing, a call never came from Carl Laemmle.

Meanwhile, like the great Rastelli, Paul juggled several projects at the same time. He kept busy. But he longed for some unique exploit, some staggering feat that would remove him from the thousands of New York strap-hangers he joined every morning to get to his office at 1600 Broadway. He dreamed of some dazzling display of sorcery that would astonish the world—and the president of Universal Pictures.

It was spring. On the desk stood a photo of his Emmy. Oh, to be in Europe now!

And then he got an idea. He *would* go abroad, somehow. He knew he could.

It was five in the afternoon. He dashed out of his office, taking three steps at a time to the upper floor. Rushing down the corridor, he bumped into Laemmle, who was just on his way out.

"Mr. Laemmle, I must talk to you!"

He looked at Paul impatiently. "What is it, Kohner? I have no time now. I'm on my way to my lawyer. See me tomorrow."

"It's terribly important," Paul insisted. "It can't wait."

"Then come along," Laemmle said. "Tell me on the way."

Laemmle's limousine was parked at the curb. The chauffeur stood waiting, cap in hand. They got inside.

"We have ten minutes," Laemmle said. Then he leaned back in the seat of the car, cupped a hand to his ear—as was his custom—and gave his passenger a nod.

"About *Foolish Wives*," Paul began. "I think the picture should have a world premiere in Monte Carlo. Maybe we can get the Prince to sponsor it. After all, we built half of Monaco at Universal City for the film. Monaco will get tremendous publicity through the picture—and the Casino is the main source of income for the principality. We should make it an invitational affair with all the royalty of Europe attending. It'll get the kind of publicity Universal cannot buy with money. And everyone stands to profit by it." He looked expectantly at the Old Man.

Carl Laemmle, notably a slow-moving man, spoke now with remarkable swiftness. "You're crazy, Kohner."

"But Mr. Laemmle—"

"Once in a while you come up with a good idea," he said. "But this one is—well, it's just *wild*. Forget it."

For a terrible moment Paul was silenced. Yet only for a moment.

"If you would send me over," he continued, undaunted, "I think I can sell the Prince on the idea. If he goes for it, he might even give you a medal."

Laemmle remained sunk in deep thought for a while. Though undeceived by flattery, he was not impervious to it. A man of inordinate vanity, his face reflected the struggle within. But he was not convinced. Not yet.

No, no—he shook his head. It wouldn't do.

"If you make me your personal representative, Mr. Laemmle," Paul went on, "I'll take a print of the picture, get an audience with the Prince and present the whole plan to him."

Laemmle seemed to be wavering, and Paul, pursuing, made one more thrust. "All you would have to invest is the trip for me to France. I've figured it out. It'll cost you four hundred and sixty-eight dollars. That's a small investment considering what Universal stands to gain."

"How do you get that figure?" Laemmle asked.

"The boat ticket is three hundred—round trip," Paul improvised. "A two-week stay, all expenses paid—figuring ten dollars a day, plus incidentals ... well, it comes to exactly four hundred and sixty-eight dollars."

"Three hundred dollars!" Laemmle protested. "That's the price of a first-class passage."

"Of course," Paul said coolly. "As your personal representative, I couldn't very well travel tourist class."

By now they had arrived at their destination. The chauffeur came around to open the door. Paul helped Laemmle out of the limousine. Silently they walked to the entrance of the building.

Laemmle stopped. "When I arrived in New York, Kohner," he said, "I was seventeen years old. My father paid the fare for steerage—twenty-two dollars and fifty cents. That was a lot of money then. All of my father's savings."

He looked wistfully up at this tall and winsome apprentice from Teplitz. "You go over to the French Lines, Kohner. Your figures were wrong. They have a first-class cabin for two hundred and fifty. Of course it's an inside cabin. You don't need a porthole, do you, Kohner?—even as my personal representative?"

And then, with a puckish smile, he vanished through the revolving door into the lawyer's building.

13

Tale of the Fiddler and the Tailor

THE TELEGRAM CAME without warning.

SAILING WITH LAEMMLE ON ILE DE FRANCE WILL
CABLE ARRIVAL TEPLITZ AFTER LANDING LOVE PAUL

Not even gone a year—and already he was accompanying Universal's powerful president on that legendary ship, the *Île de France!*

Mysterious and wonderful Paul's triumphal return seemed to us. The family gathered in the garden of our home on that warm summer evening to speculate about this new turn of events and to consider all the possibilities.

"I think President Laemmle wants to meet us," my mother said. Paul had occasionally mentioned Rosabelle. Remembering his glowing description of her, she had arrived at a simple, motherly conclusion.

"Ridiculous," my father scoffed. "The boy is too young for such nonsense. He's just keeping Mr. Laemmle company. He likes Paul and wants him around." But his face told us he might be expecting more.

"Maybe he's going to make a picture here," my nine-year-old brother Walter suggested. That idea appealed to me too.

The expected arrival of the "Amerikohner" was duly reported in the town paper. I sunned myself in the reflected glory of my older brother, becoming deeply engrossed in daydreams of my own future fame. I was already taking my first fling at writing. Poetry. Short stories. Even a script specially designed to be made into a film. With Paul's help I would sell this masterpiece and be launched on a writing career.

In the next few days the suspense became almost unbearable. Waiting for the mailman to come with a letter from Paul. Rushing to the phone, only to hear the voice of a family member asking for the latest news. The *Île de France*, we figured, had arrived in Le Havre by now. But we heard nothing from him. Where was he?

Just when our expectancy was ready to explode, another telegram appeared.

ARRIVING TOMORROW EVENING SIX O'CLOCK
TRAIN ENGAGE LOEWENTHAL

Now this was a puzzlement. There were two Loewenthals living in our town. They were brothers. One was a tailor, Theodore by name—a simple mender of clothes who had never reached the sartorial status of some of the excellent Czech master-craftsmen abounding in our spa. Theodore Loewenthal was called upon to put patches in worn-out jackets and pants, to shorten or lengthen clothes, to spruce up wrinkled garments. His younger brother Hugo held a much more exalted position: first violinist with the *Kur* orchestra. Also, with some of his fiddler friends, he had formed a chamber orchestra known as the "Loewenthal Quartet." They performed during the winter months in the local concert hall—and were hired for social events such as weddings, receptions and funerals.

Brooding over the cryptic message, my father posed the solution: "He means Hugo and his quartet. Of course. He'll be arriving with Laemmle and he wants to have a festive welcome at the station. Fritz, run over to the Herr Concertmaster and tell him that I want to see him right away."

While I ran to the modest home of the concertmaster, my father called the leading hotel in town to reserve the "Emperor Suite," which had been occupied during the time of the Austro-Hungarian monarchy by the last of the Hapsburgs—the unfortunate Kaiser Karl.

The next day started early in our house. My mother began to prepare the feast for the evening. From my room I listened to her impatient voice detailing the chores to our maids and extra help.

I felt euphoric. Indeed, I hoped to interest the president of Universal Pictures in my manuscript. But mostly I visualized the esteem in which my friends would now hold me when I appeared on the *corso* in the company of my illustrious brother and the movie mogul from faraway California.

Half an hour before the arrival of the express train—known as the six o'clock *Schnellzug*—the station was packed. Our numerous "extended family" members came in their Sabbath best. An uninvited group of my brother's school pals and a cluster of curious onlookers also appeared, for that afternoon the local newspaper had carried the story of Paul's arrival, going on to speculate whether President Laemmle might be changing his yearly stay at the famous spa of Karlsbad for the less ostentatious but equally salubrious thermal springs of Teplitz.

The Loewenthal quartet took its place at the platform where the first-class pullman usually came to a stop. They wore their dark evening jackets. I noticed that even the stationmaster had donned his gala uniform.

I watched my father, who had arranged the whole extravaganza. He was a man who hated ostentation. But that summer evening he had completely surrendered to his illusions. Suddenly I found all this ceremony ridiculous and embarrassing.

Still, even though I tried manfully to disassociate myself from my family, my heart skipped a few beats when the express train pulled into the station. I saw Paul immediately. He had opened the compartment window and now looked with stunned incomprehension at the reception party.

The Loewenthal Quartet started to play "Over There"—the only American melody then known in that part of Europe. This was only a three-minute stop, so passengers had to depart swiftly. A couple of porters rushed up to the window to lift down the baggage. Down came Paul's suitcases. Nothing else followed. Then the car door swung open and out stepped my brother—alone.

While the music went on determinedly, I broke out in a cold sweat. Seeing the sneering looks of my brother's old friends, the grins frozen on the faces of my family, I felt horribly ashamed.

A sharp, long-drawn whistle—and the express train pulled out of the station. The welcoming embraces were mute and strained.

"Where is Laemmle?" were my father's first words.

"In Paris," Paul said. "Why?"

"We thought—I mean—you cabled that you were traveling with him."

"On the boat. Yes."

"But your wire said to engage Loewenthal—"

"The tailor," Paul said. "I need to get my dark suit pressed. I have to leave early tomorrow morning for an audience in Prague, at the Hradschin Castle."

And then something quite marvelous happened. My father began to laugh. A man who rarely laughed, he now broke into a paroxysm of laughter. We all started to laugh—and could not stop. Although not quite knowing what it was all about, Grandmother laughed too. All the excitement and the subsequent misunderstanding had brought us to the edge of hysteria—to which the laughter now gave a blessed release.

After the elaborate dinner our mother had prepared, Paul told us the whole story.

Laemmle had indeed decided to send him to Monaco—but he had to wait till Uncle Carl and his retinue sailed on the yearly European jaunt. In Le Havre they had parted ways, Laemmle going to Paris and Paul, with a print of *Foolish Wives*, to Monte Carlo.

Oh yes, he had been received at the royal palace. By the major-domo (or whatever title the liveried operetta-style character held). Who was friendly but firm.

"Mr. Kohner," he had said in his best Monégasque English, "we have heard about your company's financing a film of great magnitude about Monte Carlo. I have seen the photographs of the outside of the Casino, and I must say it is a marvel of American ingenuity. Even His Royal Highness was impressed with the verisimilitude. We understand, however, that this film also shows our Casino on the inside. The focal point of your story, in fact, is the gamble. Now the gamble, Mr. Kohner, we do not want to see propagated or glorified. Certainly the principality of Monaco receives revenues from the Casino. But it happens that His Royal Highness detests the gamble. His Royal Highness would, if he could, blow up the Casino and everyone who is in there, profiting by it, to perdition—I venture this is the proper expression. We therefore regret that you have taken the trip to see us as the personal representative of the president of Universal Pictures. It is of no avail. In fact, when this film is sent to Europe we will issue a special edict forbidding its exhibition within the principality of Monaco. Thank you—and no *au revoir.*"

Defeated and feeling sick, Paul sat down on a bench outside the palace. He who was so ambitious, so eager to please, had failed in his mission—after almost assuring Laemmle that he could bring it off. How could he face his boss again? And what about the promised decoration he had dangled in front of him? Paul knew it was *that* honor, more than the premiere of a film, which had prompted the Old Man to send him to Monaco.

Just then a simple thought occurred to him: a medal is a medal is a medal.

He rushed back to his hotel. It was five in the afternoon. He put a call through to Universal's distribution office in Prague. Luckily he caught the manager just as he was about to leave.

Maxim Stransky had some leverage in the new republic. He enjoyed excellent social connections with the Hradschin Castle (the Czech equivalent of the White House). And Stransky was indebted to Paul because he had recommended him for the manager's position.

Paul told him about his predicament. He had promised Laemmle to pull off the Monaco publicity stunt. Above all he had hoped to secure a decoration for him. Some kind of medal Laemmle could display on his lapel. Now that he had failed, he found himself in a tight spot. His superiors in the New York office would rejoice, for they had taken a dim view of the whole project and said so to Laemmle. Unless Paul would be able to assuage the president's vanity by getting some singular honor accorded to him, he might find himself out of favor—and out of a job.

"Terrible. Terrible," Stransky commiserated. "But what can I do?"

"You can get me an audience with President Masaryk. Then I will try to persuade him to receive Laemmle and make him a 'Knight of the

Premislides.' Or something. Anything. Just so long as it has a medal or ribbon he can be photographed with."

"But, Paul—" Stransky stammered. "What services has Carl Laemmle rendered to the republic?"

"Quite a few," Paul said quickly. "First of all he is a yearly visitor to Karlsbad—so he's promoting a Czech spa. Second: he is going to produce a film in Czechoslovakia."

"He is—really—?"

"He doesn't know it yet," Paul said with confidence. "But he will!"

The following noon Stransky returned the call. An interview with Jan Masaryk, the president's son, was arranged. To secure the audience, Stransky—carried away by Paul's bravado—had gone a step further. He had told his friend Jan that Laemmle wanted to build a movie studio in Czechoslovakia.

This time, behind the scenes, Paul pulled the proper strings. Laemmle was received by the son of the president, and an order of merit was pinned on his chest. Jan Masaryk, raised in the United States, spoke a faultless English. He extolled the movie mogul and his achievements in a lavish fashion. Carl Laemmle beamed. And Paul Kohner, as his "personal representative," stood close by, in a well-pressed dark suit—beaming too.

And of course there were photographs taken to record this august occasion.

14

The Celebrity Business

THOUGH THE 1920s did not invent the celebrity business, they certainly perfected it. Channel swimmers, boxers, movie stars, statesmen flourished. And now film tycoons.

The reception at Hradschin Castle made a high moment in Carl Laemmle's life, giving him a recognition beyond any he enjoyed in movie circles. He was now elevated to international fame. And Paul proved clever at keeping him there. With his charm and good looks, his audacious savoir faire, his easy command of language, he excelled at conducting the business of celebrating Carl Laemmle. Photographs were released showing the little man from Laupheim shaking hands with Eckener, the commander of the *Zeppelin*. Having luncheon with the diminutive Austrian Chancellor Dollfuss. Receiving the great pianist Jan Paderewsky at Universal City. Talking to President Coolidge at the White House. Exchanging simulated blows with Jack Dempsey. Discussing movie deals with S. M. Eisenstein.

As a public relations man for his boss, Paul was able to travel stylishly, diverting himself to his heart's content in hobnobbing with people prominent and notorious. But after a while it got boring and seemed silly. He wrote Laemmle that he needed a change. He asked to be transferred to California so he could get involved in the creative part of the movie business.

Then he nervously awaited Laemmle's response. It was—surprisingly—positive. Perhaps remembering Stroheim's recommendation, Uncle Carl agreed to send Paul to the West Coast.

One morning soon afterwards Paul found himself in a compartment on the Chief—on his way to Hollywood.

Paul was fascinated with this new territory with all its opportunities and eagerly entered into whatever work was given to him.

At that time Laemmle employed the brilliant and equally eager Irving Thalberg. As head of production, Thalberg's position was formidable, especially considering his age (he was twenty-four). He had just fired the great Eric von Stroheim, who was directing a multi-million dollar picture. This move Carl Laemmle would never have made on his own, but it saved Universal from bankruptcy. Thalberg then requested a raise. With dialogue of this sort, Laemmle always grew hard of hearing and recalcitrant. Thalberg promptly quit Universal and moved over to MGM.

Pretenders to the vacated production throne swiftly came forth. Paul lost no time in offering himself to Laemmle as a substitute Thalberg. This time the Old Man did hear well.

"You're running too fast, Kohner," he told his protégé. "You know next to nothing about the production end of the business. Also—very important—if you want to be a producer you must know *what* to produce. How do you find out? From the exhibitors. That's how I started: listening to exhibitors. *They* know what audiences like. Not the film critics."

"Fine—why not?" Paul amiably agreed. "I'll talk to some of them."

Laemmle smiled slyly. "No, Kohner—not to some of them. To *all* of them. You must cover the country, state by state. The studio will furnish a car, and you can go on the road. In the hick towns you'll find out what they put their two-bits down for at the box office. Very educational, the grass roots. Of course you'll be my personal representative again."

Paul was dumfounded. Having spent almost a year as Laemmle's ambassador-at-large, he now saw himself reduced to a menial assignment. He requested time to consider the proposal.

In the following week he pondered Laemmle's offer. Maybe, he reasoned, the Old Man was right. After all, what did he really know about the country? He knew New York now. But New York was not America. If he wanted to produce films, American films, he had to get the feel of the whole nation. He slowly convinced himself that canvassing the continent would not only benefit his employer, but himself as well—pointing him in the right direction as a future producer.

Thus, like our father a generation before, my brother Paul went on the road. His territory was quite different. Our father had traveled throughout Europe, but his oldest son—in a two-seater Buick convertible—drove through the backlands of America. During one year he covered more than a hundred thousand miles, from the deep South to the northern reaches of Montana, Washington and Maine. He talked to hundreds of theatre owners and to thousands of moviegoers. And every week he dispatched his reports to Laemmle.

It was a year of painstaking education—and of painful loneliness. Once in spring he drove through the flatlands of Wyoming and came to an out-of-the-way hamlet. Suddenly he stepped on the brakes. Was it a mirage? Through a fence next to a wooden shack a branch of blue lilacs peeked out.

Paul jumped out of the car. A lilac bush grew in our garden at home in Bohemia. He had never encountered one here in America. He broke off a sprig of flowers. Inhaling the familiar scent, Paul found tears in his eyes.

15

Right and Left

THE YEAR WAS 1924.

Paul had served his stretch on the American road. Meanwhile, I had gone to Paris to study at the Sorbonne. Since inflation had ruined our father's business, this would not have been possible for me without my brother's support, both financial and moral.

Remembering this year, I am inclined to feel wistful, for it was a particularly poignant time in my own youth. Every month I received a letter from Paul, postmarked Hollywood, containing the munificent sum of twenty-five dollars. The Bank of America check, converted into francs, made a fortune for a Sorbonne student—or for almost anyone in Paris. I must confess that most of it was not spent on higher education. For the first time the enticing mysteries of love were opening up for me. But the pleasures of love are not always free. Because of my affluence I became quite popular among the Montparnassians, so Paul's dollars melted rapidly if gratifyingly away.

Once a month, in turn, I sent my brother a carefully edited report about my activities. His prompt reply kept me abreast of his own progress professionally.

After Paul's return from Main Street America, Carl Laemmle, true to his word, had assigned him to the studio's production department. Following the routine route—from production assistant to producer of two-reelers—he eventually was given his first full production job.

As his first film he chose *The Story of Hannerl and Her Lovers*, the book he had once described to Stroheim, retitling it *Love Me and the World Is Mine*. It seems strange to me now that Paul, after sounding out the preferences of American exhibitors, picked that particular slice of Austrian schmaltz served up on a tableau of a vanished monarchy. But in those days I didn't question the wisdom of his choice. Proudly I showed my friends the publicity clippings, announcements in the trade papers and eventually the first stills, which he had forwarded to me.

For the directorial assignment Paul had imported the German director E. A. Dupont, who had achieved international acclaim for his *Variété*, now recognized as a classic. The leading female part was played by Mary Philbin. An ingenue of twenty, she had won a beauty contest in her native Chicago. Believing he had discovered another Mary Pickford, Laemmle gave her a contract and was "building her up" for stardom.

One day my brother wrote that he had given Miss Philbin a ring. They were officially engaged to marry. "Stills" soon arrived from Hollywood: glossy photos of the two holding hands, gazing at each other coyly.

Mary had a sweet face. The innocence of childhood still lingered in her eyes. There was something frail, protection-seeking about the way she leaned against my brother.

But I wondered whether she could ever take Emmy's place: Emmy who hadn't wanted to go to America, and married someone else. The family wondered too. Particularly our mother. As mothers do, she entertained grandiose dreams about her oldest son. Greatness. Triumphs. Material success. And a nice Jewish girl for a bride. Like, for instance, Rosabelle Laemmle.

Rosabelle was probably very fond of Paul, who was a frequent guest in the Laemmle home. Now wouldn't the only daughter of the film tycoon be an ideal match for Paul?

Mary Philbin, on the other hand. Well, she was just an actress, and marriages to actresses were doomed to disaster. Our mother took pride in her own ancestry. The Béamts, she maintained, were of French stock. Her great-great-grandfather had actually been a close friend of Napoleon's. Then there was "my cousin Heinrich Heine"—of the banking firm of Heine in Hamburg, no less. He too had married out of his class, becoming a poet—and look to what a sorry end *he* had come.

In June Paul came to Paris. I went to meet him at the boat train. We hadn't seen each other for a couple of years. And there he was, tanned, tall, suave, wearing a light summer suit—walking calmly and debonairly along in the bustle of the arrival. He shook hands. We talked about the trip, the weather, the family. We really had nothing much to say to each other.

I took him to his hotel. That is, *he* took me along—to the George V, of course, where a suite was reserved for him. (From now on it would always be a suite, not just a room.)

I had never been to the George V, nor to any of the other "American" hotels on the Right Bank. On the Boul' Mich where I lived, I walked around in slippers. It was *my* quartier, the streets *my* home. The "other side" was for "them"—tourists, parvenus, Americans.

But a deeper gulf than the Seine, which divided the Left Bank from the Right, seemed to separate Paul and me. The years in America, the life in the movie colony, had molded him into a "Hollywood character."

He buzzed for room service. Then he began to make phone calls to Berlin, Vienna, Prague, Rome. I watched him—this stranger who was my brother. He put a big framed photo of Mary Philbin on the mantelpiece. It looked like an advertisement.

The waiter arrived with gourmet foods. I was urged to eat. But I had no appetite. The waiter opened a bottle of iced champagne. As we drank, Paul talked about the picture he had just finished. Raved about it. Said that Laemmle might make him head of production at Universal. (After just *one* picture? It sounded incredible but still I believed it.) He showed me a Hollywood trade paper with the banner headline: Paul Kohner—Is He Another Thalberg?

The phone started ringing. He made appointments: in the afternoon, for cocktails, in the evening, for supper, for next morning.

"Would you like to see where I live?" I asked him.

"Of course," he said absently. "Where is it?"

"At the Quartier Latin, close to the Sorbonne."

We went downstairs. Paul hailed a taxi. "Let's take the Metro instead," I said. He looked at me as if I had taken leave of my senses. Ride in a subway?

So we took a taxi up to the Boulevard St. Michel. Walked up four flights to my room. When I introduced him to my landlady, he was gracious. Kissed her hand. He sat down on the one broken chair and looked at me as though I were an actor he was considering for a part. He gazed around the room as if envisaging it as a set for a film of *La Vie de la Bohème*.

I had planned to show Paul my haunts on Montparnasse. The Dôme, the Rotonde, the Jockey. To introduce him to my friends. I had been bragging about him. I now decided against it. They would find him ridiculous, and he would find them weird. I resented him for having gone "completely Hollywood."

We drove back to the George V. He invited me to stay with him in his suite for the few days before we traveled home together as planned. Under the pretext of having to cram for exams, I begged off. Oh yes, exams. He understood.

On the train homeward a few days later, though, the wall between us crumbled. The gulf separating our two lives began to fill in. It was night. We had sleepers. He couldn't sleep, said he was worried.

Was it Mary? Was it his first film, as yet unscreened? Almost timorously I asked.

I had guessed both correctly. Paul wasn't sure whether he had done the right thing—giving Mary Philbin the diamond ring, asking her to marry him. In Hollywood it had seemed right. But once on the boat, doubts assailed him. They had exchanged cables daily. Her messages seemed superficial, unsatisfactory.

In Paris he had told me that our mother's disapproval over the engagement didn't bother him. But now that we came closer to home, he confessed that he was not insensitive to her judgment. His ties to the family were stronger than he had wanted to admit to himself.

Layer after layer of the Hollywood fake-front plaster began to peel off: the ostentation, the excessive pride, the buoyant display of self-assurance. Then he confided that he had gotten disturbing reports about his first film. An uncut version of *Love Me and the World Is Mine* was shown at Universal City after his departure, and some of the reactions were disastrous. He couldn't understand it, because the "rushes" had looked so good. He had, of course, enemies at the studio. Mainly relatives of the Old Man, lying in wait for him to take a tumble.

At the moment Carl Laemmle was in Europe too—actually receiving some honor in his hometown of Laupheim. Any day now he would be in Karlsbad. Paul was certain that "friends" would lose no time in informing Laemmle of his protégé's failure. He might, he thought soberly, lose his job.

Doing my best to improve Paul's morale, I told him he must trust his own judgment. He had selected a good story, a competent cast, a proven director. Even though I hadn't seen it yet, I was convinced that he had made a fine film.

It worked. Slowly, his self-confidence came back.

Once again the family assembled in full force at the train station. But no Loewenthal background music this time.

Early next morning the phone began ringing—and never stopped.

16

Love Me and the World Is Mine

Most of the calls came from nearby Karlsbad, where Laemmle and his entourage had again taken up residence at the Hotel Pupp. But it wasn't the Old Man who was calling. It was his secretary, Harry Zehner. He confirmed Paul's fears: the reports on the first Kohner production coming from the Coast were grim. Laemmle had been advised not to invest more money in distribution. Laemmle, who never quite trusted anyone in his organization, wanted to see the picture himself. A print of the film was on its way to Universal's London office.

Paul must have lain awake most of the night in his old room, brooding over his predicament. Was it possible that he had really blundered? Wasted half a million of Uncle Carl's money? If this was true, he would have to resign. Otherwise—and worse—he might be "fired." That blunt, humiliating word.

Now how could Paul, like the great Houdini, get himself out of this tight box?

Then—as always seemed to happen in moments of stress—he concocted a new trick. He called the manager of the London office and asked him to ship to Teplitz, at once, the print of the picture—which, coincidentally, had arrived there that very morning. He himself, he said, would take it up to Karlsbad to screen it for Laemmle.

A couple of days later, Paul and I picked up the precious cargo and carried it to our father's movie theatre. At the close of the evening's performance, our father, Paul and I settled down in the back row of the house to view the eight reels of *Love Me and the World Is Mine*.

It was not a very good film. Hollywood was rarely felicitous in re-creating the atmosphere of Austria and Vienna. But the picture did have its moments of charm. I was particularly fascinated by Mary Philbin, who looked like Rowena in *Ivanhoe*. Watching her performance, I kept reminding myself that this delicate Botticelli girl would one day be my sister-in-law.

When the lights came on again, Paul turned to our father. The "Kino-Kohner," who had been an exhibitor for a long time, was an expert at evaluating viewer response. Now he sat in silence. As was his habit, his thumb and forefinger massaged his lower lip. Then came the verdict: "It needs music." (This was a few years before the movies provided sound.)

45

Music?

My brother, who had sat in his chair throughout the screening like a man nursing a terrible toothache, jumped up. Suddenly the pain vanished. Color returned to his face. He caught our father's train of thought.

"Loewenthal!" he cried.

The "Kino-Kohner" smiled broadly. This time there was no misunderstanding. They both knew which Loewenthal.

Maestro Hugo was roused from bed early next morning and coaxed over to the theatre to watch the second screening of Love Me and the World Is Mine.

"Herr Concertmaster," Paul said, "I want you to arrange a musical background score. I'd like to use some of the popular Austrian tunes to 'illustrate' the film. A couple of Strauss waltzes. 'The Radetzky March.'" He hummed it for him. "When can you get the orchestra here for a rehearsal?"

"But, Paul—" Loewenthal cut him short. "This is not America. My orchestra is under contract to the city. We have to perform during the morning and evening promenade. We must also rehearse every day. How could we possibly do this for you without the Mayor's consent?"

"I will make a substantial contribution to the orchestra's fund," Paul said determinedly. "This is of the utmost importance. Please bring the musicians here as quickly as you can. I will get the permission."

And off Paul went to see the Mayor.

Had the "Kino-Kohner" proposed such an unconventional scheme, the town fathers would have turned him down. The "Amerikohner," however—he was something else. After a hasty consultation with his council, the Mayor permitted the orchestra to devote a few hours of the day to rehearse the score for Paul—whose fifty-dollar donation in those days made an impressive sum in Czech crowns.

Over and over again that day the picture was projected on the screen. Meanwhile, Maestro Loewenthal threw himself enthusiastically into this uniquely challenging assignment.

Next day Paul called Zehner and asked him to reserve the "Elite" movie house in Karlsbad for the following morning. If it would be agreeable with Mr. Laemmle, he said, he would come down and show his much-maligned production. Shortly afterwards the reply came through. Tomorrow at eleven Laemmle would see the picture.

Paul hired a big bus. And at the break of a beautiful summer day, the thirty-two man orchestra, complete with instruments, boarded it for the three-hour ride to Karlsbad. Paul took me along to help him through the ordeal. He appeared more tense than I had ever seen him. I tried hard to persuade him that he had nothing at all to fear—while all the time I was shaking in my boots.

Upon our arrival at Karlsbad the orchestra was ushered into the orchestra pit of the Elite. While Maestro Loewenthal and the orchestra were treated to a full-course "Karlsbad breakfast," Paul rushed over to the Hotel Pupp.

He found the climate glacial at the Laemmle suite. On top of the bad reports about the film came the Old Man's displeasure that Paul had ordered the print to be sent to him, not directly to Karlsbad.

Not only had Laemmle invited his whole clan to the film showing, but also an American guest who was taking the "cure" at the spa: Sol Lesser, head of the powerful RKO Theatre chain.

From my safe seat in a front row I apprehensively watched the group, headed by Uncle Carl, settling down in the rear of the theatre. The house darkened. First the credit titles appeared on the screen, and then an Austrian military regiment, preceded by an army band, marched down the *Ringstrasse*.

Suddenly out of the orchestra pit resounded the brassy strains of "The Radetzky March." Head raised, galvanized, Carl Laemmle sat up in his seat. He loved simple, popular tunes—and that was the kind of uplifting background music he was treated to for the next ninety minutes by the dedicated musicians under the baton of Hugo Loewenthal.

I myself felt stunned by the impact of the music, which somehow accelerated the slow pace of the picture itself and imbued it with a wholly different mood. The once-soggy *Love Me and the World Is Mine* now seemed to play swiftly and pleasurably. And when it came to the traditional happy ending, one could hear the sniffles of some of the female members of Laemmle's retinue.

No one moved when the lights came on. Laemmle had extracted his pocket handkerchief and wiped a tear away. Questioningly, he turned to Sol Lesser.

"Beautiful, Mr. Laemmle," said Lesser. "Very moving. I'll book it for our chain. It's one of Universal's finest productions."

Laemmle nodded, dazedly. Then his eyes roamed over the clan. Their faces were wreathed in smiles. Some of his close advisers looked embarrassed. Uncle Carl nodded triumphantly.

Then he turned to Paul. "Good job, Kohner. I am delighted. What was the name of that story you wanted to do next?"

"The Man Who Laughs, by Victor Hugo," he said.

"Whichever Hugo he is, you go right ahead with him, Kohner. And now—how about lunch, everyone?"

He jumped up with a youthful bounce and happily strode out of the movie house.

Uncle Carl and
the Theory of Relativity

THUS CAME VICTOR Hugo's *The Man Who Laughs*, starring the demonic Conrad Veidt and ingenue Mary Philbin. Next *A Man's Past*. Then *The Cat and the Canary*, directed by the brilliant German Paul Leni—one of the first guided by the rule that movies must, above all, engage the eyes.

Paul Kohner wasn't called "Producer." At Universal that title belonged to Carl Laemmle. Yet Paul did a producer's job. He chose the story, helped the writer prepare the script, picked the director, worked out the budget, selected the cast. But on the screen it merely said "Supervisor."

In our hometown of Teplitz, however, Paul was a Hollywood Super-Producer. Our father saw to that. "A Paul Kohner Production," the local paper announced, and billboards appeared on the promenade of the spa, informing the populace of the forthcoming event. Specially ordered credit stripes flashed PAUL KOHNER, giant-size, onto the screen at the "Kino-Kohner's" theatre.

American films were exceedingly popular with Europeans. And at the same time Europeans became very popular in America. Paramount imported Ernst Lubitsch and Emil Jannings. Fox got Alexander Korda, F. M. Murnau, Berthold Viertel. MGM had Maurice Stiller and his Garbo. Warner took Paul Ludwig Stein.

Paul was well aware of the great reservoir of talent in European actors, directors, composers. Exercising his future profession as agent, he tried to convince his employer to put a number of those artists under contract. Lacking the boldness of a Mayer or a Fox and more limited in funds, Laemmle usually let the best of them slip through his fingers. Yet he did sign Conrad Veidt, Paul Leni, William Dieterle, the Hungarian comedian Huszar Puffy, Rudolph Schildkraut, the great actor of the German and Yiddish stage, as well as his flamboyant son Joseph. A "European colony" began to flourish around Hollywood, centering in Beverly Hills.

Since Paul was a faithful and engrossing letter writer, I became privy to some of the fascinating doings in the Hollywood of the Twenties—and, later on, in the early Thirties. He reported on dinner parties where he sat at candle-lit tables among international beauties. Renowned novelists, poets and playwrights ambled in and out of swimming pools. From Paul's descriptions, it seemed a place where people devoted themselves relentlessly and hedonistically to a wide variety of pleasures. Not a day passed without some highly publicized figure arriving, to be welcomed and feted.

And Paul, by some sleight of hand, was always luring the famous—for talent, beauty, notoriety or genius—to Universal City. The glossy photos arrived in Teplitz showing him arm-in-arm with Pola Negri, Greta Garbo and Dolores del Rio. And handshaking with Maurice Stiller, D. W. Griffith, Sergei Eisenstein, Emil Jannings. To mention just a few. Paul still kept his skills for the celebrity business.

One day Albert Einstein came to stay for a while in Los Angeles. How do you meet Einstein? Paul asked around. Simple. You call Lilly Petchnikoff—Hollywood's Madame de Staël of the Twenties—and get invited for dinner with the Einsteins.

During the course of this arranged evening, Paul, well aware of how pleased Laemmle would feel to be host to Einstein, asked the great scientist whether he would be interested in visiting a motion picture studio.

My not-easily-stumped brother was indeed flabbergasted when the amiable Einstein told him he wouldn't dream of entering a studio. Films, he asserted, were nothing but a bad habit that had corrupted the century—just an eruption of questionable taste and *kitsch*.

This position represented a challenge to Paul. He waited. After dinner, the great man reached for the violin and gave a recital. Then Paul casually mentioned that it would be wonderful to immortalize such an event on film—by means of that marvelous new invention, the sound picture. Paul assured Einstein that Carl Laemmle would consider it an honor for his studio to make a short film of an Einstein violin concert—and give him the print as a present.

Singularly devoid of personal vanity, the scientist was not swayed. But he obviously had taken a liking to Paul, and soon agreed to pay a visit to Universal City if he would escort him around.

However, he imposed one condition: Carl Laemmle must give his word that no photos would be taken. Tired of being exploited by the news media, Einstein had become camera-shy.

To Paul's surprise, Laemmle immediately acceded. "You can tell Professor Einstein," he said, "that I fully understand his command. We won't take a single photo of him."

The date for the studio visit was set. Laemmle ordered a studio car to pick up the Einsteins. Since it was a pleasant spring morning, Paul found nothing unusual in the fact that the limousine was a convertible, the top down. In the back seat Dr. and Mrs. Einstein were joined by Lilly Petchnikoff. Paul sat next to the chauffeur.

The entire reception was carried out with panache, on a suitably grandiose scale. At the main gates to the studio, decorated with the flags of the Weimar Republic, the Universal police force stood at attention. The car stopped at the entrance. Surrounded by his executive staff, Carl Laemmle stepped forward. Greeting the scientist in German, he helped him out of the car.

It looked like a well-rehearsed scene. All that was missing were the cameras turning. But *were* they missing?

Not really. Two magnificent palm trees flanked the studio gates. And high up on each tree, well camouflaged, perched a cameraman—with his movie camera rolling.

Carl Laemmle led the Einstein party on a guided tour through the sprawling expanses of Universal City—its stages, laboratories, animal farm. On the back lot, a Western brawl was staged for the edification of the celebrated professor. At noon a festive luncheon awaited him in Laemmle's private dining room. And all the time—on rooftops, behind brushwork, on girders, rafters, catwalks—cameras were grinding away, surreptitiously recording the historic visit.

After lunch Albert Einstein was taken to the biggest of the many projection rooms on the lot. A screening of the just-finished *All Quiet on the Western Front* had been arranged—obviously to convince the reluctant moviegoer that true works of art could emerge from Hollywood's film factories.

When the party entered the theatre, the professor was guided to a seat in the back of the room. The lights dimmed. Einstein didn't seem to notice that the house was filled to the last seat. The other spectators belonged to the Who's Who of Hollywood—directors and stars invited by Laemmle to view the first showing of the film, but who came mainly to get a glimpse of the author of the Theory of Relativity.

Watching Lewis Milestone's screen version of Remarque's novel, Einstein seemed fascinated, absorbed. When the lights went on again, there was no applause. All faces turned to stare at the world-famous genius—who, visibly shaken by the film's impact, still paid no attention to the rest of the audience.

A dainty blond girl rushed up to Einstein, grabbed his hand and kissed it. "Professor Einstein," she gushed, "this is the greatest moment in my life."

Einstein quickly withdrew his hand. He stared at this impassioned admirer, then turned to his host and asked who this lady was.

Laemmle cleared his throat. He even blushed. It seemed incredible to him that any living person could fail to recognize one of the world's best-publicized faces. "That was Miss Mary Pickford, Herr Professor," he said.

"Mary Pickford? Who is she?" Einstein asked.

A short while later the limousine drove up to return the illustrious visitor to his hotel. Einstein thanked Laemmle for his hospitality. He especially appreciated, he said, Mr. Laemmle's respecting his wishes not to be photographed.

"Herr Doktor," said Laemmle deferentially—his eyes sparkling behind the thick lenses—"I promised our Mr. Kohner not to have a *single photo* taken of you. I have scrupulously kept my word."

He looked blandly at Paul, who was standing next to Albert Einstein. And he smiled.

18

Another View of Hollywood

WHILE MY BROTHER went on producing motion pictures, seven thousand miles away, at the University of Vienna, I had written a book. My doctoral dissertation, it was about the German film.

My work attracted some attention, at least within the confines of the University, for it was the first time that such an investigation—approaching the cinema as art form in a scholarly manner—had ever been admitted as a doctoral thesis. Among other rewards, I received an offer from the *Berliner Tageblatt*—one of middle Europe's leading newspapers—to travel as a special correspondent to Hollywood and report on the new production methods and changes instigated by the new "talkies."

I sailed at the beginning of October in 1929—proud of my assignment, eager to see at last the fabled town in California, happy to be joining my brother Paul and curious to meet my future sister-in-law.

When I stepped off the *S.S. Bremen* in New York, a crowd of strangers buzzed around me, pounding me on the back and yelling "Fritz!"—as if we had been playmates from kindergarten on. I was amazed and disconcerted. They saw to it that my luggage got properly checked out, meanwhile clamoring to know how I liked America—which I had only glimpsed through the porthole of my cabin. No sooner was my baggage stowed away in a taxi than the welcoming committee dissolved, as quickly and mysteriously as it had come. I never saw any of these friends of Paul's again.

I stayed in New York for just one night. A reporter from a film trade paper came to interview me. He wanted to know what people in Germany thought of the new "talkies." Fresh from the University, self-assured, I told him that the invention had absolutely no future. My doctoral thesis, after all, propounded the theory that the silent film had developed its own language, had created a new sort of visual poetry. To use the spoken word now would be to desecrate the medium. Sound films were doomed to failure.

On a bleak October day the Twentieth Century left for Chicago, where I was to change trains. A friend from my home-town, Frank Iltis, met me at an ungodly hour and took me to another station from which the Chief departed for Los Angeles.

Having heard stories of the resplendent private cars of movie tycoons and stars, I looked for them on the sidings, but they were nowhere to be seen. Trying to accustom myself to the ways of this new land, I stayed up late at night in the smoker, where men sat around trading jokes and aiming at the spittoons.

Three days later I arrived at the Union Station in Los Angeles—a small adobe building. So this was "Hollywood"?

Paul, though, was there on the platform to greet me. We hugged each other. Checking his watch, he said that we were invited to dinner at writer Hans Kräly's. It was in Beverly Hills, so we must hurry.

My first ride in a car along Sunset Boulevard that evening is as vivid still to me as if it were happening right now. But it wasn't at all what I had expected. Everything seemed so unglamorous. Here and there frazzled-looking palm trees. Food markets lit up at night. Few people on the streets. Negroes, Mexicans. Noticing my bewilderment, my brother said, "This is just 'downtown.'"

He was nervous. He kept checking his watch. "Jesus, we're late." He pressed a button on the dashboard—and an infernal shriek howled through the night. Cars pulled to the side to let us pass. Our swift passage impressed and puzzled me. "I'm an honorary sheriff of the Universal City police force," Paul explained. "In case of emergency I can get away with it."

"But what is the emergency?" I asked, dumfounded.

"I told you. We are invited to Hans Kräly's house. Dinner is always served at eight sharp."

In those days Kräly was a highly paid screenwriter. A former opera singer, he had struck up a friendship with Ernst Lubitsch when they were both fledgling actors in a provincial German theatre. After Lubitsch's quick rise as a film director, Paramount brought him to Hollywood. He in turn imported Hans Kräly, who wrote many of Lubitsch's films.

We arrived at Kräly's home on Rodeo Drive shortly after eight. My brother dashed into the Spanish hacienda like a doctor on an emergency call. I followed him in. A butler—black, in a white jacket—took my coat. A group of people hovered around a bar. Paul greeted everyone with a lot of backslapping.

I stood around. Oh, yes—my brother. Paul introduced me. Hello, hello. I shook hands. Then they returned to their drinks. I was shocked. Was this how one greeted the correspondent of the *Berliner Tageblatt*? I wanted to talk to someone, but no one would talk to me. A latecomer entered, a man with military bearing, smiling affably. He introduced himself: Albert Conti. He was an actor, from the days of the Austro-Hungarian monarchy. And unlike the others, he seemed to be a real person.

The butler announced that dinner was served. We went into the dining room. Candlelight. Place cards. Mrs. Lubitsch at the head of the table—flanked by her husband and Kräly. I sat next to a Dr. Redlich, a fellow correspondent, who wrote for the *Berliner Film Kurier.* He was tall, tight-lipped, smiling diffidently as though his head were full of incommunicable wisdom.

Silently we ate the fish. The butler poured the white wine. I watched my brother self-consciously dissecting the fish. People seemed so *wary* of one another.

I began to identify the faces around the table. The aristocratic-looking Alexander Korda and his beautiful wife Maria. The Hungarian playwright Ernest Vajda. The director Paul Ludwig (Lulu) Stein and his rolypoly wife Olli. Lubitsch and his puckish assistant, Henry Blanke.

Mrs. Lubitsch, a charming blonde from the Rhineland, whispered something into Kräly's ear. "Ha-ha-ha—" Kräly exploded. Everyone seemed to wake up.

"Let's hear it, Hans!" Albert Conti said.

Kräly repeated what Mrs. Lubitsch had whispered. Some double-entendre, a joke. All laughed. The ice was broken. At least conversation started.

Now everyone had an anecdote to tell, some "inside story." Yet the laughter that followed each story was not pleasant.

The main course was served. Filet mignon. A red wine. More studio gossip. My brother too told a story—trying to be part of the group, trying to be like *them*, but somehow not quite succeeding. No one bothered at all with me, even to look at me.

I wanted to leave. Was this indeed the *crème* of the "European colony" which Paul had described so glowingly to me? I wondered gloomily how I would fit in or ever feel at ease among them. After a seemingly interminable and boring evening, Paul and I left.

(In the following months there were many such evenings. I began to realize that fear caused the guarded behavior of all those harassed Hollywood toilers. The onslaught of sound pictures had upset the power structure. No one knew what was going to happen. The higher a man's position, the greater his fear of losing it. Fear abounded everywhere connected with the film factories, naturally extending into the social sphere. Fear inspired the wanton boss flattery as well as the condescension toward an inferior. Gathered around Kräly's table on that first evening were men who belonged to different strata of insecurity. Of all of them, Ernst Lubitsch, in the highest position, was the most scared. Kräly came next in line. "Lulu" Stein worked on "low-budget" films, so was frightened. And at the time Blanke was Lubitsch's first assistant: wholly dependent on the stability of his boss's status. Since Redlich was a newspaperman, he couldn't be trusted to mind his own business. Neither, apparently, could I.)

"Did you enjoy yourself?" Paul asked me on the way to his home.

"Not at all," I told him frankly.

He glanced sharply at me. "That's too bad," he said. "The dinner party was actually given in honor of your arrival."

I was amazed. "But nobody even looked at me or talked to me," I said. The whole episode seemed grotesquely ironic.

"I noticed that," Paul said. "But remember that everyone in Hollywood is tense right now. A lot of people are acting strangely. Suspicious of friends. Shy of strangers."

"Why?"

"It's the 'talkies,'" Paul answered. He began to explain how things were "in flux" in all the studios, and very much so at Universal. Undecided whether to join the talkie bandwagon or not, Laemmle had cut production. At the moment, Paul said, he was "off the payroll"—whatever that meant. And whatever it meant, it surely explained his restlessness, his anxiety, his near-outsider demeanor at Hans Kräly's house. He was decidedly on the social fringes ever since his position of power had taken a downward turn.

Well, at least here I was, driving through Hollywood to Paul's place. Of course I expected to see one of those magnificent mansions seen in innumerable photos depicting the Hollywood life-style. I anticipated the pleasures of the requisite swimming pool, steamroom, king-sized bed. My brother, after all—despite this temporary setback—was a "producer," a man of considerable substance in the film industry.

The car came to a stop on Harold Way in Hollywood—a pleasant, tree-lined street with a row of small frame houses. The building we now entered—each of us carrying a suitcase—was a boardinghouse. My brother lived in a single room containing the accustomed "Hollywood bed," a large closet, a small desk and a chair. The nearby room that had been readied for me was as small as a train compartment, with space for little more than a narrow couch, a dresser and a cheap wardrobe closet.

Though dog-tired, I sat up late that night in Paul's room, listening to his tales of woe. It struck me that until I arrived, he had nobody to whom he could confide his insecure feelings and sorrows; that to all others, perhaps, he always had to maintain his mask of self-confidence and success.

"I'm a low man on the totem pole at Universal," he started out. "Though I'm a producer, most of the credit goes to Junior Laemmle, who's the production head now. My salary is puny compared to those in other studios. But I cannot demand more money, nor do I dare to quit. I probably couldn't get a job anywhere else because everyone around Hollywood believes that I'm a nephew of the Old Man. I have done nothing to contradict that rumor. And now the very word 'nephew' has become a joke here. At the moment, with the big switch to the talking pictures, the studio is in chaos. In a time of great change like this, when no one knows in which direction to move and how, it's standard procedure to put everyone with no immediate assignment or project on 'layoff.' Unfortunately, I don't even have a contract. Laemmle never gave me one—and I never asked."

Paul, of course, had never revealed any of these feelings and complaints to our family. When he traveled he did it like a nabob—with trunks full of Hollywood wardrobe changes and a host of magic tales. He knew he was casting a spell over us. There was no doubt that he loved his family. Cared for it both deeply and extravagantly, always bringing expensive presents when he appeared. He supported me, supported our younger brother Walter's schooling, paid for everybody. He never let on that all his savings were squandered on those impressive transatlantic jaunts.

He looked forward to the trip to Europe and to the small town where his presence conveyed an atmosphere of fantasy. Our father paraded his successful son around, traveled with him to Prague, saw to it that he was interviewed and photographed. He basked in his son's glory. The "Kino-Kohner" was a self-made man who had left home at the age of twelve, with hardly any schooling. And while he had made great strides in the world, considering his humble background, the prominence attained by his son now gave him a real *raison d'être.* Of course he took pride in me too and in my academic achievements. And he loved Walter, our youngest brother. But Paul—well, he was more obviously an extension of himself; and more the "salesman" type. He was the one who had already "made it." No wonder my brother implored me now not to say a word to the family about the true state of his affairs, which would destroy our father's glorious illusions.

There was one thing, though, that he did ask me to write them about. A bit of news that would please them—particularly our mother. A few days before, his engagement to Mary Philbin had been broken off. And this, he admitted, had lowered his social standing a few notches more.

That first night in my temporary quarters I barely slept. Try as I might, I could not rid myself of the terrible gloom that had settled over me. And within me some private panic was uncoiling. Would *I* be able to help my brother get through this crisis in his life? As the only representative here of his own family, perhaps there were things I could do—if only listen with concern whenever he unburdened the shadowy side of his Hollywood career.

Paul had shown me a couple of trade papers which reported in prominent places the arrival of the "noted brother of Paul Kohner." I might be able to use my position as a freelance correspondent to work to my brother's advantage. In small ways I could do my part in boosting his fallen prestige. For example, I could write my first interview from Hollywood featuring Paul's boss, Carl Laemmle. I wanted to begin to pay back, in some form, at least some of the debts I owed Paul. My determination gave me a new strength and incentive.

The following morning I set out to interview the president of Universal Pictures.

19

By-Line Hollywood

T HE LAEMMLES, FATHER and son, finally decided to convert their studio set-up to producing "talkies." They realized that they needed men better read than they to choose material for the new films. No longer would moviegoers settle for the simple, sentimental fare of the silent screen. Adding spoken narrative, dialogue and musical scores gave the cinema new dimensions—and new requirements. A more sophisticated literature was now on call.

Paul was among the first on their staff to be reactivated. Carl Laemmle Jr. asked him to make a list of "literary properties": novels, stories, plays which Universal might acquire for production—especially those in public domain, for which they need not pay authors' royalties.

Paul went immediately to work. Within a week he had assembled and submitted a list of titles, complete with synopses, to the Front Office. And then he waited. At last, impatiently, he inquired whether anyone had yet reviewed his research project. He was told to "stand by."

He already knew that bit. It was not for him. He paced around the lot like a man possessed. But at least he was in the running again. The gloom of the layoff period had ended.

One evening he waited at the door of Carl Laemmle's office, knowing the precise moment the Old Man would leave. The ride to his home in Beverly Hills, which took about twenty minutes, was the best time to get the boss's ear—alone.

"Well, Kohner," Laemmle said, cocking his head, "I see you've got something up your sleeve."

"I have had no word on my recommendations," Paul said.

"Sorry about that," Laemmle said. "But all production decisions are up to Junior, you know. I'm just the elder statesman. He'll get to your list when he can."

"You're still the head of the studio," Paul asserted. "Anyway, forget my list for now. Here's an idea that could bring Universal millions."

"Go ahead." Laemmle characteristically cradled his ear with his hand and gave Paul his undivided attention.

"Because of the talkies Universal is losing the world market," Paul said. "Half of our revenues in the past came from foreign countries. We must make our new sound films attractive to other than English-speaking territories."

"How?"

"By making versions in *different languages*. They can be done at the same time the English versions are shot—and at very little additional cost."

Then he explained the plan he had worked out.

"A very interesting idea, Kohner," Laemmle said. "Why don't you submit a budget?"

A few days later Paul moved into a bigger office. He had a new title: Supervisor of Foreign Production.

The studio was just about to wind up its first lavish and expensive sound picture: Paul Whiteman's *King of Jazz*. Paul's initial assignment was to produce versions of the film to be shown in foreign countries by supplying a different Master of Ceremonies for each language. He hired prominent German, French, Spanish, Italian and Japanese actors, who stepped before a curtain and introduced the film in their native tongue. Although the whole process took only a few days to shoot, the finished films looked like a picture specially done for each country. It was impressive—and inexpensive.

The Spanish *King of Jazz* was so well received that the studio decided to do other films designed for the Latin-American market. Out of the rich reservoir of Spanish-speaking actors in southern California Paul swiftly recruited complete Spanish casts for other films. Following the English takes of scenes, Spanish versions were shot. For the substantial German market Paul imported well-known German actors. The French were given the same procedure.

The Laemmles were well pleased with the results. The investment in these foreign versions was minimal, the box office considerable—and the competition for the world market got left far behind.

Paul received a salary raise of twenty-five dollars.

He had arranged for an office at Universal studio where I could work. He even supplied me with a brand-new model-T Ford so it would be easier for me to get around, from my flat in the middle of Hollywood out to Universal City, or on interviews, or to socialize.

Throughout countless interviews in palatial homes, at well-cultivated ranches, among beautiful flowerbeds on vast lawns or in huge swimming pools, I listened to the outpourings of the inflated egos of the "stars"—of Douglas Fairbanks, Harold Lloyd, Mary Pickford, Buster Keaton, Dolores del Rio, Ramon Navarro, Gloria Swanson, Pola Negri: talented people whose need for self-expression churned fiercely when asked to talk. It seemed as if they were, indeed, not quite sure who or what they really were; and that by speaking out they might achieve some special identities of their own that could confirm or even contradict the well-known profiles that the studio publicity departments released for public consumption.

I went stark naked with Fairbanks into a steamroom, played toy trains with Buster Keaton, sat up with Charlie Chaplin at Henry's till the morning hours. I also spent nights on end in the homes of kind, hospitable people where interminable gin rummy and poker parties crisscrossed with "orgies" of the 1929 vintage.

But my first year in Hollywood brought on a long siege of melancholia. I thoroughly disliked what I was doing. I spent ten months trying to scratch enough money together to return to Europe.

The magical aura that had always surrounded my brother now seemed to evaporate. I began to see him in more human dimensions. Was he just a frightened prisoner of his weekly paycheck? Had he accepted completely the platitudes of the motion picture industry? Why did he prostrate himself before his bosses and treat with a respect not due them others in positions of power? What was the evil spell cast by this Hollywood, that it could make natural princes servile?

Paul explained his behavior with the Laemmles as loyalty. Carl Laemmle had opened the gates of America for him, and he felt beholden. One day, he was sure, he would achieve some breakthrough. But in the meantime, he just had to go along with things. To keep looking for the main chance, wherever it might lie.

Unjustly condemning my brother for shattering the idol I had made of him, I began to hate not only what he was doing to himself, but the very place where he made his living. The perpetual sunlight, the palm trees, the kept lawns, the big cars, the endless parties—everything.

Yet much of the time I too acted like a Hollywood minion. To get my by-line on stories and earn my fare home, I had to smile. And act as if the magic there was real—and quite wonderful.

Vaverka of Prague

MOST OF MY brother's friends of that Hollywood era of the early Thirties now occupy the territory of the dead.

Like Antonin Vaverka.

I had often observed his granite-hewn face in my producer-brother's waiting room at the studio. When it was announced that Paul Kohner had been put in charge of "foreign versions" of films, the hundreds of alien actors who had made their way to Hollywood, but seldom landed a job, began to trudge out to Universal City. For hours and days on end they waited, trying to curry the favor of an all-powerful secretary, who might open for them the door to Paul's office.

One of only a handful of fellow transplanted Czechoslovakians, Vaverka elicited Paul's special sympathy. Once in a while Paul was invited to the Vaverkas' small apartment on Cahuenga Boulevard, where Mrs. Vaverka, an exquisite cook, prepared Czech food.

Paul would have liked nothing better than to give Antonin a few days' work—and he did indeed maneuver to use him here and there. But now with the arrival of the talkies, the old actor's plight became acute. Even though he had been living in Hollywood for almost eight years, he spoke only *one* English sentence: "I am Antonin Vaverka, Czech actor of Prague National Theatre."

Things had been different for him in the "silent days." Not that Vaverka ever had an easy time of it, but the small Czech colony to which he belonged stuck closely together. When things really got bad they called Paul. Once in a while he could provide the neediest with work as "extras," but more often he handed out small checks to keep the most desperate from starving.

Among this Czech group Antonin Vaverka was the only genuine actor. He had indeed played on the stage of the prestigious National Theatre in Prague. Furthermore, he was a paying member of the Screen Actors Guild and had played small parts in silent films.

With his amiable blue eyes and grey sideburns, Vaverka bore a certain resemblance to the late Austrian emperor Kaiser Franz Joseph. This look-alikeness had inspired the latent agent in Paul to take action one day.

"How long would it take you to grow a full 'Kaiser' beard, Antonin?" he asked Vaverka.

"About three weeks."

"Grow it," Paul said.

Then he called Eric von Stroheim, who was his close friend ever since their meeting in New York.

"How are things going with *Merry-Go-Round,* Von?"

"Looks like I'm starting in four weeks."

"I loved the script," Paul said. "By the way—do you have an actor to play the Kaiser?"

"Not yet."

"Then stop looking. I've got him."

Stroheim was notorious for demanding absolute verisimilitude even in the tiniest details. Kaiser Franz Joseph had a small but most significant part in the film. It would have been easy enough to hire an actor resembling the late emperor and tack a beard on him. But Paul knew that Stroheim, still a faithful vassal to his one-time emperor, would insist on a *real* beard and on an accurate portrayal of his Kaiser.

"Where is he?" Stroheim demanded.

"You must wait three weeks, Von. But believe me, I'll bring you the *only* Kaiser Franz Joseph you'll find in Hollywood."

In three weeks to the day, Antonin Vaverka was Emperor Karl Franz Joseph. Paul had outfitted him with an authentic Austrian uniform, complete with golden tresses, medals and imperial insignia.

Paul personally escorted him to Stroheim's office. When Vaverka walked in, the ex-cadet stared at him, stupefied. Then Stroheim jumped up, assumed military bearing and saluted his risen-from-the-dead emperor.

The part was well paid. Suddenly Vaverka was in demand. In the wave of films set against the background of the old middle-European monarchy there were portions specially designed to accommodate his portrayal of the Kaiser. Stroheim used him again in *Wedding March,* and Paul put him in *Love Me and the World Is Mine.*

Antonin Vaverka saved every nickel he could. His peasant slyness told him that the Kaiser gold-rush would one day come to a halt. As indeed it did with the advent of sound pictures. There was one more small nugget for Vaverka when Paul hired him to M.C. the "Czech version" of *King of Jazz.* Resplendent in tails and stiff white colar, Antonin Vaverka appeared in front of a curtain and introduced the film in the Czech language. He had made the translation himself, and Paul accepted it in good faith. This was the high point of Vaverka's Hollywood career.

When the version was finished, Paul invited Dr. Felix Janowsky, the Czechoslovakian consul in Los Angeles, to view the film.

"Well, Dr. Janowsky," Paul asked when the lights in the projection room went on, "how did you like it?"

"A fine film," said the consul.

"Would you say it will do well in Czechoslovakia?"

"I am sure of it," the consul replied. "Especially when you cut out Mr. Vaverka."

Paul was stunned. "But—Vaverka told me he was a popular actor in the republic. That he had played at the *Narodni divadlo*—"

"That is possible," said Dr. Janowsky. "Maybe a long time ago. However, now—well, I hate to say this about one of our people—but I did not understand what Mr. Vaverka was saying. It *sounded* like Czech, but believe me, Mr. Kohner, it was not my mother tongue."

Paul took the consul's advice. The M.C. introduction landed on the cutting-room floor. This was the actor's last appearance in front of a camera. From that time on he never got another assignment.

When all their savings were gone, Mrs. Vaverka hired herself out to homes that enjoyed Bohemian cuisine. One day Vaverka came to Paul's office. He begged Paul to help him get back to Prague. There he would find work as an actor at his home base, the National Theatre. Paul gave the Vaverkas the money for the return to Prague. With tears on his imperial face, the old actor swore he would pay back every penny.

Some months later a letter arrived. Vaverka's dreams of a new career had come to nothing. The feeling of shame at his failure had become an illness. He could not bring himself to write. But now that he was receiving a pension from the National Theatre, he was able to start paying off his debt to Paul.

Soon thereafter Paul received another letter—this one from Mrs. Vaverka. Antonin, she wrote, was disenchanted with Prague. He now had only one wish: to go back to Hollywood. The Vaverkas had saved money for the trip, and if Paul could get them a job, *any* job, they would return on the next boat.

But how could Paul possibly help the Vaverkas? One evening, discussing their situation with his friends, someone had an idea.

"You need servants, Paul. A cook, a butler—a gardener."

Paul had just rented a Spanish-style home, complete with servants' quarters. The idea appealed to him. He remembered Mrs. Vaverka's boiled beef and dumplings. He wrote them to come back. They would both have jobs in his house.

A week later in Prague Antonin Vaverka got up early. It was a lovely spring morning.

"Blatta," he said to his wife, "I had a wonderful dream. I dreamed we were back in Hollywood. We lived in a beautiful Spanish house. I worked in the garden among the flowers and you cooked in the kitchen. I smelled the *polivka* you were preparing, even. It was heavenly."

To celebrate the fine morning, he put on his best "Hollywood" suit, took hat and cane, stuck a flower in his buttonhole and went out for a stroll. Jauntily, he swung his cane as he crossed the Wenceslav Square. He didn't see the tram that was just turning the corner.

At noontime a policeman knocked at the Vaverkas' door. Antonin, he informed his wife, had been hit by a streetcar and had died in the ambulance on the way to the hospital.

The next morning Paul's letter arrived.

21

Enter Lupita

During my stay in California I often wondered about my brother's love life. He hardly ever "dated." Of course he took starlets to "openings" and to restaurants, to be "seen," photographed. But this was all part of the Hollywood scene. You had to create and sustain some "image."

Mary Philbin, his ex-fiancee, had certainly projected the virginal image. Even off the screen. The two of them together looked like a perfect valentine. But that sweet courtship had come to a sour end. Paul depicted the finale for me.

One day a "friend" told him he had seen Mary driving in a car with Big-Boy Williams, a very popular cowboy actor.

"Do you happen to know Big-Boy Williams?" Paul asked Mary casually during dinner.

She blushed.

"Well, do you?"

She nodded.

Paul drove her home. "I'd like to have my ring back," he said.

Again blushing, Mary slipped the ring off her finger.

His eyes followed her as she walked between the blossoming honeysuckle bushes toward the entrance of her house—ethereal as a sunbeam. And that was the last he saw of Mary Philbin.

Then he entered into a barren time. Evening after evening I watched him having dinner with the "boys" and then settling down to an all-night gin-rummy session. To me it was a waste of a good man.

Shortly before my return to Europe Paul and I had a dinner date. He seemed in high spirits. Something good must have happened. A new assignment? A promotion?

"We'll be picking someone up," Paul said as we drove along Cahuenga.

We pulled up on a side street, and Paul disappeared into a bungalow. I sat in the car, waiting. Curious. A short while later he emerged with a girl. In the door frame stood an elderly woman, waving after them.

I stepped out to let the girl sit in front with Paul.

"This is Lupita," Paul said.

She smiled. She looked no more than high school age. And Paul was in his late twenties. She had luminous dark eyes, black hair and a remarkably good figure. I couldn't take my eyes off her as we drove to Musso & Franks on Hollywood Boulevard. She didn't say a word all the while.

Lupita was Mexican, I learned, and had only recently arrived in Hollywood, accompanied by her grandmother. This was the first time she had ever been permitted to have dinner with a man—alone. Or rather with two men. Obviously I was asked to tag along as chaperone.

In the restaurant I watched my brother trying to communicate with this artless girl. There was that lovely corsage he suddenly produced and pinned on Lupita's summer dress. There was the ceremony of ordering—guessing her preferences exactly. And there was his soulful gaze at the beautiful young woman which expressed his total devotion.

Then came a revelation. I suddenly realized that my brother, like this charming creature, possessed a singular innocence that enhanced the romantic courtship. By his own choice, in this uninhibited center of venery, where sex was as available as a bottle of Coca-Cola, Paul played a pure Parsifal in search of the Holy Grail.

After dinner we took Lupita home. Delivering the precious package to her duenna, we went inside. Grandma Sullivan was a tall woman of Irish descent who spoke English well. She had penetrating blue eyes and carried herself like a queen. Though well advanced in years, she moved in an aura of beauty—the beauty of spirit and serenity. Regally, she asked us to sit down for a while. After a cup of tea and some homemade cookies, we left.

"What do you think?" my brother asked.

"A lovely girl."

"And a fine actress."

"Actress?"

"An absolute natural. I made tests of her. She'd be excellent for the Spanish version of *The Cat Creeps.*"

"She can't be older than sixteen," I said.

"Seventeen."

"How did she ever get here?"

He told me.

Robert Flaherty, the director of *Nanook of the North* and *Moana*, had been sent by Fox Films on a talent search to Mexico. In a private boarding school he spotted Lupita Tovar, daughter of a railroad official. She had never had any dramatic training. She just happened to be a soul-stirring beauty. For the silent films one did not need a talent for acting. To look beautiful was enough. It was the director's task to turn beauty into talent. Which sometimes happened.

Lupita, with a dozen other girls selected by Flaherty, did a screen test. She was not surprised later when she was summoned by her school's headmistress and informed that she had won a Hollywood contract. She merely fainted.

Her parents were called to the school and told the good news.

Movies? Never! the father said. It took some pleading and scheming by Mama Tovar to change her husband's mind. Only when the maternal grandmother agreed to accompany Lupita to Hollywood and act as her guardian did Señor Tovar relent.

Lupita's arrival in Los Angeles was not exactly auspicious. No one came to welcome her at the station. Grandma Sullivan enterprisingly took a cab straight to the Fox studio. After waiting with her charge for several hours, she was finally received by the casting director. Ah yes—Mr. Flaherty's Mexican discovery! What's the name? Lupita Tovar. Sounds okay. One wouldn't even have to change it.

Grandmother and granddaughter were installed in a small bungalow on Western Avenue, not far from the studio. Unfortunately, the era of silent films had just ended. Unfortunately for Lupita—because exquisite features and an attractive figure suddenly were not enough. So she sat out the routine term of six months at Fox without doing anything at all. Lupita Tovar, aged seventeen, now faced the grievous prospect of returning to Mexico without even having gone in front of Hollywood's cameras. She had expected, after all, to make some kind of imprint.

But Lupita Tovar did speak Spanish. Beautifully. And out at Universal studio, she heard, they were hiring Spanish-speaking actresses. She took the streetcar to Universal City. And there, among hundreds of compatriots, she sat waiting for the producer to appear. Who happened to be Paul Kohner.

When Paul walked into the crowded room, his eyes accosted her instantly. He beckoned her into his office. Lupita told him her story. He listened attentively—not understanding one word. While she spoke in a mellifluous voice of her disappointments, he experienced a sudden and overwhelming emotion for this ingenuous Mexican ingenue. She appealed to his knightly streak, his gallantry, his incorruptible romanticism. He wanted to help her.

He gave her the Spanish script of *The Cat Creeps*. There was a part in it that seemed to fit Lupita perfectly. Her reading of the script was merely a formality, he knew. In his mind, he had already signed her for the role.

When I left for Europe, I had the definite impression that Paul had started a new courtship. His letters to me indicated that I was correct.

From the time of their first meeting, it seems, they were frequently inseparable. Paul became Lupita's *minnesinger*. For hours he read poetry to her—German poetry, of which only the sound could have pleased her. Rilke, Heine, Hoelderlin. As he looked into her dark eyes he felt a happiness he had never known before—not with Mary, not with anyone. Because Grandma Sullivan watched strictly over her grandchild's every step, their courtship was full of scurrying and conspiracy.

But Paul did more for Lupita than woo her with poetry. He promoted her career. He pressured Universal to take her under contract. Soon she played leads in Spanish versions. Her appeal on the screen was the same that had moved Paul—that of feminine vulnerability. The films produced under Paul's supervision proved to be highly successful in Latin America.

One day a Señor Alarcon, the distributor of Universal Films in Mexico, appeared. In his attaché case he carried a movie script based on one of Mexico's most beloved romantic tales: *Santa*. He asked Lupita to read it. Lupita had naturally read the novel already, for generations of Mexican schoolgirls had shed tears over the heroine.

If Lupita took the leading role, Señor Alarcon said, there would not be much money in it; but she would have the honor of portraying a young woman dear to the hearts of all Mexicans, in the first talking picture to be produced in her native country.

The thought of separation distressed Paul. But his talent agent's instincts told him that this was Lupita's big break. His good sense also convinced him that a parting would test the strength of their relationship. So he advised her to accept the offer.

Santa was made into a memorable movie. Today, almost a half-century later, it is a classic—Mexico's own *Gone with the Wind.*

Sons and Father

ALL HIS LIFE our father had exerted great efforts to keep fit. Sleeping with wide-open windows summer and winter. Taking ice-cold showers. Walking for miles each day. Staying away from the doctor's office.

But our seemingly indestructible father suddenly fell ill. In good health until now, he suspected that something definitely dangerous and likely to be final was taking place. Something that neither time, a bottle of schnapps nor a steambath could heal.

It was the beginning of the Thirties. Recently married, I was living in Berlin. My mother phoned me to say that my father was very sick. He had lost a great deal of weight, his color was yellow and—most alarming—he had no appetite. The family doctor had suggested taking him to Vienna, which at that time had the best medical school in Europe. I persuaded her, however, to bring him to Berlin, where there was a brilliant diagnostician whose reputation overshadowed all the famous physicians of Vienna. Surely the great professor would diagnose the disease correctly and find a cure.

The first sight of my father, whom I hadn't seen for a few months, shocked me. He looked like a dying man. Gone were his imperiousness, his firmness, his inner strength—or whatever it is that enables people to overcome bodily or spiritual misfortune. Instead, his face showed unhappiness at having been uprooted from his surroundings and defiance at being brought to a city he disliked.

I took him straight to the hospital, where he was immediately received by the august German professor. After a long examination he had no diagnosis to offer. He said he would have one shortly. Meanwhile my father was to be bedded down for a period of observation.

Sadly I watched this lusty, always vital man wasting away in his hospital bed—tubes stuffed into all apertures but never complaining for a moment, trying valiantly to swallow a few bites of food, pinning all his hopes of recovery on the eminent man of medicine, whom he entertained with some of his best jokes. I felt closer to him than I ever had before, perhaps since our roles had changed. I was the man now and he the child.

After a couple of weeks of "observation" and "testing," my father had lost another twenty pounds. One afternoon I walked into the professor's private office and asked him whether it wouldn't be a good idea to take my father home to Teplitz.

"Certainly a good idea, Herr Doktor," the professor said, as if talking to a colleague. "I'm afraid I cannot be of much help. One could, of course, open him up. But why should I subject him to more suffering? I know precisely what we would find. To operate would be too late anyhow. A lovable man, your father," he added wistfully. "I shall miss his jokes."

In the absence of my older brother, I felt it my filial duty to give my father the bad news. I had figured out an elaborate scheme to cushion the shock, but as soon as I started out, my father was—as always—way ahead of me.

"I'm glad to be going home," he said. "I would never have forgiven you if you'd let me die in this awful city."

On the train home I wrote Paul, giving a detailed account of the situation and the professor's opinion that our father was obviously dying. A letter to Hollywood took from ten days to two weeks, depending on ship and plane connections. I fervently hoped that my older brother would be able to see him once more before the end.

We arrived in Teplitz in the evening. A sad family procession followed my pitifully diminished father to his home. With us was our doctor, a general practitioner, who also happened to be my recently acquired father-in-law. He knew the family as intimately as only a small-town doctor could. (He had delivered all three of us brothers.) He listened now to my report of the eminent professor's verdict. A man of touching modesty, he had not asked to take charge of my father's "case." But now he went into action.

He threw all of us out of the room so he could conduct his own examination. He pressed his ear close to my father's chest and listened. He did not have at his disposal many of the sophisticated instruments used for examination in the big cities. He believed in what his fingertips and ear told him. And they had told him that my father was by no means a terminal case.

"I suggest that we *do* operate," he said finally. "We can do this here as well as anywhere else. We have an excellent young surgeon at the hospital. It doesn't have to be today or tomorrow, but we shouldn't wait too long."

My father was much cheered by this verdict—as every doomed patient is when offered the tiniest flicker of hope. In fact, we all cheered up, believing that a miracle might be possible.

Hope sustained us in the week that followed. My father forced himself to eat and drink so as to gather strength for the ordeal ahead. And every day he asked me to run to the post office. I knew how much a letter from Paul would mean to him—to all of us in fact. Yet every morning the clerk at the small post office commiseratingly shrugged his shoulders. Nothing from Hollywood.

My father took a turn for the worse. A date was set for the operation.

On Friday evening I sat by my father's bed. Surgery was scheduled for Monday morning. Suddenly he was seized by an intense anxiety. Fear then spread over the whole household. My father had always been the firm head of the family: our secure rock, the stern administrator of our lives, our center. His indomitable presence now seemed to be leaving us.

The phone rang. Since my mother was preparing dinner in the kitchen, I went to answer it.

"This is long distance," a girl's voice said. She sounded quite excited. "I don't know if this is an April Fool's joke"—it was the first of April—"but a call is supposed to be coming through from Hollywood in America!"

"No," I said. "It is not a joke. It must be my brother calling."

The operator giggled. "We've never had a call come through from America. And Hollywood—my God—isn't that even farther than New York?"

"About three thousand miles farther," I said.

"*Jesus Maria!*" she cried. "I hope it'll work. I must tell the newspaper about it."

"How long will it take?" I inquired.

"How should I know?" She giggled again. "But I'll stay up all night if I have to—just to hear that Hollywood operator's voice."

I hung up the receiver and waited a while to control my excitement.

"Who was it?" my father asked.

"It's a call from Hollywood. The operator said it'll come through soon."

A wide smile spread over his ravaged face. "Paul," he said.

For a moment, watching that enormous glow of pride, I felt a twinge of jealousy. He called my mother to tell her the incredible news. His Paul was telephoning from the other side of the world.

But then—was it so incredible? Everything was possible with Paul the magician.

When the call finally came—about ten that night, the phone ringing insistently like a fire alarm—my father got up and marched unaided into the hallway. "Yes, my boy, I can hear you well," he said, his voice strong. "This is wonderful—but it must cost a fortune. . . . I know, *you* never mind the money, but *I* do. . . . Yes, they will operate on me Monday. . . . What is it? I should *wait?* . . . You mean, you will come here—in ten days—?"

An unbelieving smile came over his face. "Well, this is wonderful news—" He couldn't go on. He handed the receiver to my mother. She herself was too choked with emotion to talk so passed it to me. I heard my brother's voice coming clearly over a distance of seven thousand miles.

Next morning the doctor came. He thought that the operation could be postponed for a week. He would arrange it with the surgeon.

And in that week my father, anticipating Paul's return, seemed to get better before my very eyes. He had a radiance about him. He even started eating things he hadn't touched for a long time—contraband food, too. One evening he asked for a glass of beer. I dashed down the street to the corner inn to get it for him—and then watched him drink it down to the last drop.

Paul arrived ten days after the phone call. He had flown to New York on one of the first passenger flights across the American continent, then spent six days on the *Queen Mary* before taking the train to Teplitz.

Paul came rushing into the bedroom, arms outstretched. A sudden wave. They hugged each other. Hard. Tears on their faces.

"You look well, Papa," Paul said.

Our father laughed, cried. Now he didn't mind the operation. He was, in fact, looking forward to it.

A couple of days later they operated on him. Waiting for the operating-room door to open, Paul and I milled about for hours in the hospital corridor, joined by our brother Walter, a student then at the Reinhardt Theatre in Vienna. Four hours later our father was wheeled out on a stretcher. His face so small, so ashen, so dead. We stared down at him. The attendants took him to a room, lifted him onto the bed.

My father-in-law entered the room. He had been present during the operation and still wore the white hospital coat. He looked exhausted.

"There was quite a big stone in the bile duct," he said. "We took it out and the gall bladder too. But otherwise—no trace of cancer, not the slightest trace."

Our taut nerves began to unwind. We could hardly believe the good news. Not until the young surgeon walked into the room. He held up a small bottle. A single yellow marble bubbled in the formaldehyde.

"Your father will be all right," he said. "And you might want to tell my distinguished colleague in Berlin that there are more things in heaven and earth than are dreamt of in his Germanic medicine books."

He obviously enjoyed his achievement—a major triumph for a surgeon in a small town in Czechoslovakia.

23

Burning Secret

THE 'FOREIGN VERSIONS' of Universal films produced by Paul were surprisingly successful. So successful, in fact, that almost half of the company's revenues now came from the foreign market.

Paul's stock at Universal Pictures rated high. And though his salary was small compared with those of executives in similar positions elsewhere, he not only had his boss's ear but also his confidence.

So when the alarming letter about our father's illness arrived, he went directly to Laemmle.

"I've been thinking," he said, "about the excellent box-office returns from our foreign exchanges—especially from the German market. Maybe we should explore the possibility of producing pictures right in Germany. It would be much cheaper. And we could reverse our procedure here by producing films there for the American market."

"Sounds like a good idea, Kohner," said Carl Laemmle. "Go and explore."

As soon as our father was out of danger, Paul took off for Berlin. He stayed a week, investigating film-production facilities there. He ascertained what he had anticipated: that pictures could be produced in Germany at a fraction of the cost in America. He went back to California on the fastest boat, his portfolio stuffed with facts and figures. During the voyage he worked out budgets for several films he wanted to produce.

Immediately after his return he proved to the Laemmles' satisfaction that setting up a complete production organization in central Europe would be an excellent move. And it would give Universal the jump on its competitors. No other studio had an executive so thoroughly familiar with the European film scene and market as Paul Kohner. Even Laemmle Junior enthusiastically endorsed the project.

Two weeks later he was returning to Berlin—this time for a long stay.

During his two-year term as the head of the European Universal Pictures, he produced about a dozen films in three versions: English, French and German. They were generally successful both artistically and financially.

His most ambitious project was the epic *S.O.S. Iceberg*, for which he had hired director Arnold Fanck. Movies shot exclusively in the outdoors, capitalizing on the magnificent Alpine scenery, were the trademark of "Dr." Fanck. As "discoverer" of this genre, he all but monopolized it throughout the Weimar era in Germany. A geologist, he was infatuated with mountain climbing. In his zeal for proud peaks, perilous ascents, Alpine storms, avalanches and downhill ski runs from high altitudes, he brought the out-of-doors onto the screen at a time when most films offered only studio-built backgrounds.

S.O.S. Iceberg was a Fanck idea. As with all his films, the plot was simple. En route to the North Pole, a plane carrying a group of scientists (among them Leni Riefenstahl, one of Hitler's favorite actresses) is forced down somewhere on the vast frozen icecap. The people take refuge on an iceberg—from which, after many hair-raising adventures, they are finally rescued by a flotilla of Eskimos in kayaks.

The cost of the film went over a million dollars—a steep expenditure for Universal. But the brilliant scenery and photography by the German cinematographer Sepp Allgeier made up for a synthetic and predictable story.

Another notable film that Paul produced was *The Rebel*. A story about the Tyrolian revolt in 1808 against Napoleon's occupation army, it was released shortly before Hitler's takeover. The Nazi press cunningly drew a parallel between themselves and the rebellious student (played by Luis Trenker) who called for a "national uprising" against a hated enemy. To them Napoleon symbolized the "system." And the student had all the "admirable" traits of a Hitlerite. As the Nazis prepared for the ultimate assault on the crumbling republic, Dr. Goebbels made excellent propaganda use of the film—much to the disgust of Paul, who had set out to do an exciting historical film, only to find himself the champion of a cause he naturally abhorred.

Meanwhile, in Berlin too, I had started my career as a screenwriter.

One day I had a phone call from Paul. He asked me to see him right away. Since it sounded urgent, I left my work and dashed to his office.

"I want you to read this script and then tell me what the story reminds you of," he said.

After reading a few scenes I was struck by the similarity to a novel by a famous Austrian writer.

"The story has been lifted from Stefan Zweig's *Letters from an Unknown Woman*," I told him.

"Of course," Paul said grimly. "I just needed a confirmation. You must not breathe a word to anyone about this."

"I don't understand—"

"It's quite simple," Paul explained. "The writer of the script stole the Zweig story. *In toto.* Just changed the names. And no one in Hollywood is aware of it."

"But what can *you* do?"

"Buy the story from Zweig to protect the company from a lawsuit."

That evening Paul left for Salzburg to see Zweig. Two days later he was back. He told me that not only had he bought the film rights to *Letters from an Unknown Woman*, but he had also acquired them for the short novel *Burning Secret*.

I had always loved Stefan Zweig's work. In the writer I had found a potent spiritual mentor who guided my vision to the beauty in simple daily occurrences. I considered his *Burning Secret* a masterpiece. So I became quite excited when I heard Paul's news.

"What do you plan to do with *Burning Secret?*"

"Make a film out of it," he replied.

"But who will write the screenplay?"

He now looked straight at me. "Well," he said, "you know all the screenwriters here. Who do you think would be best qualified?" And he smiled.

Magically, he had once again opened a potato sack for me.

Because Hitler's takeover in Germany seemed inevitable, film producers knew that a tremendous economic and artistic upheaval was imminent. A sense of urgency prevailed among all of us connected with the cinema: especially, of course, those who were Jewish.

With a fury I went to work on the screenplay. I followed the Zweig novel closely, believing that the raw material would be understood and appreciated by any audience. For *Burning Secret* tells the story of a twelve-year-old boy's awakening to the "facts of life."

To my surprise, I finished in less than six weeks. I somehow felt the writing process should have been more agonizing. Since Paul liked my screenplay, production started almost immediately. Robert Siodmak, considered one of Germany's most brilliant avant-garde directors, was chosen to direct. The leading parts were taken by two popular actors, Willy Forst and Hilde Wagener.

The film's premiere was scheduled for March 31, 1933. On the following day, as part of Hitler's "new order," the first Nazi-organized onslaught against German Jews and boycott of their business establishments was to take place. We felt rather uneasy.

All of us who had contributed to the picture were invited to the formal opening of *Burning Secret* at the Atrium Palace, one of Berlin's most distinguished movie theatres. Besides the director and performers there were Allan Gray, the composer; Max Colpe, the lyricist; Alfred Polgar, who wrote additional dialogue—and me.

The customary American procedure of "previews" was unknown in Germany. That evening the film would meet its first audience. And while we thought we had made a fine movie, there was no telling how an audience would respond. To add to our own nervousness, an uneasy apprehension pervaded the whole theatre. One would have to be willfully blind and deaf not to sense the unmistakable signs of some momentous happening.

The house lights dimmed. The titles began to flash on the big screen. I had, of course, seen the picture in its final "cut" at the projection room. And now my heart climbed up to my throat in the expectation of seeing my own name on the screen as adapter of the literary chef-d'oeuvre.

But there were no names. Except for the picture's title and the cast listing, no other "credits" appeared. My wife and I looked at each other in disbelief. What was happening? Turning every possible explanation over and over in my mind, I could only conclude that some fantastic act of sabotage had been carried out at the last moment. But how? And—more importantly—why?

During the next two hours I became acutely aware that the audience was reacting to the film in a most unusual manner. I sensed in the viewers an intense response, an eagerness both to embrace the work and to pay its creators homage.

When the lights came on again, the audience started to applaud. First warmly, then lavishly—at last thunderously.

This was, I suddenly understood, more than unreserved approval for a well-done film. It was a spontaneous demonstration protesting a humiliating act of suppression perpetrated against the movie's creative staff, who had been denied official recognition.

When the stars appeared in front of the curtain, the audience yelled: "Director! Author!" The players looked helplessly toward the wings and then shrugged, embarrassed.

Long after the actors had retreated, the audience stood clapping and shouting and stamping, voicing their anger and defiance. The commotion showed no sign of diminishing.

In the foyer I sighted Paul. He looked ashen. Taking me aside, he told me what had happened. Universal Pictures in Berlin had received a threatening call from the office of Dr. Goebbels, Hitler's powerful minister for propaganda and editor-in-chief of the biggest Nazi newspaper, the *Angriff*. Unless all the names of the Jewish contributors to the film were eliminated, the picture would be banned from distribution throughout Germany. The frightened distributors, seeing no other way out, complied by ordering the deletion of credits. Meanwhile Paul had made some desperate but useless efforts to contact Dr. Goebbels, whom he knew personally, and who more than once—especially after viewing *The Rebel*—had asked him to continue his production work in Berlin.

All of us most responsible for the movie *Burning Secret*—director, composer, lyricist and myself—were up together much of the night, administering extreme unction to our careers in Germany. Absent from the scene was its Jewish creator, Stefan Zweig.

After the wake we went out in the street to get the morning papers. Most of the German newspapers were still in "liberal" hands. From them the film received glowing tributes—with all our names prominently displayed. But it was the swan song of the free German press. After that day—April 1, 1933—all "racially incriminated" editors were summarily dismissed, together with their liberal and leftist columnists and reviewers.

And even though a "deal" had been made between the Nazi propaganda ministry and the film's distributors, *Burning Secret* was banned from all German movie theatres as *fremdstaemmig* (of alien origin). Paul smuggled a print out of the country to the still-free city of Vienna, and there, at least, the film received a short-lived acclaim.

The Voice of the Pope
and the Voice of Kiepura

A NOT SO FUNNY thing happened to Paul on the way to the train that would take him to the relative safety of Vienna.

Driving to the Berlin train station on April 1, 1933, he caught glimpses of S.S. and S.A. men beating up old Jews on the *Kurfuerstendam*, of store windows being smashed and painted with signs that said "Jewish Shop," "Don't buy from Jews" and *"Juda verrecke!"* (Jew perish!).

He boarded the Berlin-Vienna Express and entered a compartment. There was one other passenger in the first-class section—an ascetic-looking man in a Catholic priest's habit, who was reading the morning paper. As Paul came in, he looked up and eyed him cautiously, then returned to his newspaper. Paul seemed to remember the face. Yes, there was no doubt, it was the papal nuncio to Berlin, Cardinale Pacelli. Paul had met him at a reception given by the Austrian ambassador to Germany.

"Your Excellency—" Paul addressed him once the train was going full speed—"I had the honor of meeting you at the Austrian Embassy."

The nuncio said this might be the case, though he didn't recall it. But he dropped the paper, indicating that he was not averse to polite conversation. "I'm on my way to Rome to see the Holy Father," he said. "I will be there for Easter. And where are you heading, sir?"

"I'm returning to the United States via Vienna," Paul said. Then he told him what he had witnessed on the way to the station.

The cardinal acted upset and compassionate and said that one reason for his trip was to report to His Holiness the alarming events following in the wake of Hitler's takeover.

"Mr. Laemmle gave the order to shut down Universal's film production in Berlin immediately," Paul told him.

"I well understand," the nuncio said. "Mr. Laemmle is perhaps of Jewish origin?"

"Mr. Laemmle is a German Jew from Laupheim in Wuerttemberg. What is happening here is of deep concern to him."

Cardinal Pacelli nodded gravely and went back to his newspaper.

It was a ten-hour train ride from Berlin via Passau to Vienna, and there wasn't much one could do in the small compartment except read or try to sleep. Paul did neither. He sat and studied the nuncio's sharp, pale face, the steely grey eyes glued to the paper. As he turned away from his vis-à-vis to stare out into the spring-blossoming landscape, an idea took shape. He got quite excited, but knew that the proper moment to propose it hadn't come yet.

The conductor opened the door to the compartment, announcing that lunch was being served in the dining car. The papal nuncio looked up from the paper, then curtly declined. He opened an attaché case and took out a few crackers.

Paul's appetite was fierce but he controlled it. "Your Excellency," he said, watching him munching his crackers, "I would like to submit an idea. You might want to take it up with the Holy See during your visit in Rome."

The papal emissary turned a wary eye on his fellow traveler. "Yes—?"

"To my knowledge, the Holy Father's voice has never been recorded for talking pictures," Paul continued. "And I don't think the interior of the Vatican has ever been photographed by a movie camera. If the Holy Father would give our company permission to do a film on life in the Holy City, he could transmit in it his own message of peace and hope to the whole world, reaching millions of people all over the globe."

Pacelli stopped munching his crackers. "And in which language would the Holy Father address the world?"

"In any language he chooses—and we will dub the others."

"Dub?"

Paul explained the dubbing process to him.

The papal nuncio took off his steel-rimmed glasses and started to clean them slowly. "And why would your Mr. Laemmle be interested in promoting the cause of Catholicism?" he finally asked.

"Peace and hope are universal concepts. And we need them—especially now."

"True, true," said the nuncio, smiling thinly. Paul sat tensely, awaiting a further response.

"It is a good thought, Mr. Kohner," his companion concluded. "I hope I have an opportunity to discuss it during my visit to His Holiness."

"And when will you be back in Berlin?"

"In about ten days."

"Then if you permit me, I shall keep in touch with you. I can easily postpone my departure for the States."

"But, you understand, I cannot make any promises. I can only bring matters to the attention of His Holiness."

"I understand fully."

The nuncio—and future Pope Pius XII—withdrew behind the protective darkness of his overcoat to take a nap.

Paul went to the diner. Instead of lunch, he ordered a paper pad. On it he composed a cablegram to Laemmle that reported on the meeting with the papal nuncio and even laid the groundwork for a complete scenario. Carried away by his innate optimism, he only casually dropped a line at the end of the cable saying that the whole project depended, of course, on getting the Pope's consent.

By the time he finished writing, the train had pulled into the border station of Passau. He used the one-hour stop to dash to the nearest telegraph office and dispatch the cable to Hollywood. The telegraph clerk was stunned. Never in all his life had he figured out the cost of a 200-word telegram. And to America, yet.

In Vienna Paul took up residence at the Hotel Sacher. Twenty-four hours later Laemmle's answer arrived.

EXCELLENT PROJECT KEEP STRICTLY CONFIDENTIAL
STAY EUROPE TILL DECISION LAEMMLE

And now a nagging time of waiting started. To be sure, there are worse places in which to bide one's time than Vienna in the spring. For instance, the State Opera was right across the street from the hotel, so Paul, an opera buff, attended every performance.

The rage of Vienna then was the Polish tenor Jan Kiepura. Kiepura's voice was considered the richest, the most exciting, in all of Europe. Paul heard him for the first time as Rodolpho in *La Bohème*, and no sooner had the last curtain come down on applause of ecstatic proportions than he was hurrying backstage.

So far Kiepura had not succumbed to the blandishments of agents and impresarios who made him spectacular offers if he would go to the States. But when Paul approached him he listened. He listened because

Paul was not just another middleman—but the production head of a well-known film company.

"Would you consider coming to America to make a movie for Universal?" he asked.

"That depends. I am under contract to the State Opera. The only time I could do it would be during the summer months."

"I think that can be arranged," Paul said—and dashed off another cable to Uncle Carl.

Kiepura's fame had not reached Hollywood yet, so Laemmle had to rely on Paul's judgment. Thus the answer that came was ambiguous. On the one hand he wanted to outdistance his competitors; on the other he didn't wish to pay a six-figure salary.

"CAN YOU SEND RECORDS WITH KIEPURA'S VOICE?" he wired.

Paul didn't feel comfortable with this approach, and neither did Kiepura. Besides, just at that moment another film offer for the singer came along—from MGM. Paul knew he had to act fast.

By then he had become a steady after-theatre guest of Kiepura and his wife, Martha Eggerth, a famous operetta star. One evening after an opera performance, he asked Kiepura, "Would you be willing to sing for Laemmle over the telephone?

"You're joking."

"No—I'm serious."

Kiepura had had a few drinks—which helped him decide. "Okay. Call him, I'll sing for him."

Past midnight in Vienna, it was afternoon in California. Paul figured that Uncle Carl would be at his desk in Universal City. His hunch was correct.

"You're very free with my money on cables and calls," Laemmle said edgily. "What is it this time, Kohner?"

"I'm talking from Mr. Kiepura's suite," Paul said. "He has just received an offer from MGM, and we'd better sign him right away if we don't want to lose him."

Whenever Laemmle was apprised of another studio's interest, the gambler in him surfaced. "How much have they offered?"

Paul named the figure.

"We cannot top that," said Laemmle curtly.

"I know. But here is the situation: Kiepura wants to do a picture with *me*. He'd be willing to forgo the higher offer. To cut a record and send it would take two weeks, Mr. Laemmle. So I have induced Mr. Kiepura to give you a sample of his voice over the phone. He'll sing one of his most popular songs—and I'll accompany him on the piano."

Laemmle seemed so startled that he didn't remonstrate. Paul turned the phone over to the tenor, seated himself at the piano. And Kiepura—holding the instrument like a microphone—belted out the current hit *"Heute Nacht oder nie"* (This Night or Never).

After Kiepura finished singing, he gave the receiver back to Paul.

"Well, Mr. Laemmle, what do you think?"

Instead of answering, Laemmle asked, "What sort of deal can you make?"

The figures were all prepared. Paul read them off a pad.

"Is that the best we can do?"

"It's practically half of the MGM offer."

"Okay, Kohner," Laemmle said grudgingly. "Close the deal. But remember—it's your head."

One deal made—and one more to go. Paul now waited to hear from the papal nuncio.

During his stay in Vienna he had phoned the papal office in Berlin several times. When Pacelli's secretary told him that the nuncio was on his way back from Rome, Paul took the next train to the German capital.

The morning after the nuncio's arrival, Paul called to ask for an interview. The alertness of the secretary's response clearly indicated that the news was good.

"I have submitted your proposal to His Holiness," Pacelli told Paul. "The Holy Father is willing to appear on the screen. He has instructed me to initiate the preliminary steps. I assume that first a scenario, or whatever you call it, will have to be written and then submitted. Am I correct?"

"Correct," Paul said jubilantly.

"Then we will see more of each other," the nuncio said—and dismissed Paul with a friendly nod.

This was the kind of organizing project that Paul enjoyed. Again he had produced a rabbit—and the rabbit was already off and away.

He traveled to Rome to make the initial arrangements. He hired an Italian writer to do the screenplay. Painstakingly he searched for an Italian crew, swearing everyone to secrecy. He cabled almost daily to Hollywood. The code word "Rome" was established for the exchange of messages.

Not all the cables were addressed to Carl Laemmle. Many of them went to Lupita Tovar. Paul also wrote long love letters—and got short replies in a laboriously acquired school English, telling him about her studio work, her longing for him, her occasional dates with his friends. Moody with frustration, he suffered waves of self-pity, jealousy and yearning.

His stay in Europe was now prolonged for an undetermined stretch of time. After several days of wrangling with himself, he finally made the most important long-distance call of his life.

It was early morning in Hollywood. Roused from sleep, Lupita thought that one of Paul's friends was pulling a practical joke on her.

"But it's really me—" Paul insisted, across thousands of miles of humming wire. Abandoning all the proper opening phrases he had prepared, he simply stammered: "Will you come over here and marry me?"

There was the barest moment of hesitation. "Of course I will!" Lupita said.

Two weeks later she arrived in Berlin. Which by then was wholly

Hitler's Berlin, in Hitler's Germany. Nineteen-year-old Lupita, speaking only Spanish and a smattering of English, felt strange and confused.

Paul took her to Teplitz, to meet the family before their marriage. Her youth, her foreignness, her stunning beauty, created a small-town sensation. To please our parents my brother persuaded her to convert to Judaism. Just a formality, he assured her. Some instructions from the local rabbi in Jewish lore in preparation for the Jewish wedding ceremony.

At the wedding, which took place in our home, the learned rabbi had availed himself of the services of the only Sephardic Jew in the community, who had translated the rabbi's speech into Spanish. The bride listened—in utter consternation. Sometimes she seemed to hear the sound of her mother tongue, but Ladino—a medieval Jewish Castilian dialect—wasn't exactly Spanish.

Immediately after the ceremony the pair returned to Berlin.

Project "Rome" was going well. The finished script was submitted to Cardinal Pacelli. After a few minor changes, it received papal approval. Paul made another trip to Rome to set up a shooting schedule. Cables sped back and forth. Finally everything was set for the start of production.

One morning, just as Paul was packing his suitcases to move to Rome, the nuncio's office called. The secretary told him that a small matter the nuncio had not previously introduced must now be dealt with. Could he come and see him? Paul went at once to the papal office.

"The Holy See," the secretary there said amiably, "would like to know what sum of money the American film company has in mind."

"Sum of money—for *what?*" Paul inquired apprehensively.

"For granting your company access to the Vatican and—most of all—for giving Universal Pictures the rights to record and reproduce the Holy Father's voice."

Silence. An exchange of money had never been discussed in the negotiations. Paul had simply assumed that the filming would be done without charge.

"What sum did the papal nuncio have in mind?" he asked tightly.

"One hundred thousand dollars," said the secretary coolly.

"Well—" Paul cleared his throat. "That seems a rather large sum for a small film. I will relay your request to Mr. Laemmle and then let you know what he says."

He sent a wire off to Hollywood to inform Laemmle that the Vatican expected a contribution to the Church in the amount of fifty thousand dollars. He felt that this figure would make an acceptable counter offer.

He waited for Laemmle's reply. The next day, when no answer came, he put a call through to California. Mr. Laemmle, he was told, was on his way to New York.

Paul waited another day, then sent an urgent cable to the New York office.

Still no answer.

Frantically he raced between his hotel and the telegraph office, thinking of all the possible reasons for the silence. Intramural intrigue at Universal. Laemmle's annoyance. Nazi interference with communications.

On the third day he phoned New York. Laemmle had not yet arrived. He told an executive there to urge Laemmle to respond to his messages immediately.

Another forty-eight hours of waiting. Finally a cablegram arrived. It contained two words:

FORGET POPE

25

Next Time We Love

HOLLYWOOD IS NOT a place to which one can easily return in less than triumph. Paul had been away for over two years. He didn't know what to expect there. The pictures he had produced in Europe had been successful—but mainly in Europe. Only *S.O.S. Iceberg* had been released in America, barely recovering the huge initial investment.

Paul was surprised, therefore, by his cordial reception at the studio.

Universal was in trouble. The change from the silent movies to the "talkies" had been made—but not as successfully as by the other "majors." Universal was essentially a family business, with production responsibilities shared by Carl Laemmle Jr. and Stanley Bergerman, Rosabelle's husband. And as so often happens with families, there were strong currents of jealousy and rivalry. Now this somehow worked to Paul's advantage. He found the younger Laemmle amenable to his re-entry into home-base production. And he was asked to look through story properties and select one to film.

Paul picked a novel by Ursula Parrot, *Next Time We Live*. A screenplay was written, then submitted to Margaret Sullavan, the actress-wife of his old friend William Wyler, who by now had become a prominent Hollywood director. She liked it, so he succeeded in luring her—a much sought-after star—to Universal. For the male leads he chose two unknowns: James Stewart and Ray Milland.

Released under the title *Next Time We Love*, the picture got excellent reviews and pleased American audiences.

But it wasn't enough to bail Universal out.

The family enmities persisted—and worsened. The junior Laemmle had literally grown up at Universal City. The studio was his schoolroom, his father the instructor. Throughout the years, Laemmle had never taken a trip abroad without having his son at his side. The boy became familiar with every facet of the company's operation. He watched, thought, breathed, *lived* movies—knew no other world. He felt—perhaps rightly so—that *he* alone should head production.

Surveying the sagging box-office charts, Laemmle Junior put the blame squarely on his father's stubborn refusal to assign Bergerman to a position that would better fit his capabilities. Then one day, at the end of a vituperous argument, Laemmle unceremoniously divested the crown prince of his powers.

That was easy to do. No one at Universal had a contract. Not even Laemmle Junior.

All this happened on a Friday afternoon.

On Saturday morning, Carl Laemmle called Paul. "I'm going to Caliente for the weekend. Like to come along?"

It sounded more like a plea. "Of course, Mr. Laemmle," Paul said. And packed his suitcase.

Sitting alone with Laemmle in the chauffeur-driven car, Paul saw how upset the Old Man really was. Hiding behind the tough little man from Laupheim was a not-so-tough Jewish father. His self-assurance had vanished. Obviously he regretted his action toward his son, but pride stood in the way of an apology.

In which ways or moments can two human beings really relate to each other? Generally, the process is gradual. But now, in his distress, Carl Laemmle regarded his protégé for the first time as a friend. His face revealed a desperate and wordless appeal for help. Paul, immediately sensitive to the change, offered to do what the older man could *not* do. He asked Laemmle's consent to try to bring about a reconciliation.

"I'd appreciate that," said Laemmle, the tired eyes behind the thick glasses watering. "Maybe Junior could come to Caliente and see me."

The car was just going through La Jolla. They stopped, and Paul made a dash for the telephone. When he returned, he could inform Uncle Carl that his son would be with him that evening.

Laemmle seemed overcome with relief and gratitude. "I've always looked upon you almost as a second son, Kohner," he blurted out. "And now you've acted like a good son to me. I'm in your debt. And I'll do something about it as soon as I'm back at the studio. You have never had a contract with us. I'm getting on. And as my dear mother said, 'A young man can die, an old man must die.' I will give you a long-term contract with Universal that will protect you in case something should happen to me. How much do we pay you now?"

"Five hundred," Paul said—quietly amused, because he was aware that Laemmle knew the salary of the least of his office boys.

"I'll raise you to seven hundred and fifty," Laemmle said magnanimously. "And I'll give you a seven-year contract with a two hundred and fifty dollar yearly raise. How does that sound to you?"

Not quite believing what he had heard, Paul replied that it would please him enormously.

"Who knows?" Laemmle went on expansively. "One day you might even be running the studio."

Then he cocked his head and beamed at Paul. My brother had never seen him so delighted with himself.

Exit

A FEW MONTHS LATER, Paul was having dinner with Preston Sturges at the Brown Derby on Vine Street—the "in" place for "in" people.

He had just made a contract with Sturges to write and direct his new production, *The Song of Joy*, a musical which was to star Martha Eggerth. Sturges was in great demand in Hollywood, and Paul felt fortunate to have signed him. His talents as a director for both the macabre and the lighthearted along with his charismatic charm as a human being were already legendary. His talk, festive and brilliant, kept a hundred colorful friends flocking around him.

Frank Orsatti stopped at their table to say hello. He was a talent agent—one of the first around town. Partly because of his personal friendship with MGM's Louis B. Mayer, he wielded great power.

"How are things, Paul?" Orsatti asked, flopping down in the leather-upholstered booth. "I hope I'm not butting in."

"You are," Preston Sturges said curtly.

"Well, you boys better look for a new location to do your work in," Orsatti said amiably. "I hear Laemmle has sold Universal."

"You're crazy," Paul said.

"It's not official yet. But get your ass out fast."

"How the hell do you know?" asked Sturges.

"I just know, smart-ass," Orsatti retorted. And having delivered this invidious news item, he grinned and walked away.

Paul's face was drained of color.

"Jesus, Paul—" Sturges said. "If anyone would know about this, it should certainly be you. When did you see the Old Man last?"

"A couple of hours ago."

"And he didn't mention anything?"

"Not a word."

"Screw Orsatti," Sturges said.

Early next morning Paul waited in Laemmle's outer office. He had slept little. Whenever under strain, he would keep twirling a gold chain around his right index finger. This day he must have whirled that chain a few hundred times before Laemmle appeared—smiling his benign smile and beckoning his secretary, Jack Ross, to follow him into his private office.

"I must talk to you, Mr. Laemmle," said Paul, almost pushing Ross aside. "Alone."

Warily, Uncle Carl retreated behind his desk and dismissed Ross. "What's on your mind, Kohner?"

"I heard a weird rumor last night," Paul said. "About the sale of the company."

Carl Laemmle's face broke into a wide grin. "Just a rumor."

"Then it's not true—?"

"Well, there *is* an offer," Laemmle said pleasantly. "You know we're not in the best shape financially, and I needed half a million right away. The bank refused. So I gave someone an *option* to buy us out. But don't worry, Kohner. This man will never come up with the balance—five million in cash. Never."

Paul stared at the old man incredulously. "You want to sell Universal—for *five and a half million dollars?*"

"Cochrane thought it was a respectable deal. In fact, he told me it was an excellent offer."

"Who made it?" Paul asked.

"A group. A syndicate headed by Charlie Rogers. But you can be quite certain that they won't be able to raise that sort of money."

But "quite" wasn't good enough for Paul. Stunned by the pitifully small figure Carl Laemmle had put on his empire, he was sure that anyone with any business sense at all would manage to close that deal.

"Did you discuss this with Junior?"

"Of course."

"And what will happen to him if the option is picked up?"

"He'll stay with the studio, of course. He's got a long-term contract now."

A contract. Long-term. Yet Laemmle had never made good on the promise given to him on the way to Caliente. Paul had felt reluctant to remind him, hoping that Laemmle would remember on his own. He was still drawing five hundred dollars on a week-to-week basis.

His whole livelihood was suddenly at stake.

"How about *me*, Mr. Laemmle?" he asked. "What will happen to me if the sale goes through?"

Laemmle chuckled. "*You*, Kohner? A man like you—with your experience, with your knowledge of the European market, and just having produced a successful picture—why, they'd be fools to let you go! Besides, if the deal should materialize—which as I told you is highly doubtful—I will talk to Charlie about you. So don't worry."

"But I *do* worry," Paul said bitterly. "I'd say this is the moment to give me the contract you promised."

Laemmle was cupping his right ear with his hand. Actually, he had heard quite well, but he needed time to formulate his answer.

"Contract? What contract?"

"The one you promised me when we were going to Caliente."

"You don't have to yell," Laemmle said sharply. "I can hear you. Unfortunately, the agreement stipulates that the syndicate must honor existing contracts only. I have no legal right to draw up new contracts during the three-month option period."

Suddenly Paul found himself reaching out for the big alabaster ashtray on Laemmle's desk—and smashing it down on the glass top. Then he ran out of the office.

He went to the parking lot, got into his car and sat there for a while, trying to calm down. He was trembling. He felt ashamed of his outburst, remorse for having turned against his benefactor—the man who had brought him to America, and to Hollywood.

But he couldn't make himself go back and apologize. What now? Should he drive home? He didn't want to tell Lupita yet of this final humiliation.

A car pulled into the parking place next to his. Paul recognized Frank Orsatti.

The agent walked over to him. "What's the matter, Paul?" he inquired. "You don't look too hot."

"I just quit," Paul said.

"Aha! Didn't I tell you?"

"I still can't believe it," Paul said.

"It'll be tough on you to work somewhere else—after all those years with Uncle Carl," Orsatti said. "You got an agent?"

"Never needed one."

"How would you like me to get you a new deal? Like—with MGM?"

"Why not?" Paul said defiantly. "The sooner the better."

An Expensive Lie

IT WAS SAID in those days that only three people could get through to MGM's boss, Louis B. Mayer: the President of the United States, William Randolph Hearst—and Frank Orsatti.

Thus when Orsatti dialed Mayer's office requesting an appointment, he got it immediately.

"How much did you make at Universal?" Orsatti asked Paul on their way to the studio.

"Five hundred."

"That's all?" Orsatti stared at him.

"That's all."

"Jesus!" Orsatti moaned. "Is it possible? Now, if I can close a deal for you with L.B., we've got to up that figure. At least two hundred and fifty. I know Mayer's way of thinking. If he hears you only made five hundred, he wouldn't be interested in you."

"If Laemmle had made good his promise to me, I would have been making seven hundred and fifty some while ago," Paul said bitterly.

As they waited in the outer office, Paul looked around him. Mayer was leaving that night for New York and Europe, so there was a constant coming and going of secretaries and other personnel.

Finally they were ushered into Mayer's office. As Orsatti started to extol Paul Kohner's talents like a sideshow barker, Mayer cut him short. "Sorry, Frank, but I've got to leave for the station. The train won't wait for me."

"Why don't you let Kohner go with you? You can talk to him on the way."

"Okay," said Mayer after a moment's hesitation. "Come along."

So Paul accompanied him to the waiting limousine. He knew that he had about forty minutes to sell himself. It had been a trying day for him, and he felt low. On the other hand, he was always sparked by challenges like this. How often had he sat in Carl Laemmle's car selling him actors, directors, stories, business plans?

"Tell me about yourself," Mayer asked as they started toward the downtown railroad station.

Paul did. He gave Mayer a synopsis of his professional background. He said he had quit Universal when he learned that Laemmle was about to sell out.

Mayer had a keen eye for talent of many kinds. He was clearly impressed with Paul's knowledge of the production end of the film business.

When they arrived at the station, Mayer invited Paul into his fully equipped office in the pullman car. The train was releasing steam, impatient to depart.

"When could you start working for us?" asked Mayer.

"Right away."

"What was your salary at Universal?"

For one beat Paul hesitated. Then he said, "Seven-hundred-fifty."

"We'll pay you the same. For one year. One thousand the second year."

And without waiting for Paul's consent, he dictated two notes to his secretary—one addressed to Eddie Mannix, the studio's business head, the other to Frank Orsatti. He specified the terms of the deal with Kohner: a straight two-year contract with options for future service.

Then Mayer dismissed Paul with a curt nod.

The train pulled out of the station.

Paul's magical salesmanship had worked again. But he felt uneasy. He couldn't get rid of a nagging thought that he had twisted the truth. And though he knew he had only acted on his agent's shrewd advice, his conscience still bothered him.

Later in the evening he called Orsatti and briefed him on the meeting with Mayer. Hoping for reassurance, he certainly received it lavishly.

"Anyone in your place would have done the same," he told Paul. "Don't lose sleep over it. Besides, no one will ever find out, believe me."

A few days later Paul reported at MGM.

He was given a producer's suite in the Thalberg building. At noontime a brass plate with his name appeared on the door.

Slowly he began to unwind. Announcements of his new position appeared in the trade papers. His friends and co-workers at Universal called to wish him well. But no call came from Carl Laemmle. (A few months later, after the deal with Roger's syndicate was indeed consummated, Paul paid a visit to his former boss. He expressed regrets over that violent outburst—and was forgiven. In fact, Uncle Carl generously congratulated Paul on his move.)

Paul sat in his plush office, waiting. He ate luncheon with fellow producers at the VIP table in the commissary. Introduced around, he felt welcomed. In search of a property for his initial production at MGM, he began to read story materials. And on payday Orsatti delivered in person Paul's first salary check. All was right again with Paul's world.

When he came into his office on the following Monday, his secretary told him that Eddie Mannix wanted to see him. Next to Mayer, Mannix was the most powerful man at the studio. A rugged Irishman whose professional career had begun as a bouncer in an amusement park, he was noted not only for physical strength but also for his blunt language.

As Paul entered his office, Mannix fixed a chilly eye on him. "I've dictated a draft of your deal with us, Kohner," he said grimly. "I have adjusted one point. Your salary."

There was a pause. Then, "You know what I'm talking about?"

"Mr. Mannix—" Paul began, but got no farther.

"You told Mr. Mayer that your salary at Universal was seven hundred and fifty a week?" Eddie Mannix leaned forward. "You were lying, Kohner."

It was the worst trap Paul had ever gotten himself into.

"Your highest salary at Universal was five hundred," Mannix went on, relentlessly. "And that's the salary we're going to pay you. For two years. That is the time commitment Mr. Mayer made. Why, I don't know. But it's not my department."

Paul felt faint. "I'm sorry," he mumbled, "but my agent—"

"That's all, Kohner," Mannix said in a gravelly voice. "If I were Mr. Mayer I would not honor this contract. But I am not Mr. Mayer. All *I* can do is see to it that you never get a production assignment as long as I'm business manager here."

The next few hours were the bleakest in Paul's career. His first thought was to walk off the lot—resigning before signing the contract. But there were economic considerations. While his salary at Universal had not measured up to his high status as a producer, it was still a respectable sum of money. And he had no savings. He lived well. After their return from Europe, he and Lupita had rented a small estate on Toluca Lake. He was generous and supported his family in Teplitz. And he also gambled at high stakes. No, he could not sacrifice a $25,000 a year income!

The only thing he could do, Paul decided, was to work hard and try to cancel out this unfortunate mistake in judgment. And in a way he felt relieved now that the lie had been exposed.

Orsatti promised to talk to L. B. and take the blame himself. But he never did, for by the time the MGM boss came back from Europe the incident seemed to be forgotten.

Week after week Paul submitted scripts he wanted to produce. They were returned—all unacceptable. "Not a bad idea, but—"; "Too costly"; "We had no luck with Austrian schmaltz"; "Interesting, but not for right now"; and so on.

Then a summons came from the Front Office. There L. B. Mayer introduced Paul to Ben Goetz, a highly respected man in the industry who up to then was the head of the largest Hollywood film lab.

"We're going to open a studio in London," Mayer explained. "Mr. Goetz will be in charge of production. With your knowledge of the Continent and your experience in producing abroad, you could be of great help to him."

Paul quickly saw this as an excellent opportunity to re-enter the film production field in Europe—if he wanted to. He asked for time to consider the proposal.

He stalled. Sitting around Ben Goetz's office for a few weeks, he helped him plan the British production set-up. Goetz—a gentle, considerate

A Paul Kohner Album

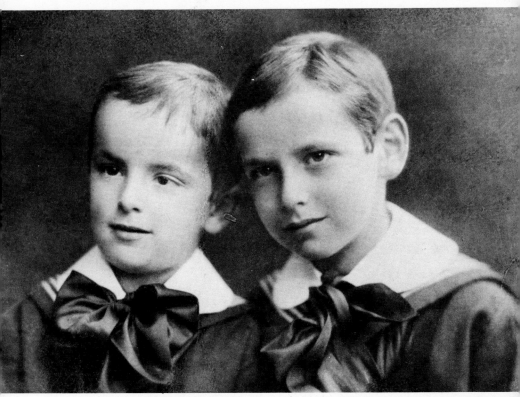

Frederick Kohner (then Fritz) and Brother Paul, the Magician

The Magician as a Youngster,
Apprentice, and Practitioner

The "Greenhorn" on New York's Broadway in 192

A second Thalberg?

Paul as Universal's casting director with the great George Arliss

The Kino Kohner on a visit to the U.S. in 1921. From left to right: Paul, Fathe
Kohner, D. W. Griffith, Arthur Robitschek, representing the Filmscha

ino Kohner" in his brief bid for a Western sheriff's role with Harry Carey

Hollywood Al Fresco (circa 1927): Among the celebrities are Maurice Stiller, Maria Korda, Mary Philbin, Emil Jannings, Conrad Veidt, Director Paul Leni, and, in the background, Ernest Laemmle and Carl Laemmle, Jr.

Lupit.

Hollywood Rococo: From left, German Consul-General von Hantzig, Dolores del Rio, Ernst Lubitsch, Maurice Chevalier, Yvonne Valet (Mrs. Chevalier), Paul Kohner, Vilma Banky, Carl Laemmle

On the set of *The Man Who Laughs*: Conrad Veidt, Mary Philbin, von Stroheim, Producer Paul Kohner, Director Paul Leni

Paul Kohner and Carl Laemmle—the Apprentice and the Maste

"rofessor Einstein, may I introduce President Laemmle?"

With German Ace Ernst Udet

With Austrian Chancellor Engelbert Dollfuss shortly before the Chancellor's assassination. (In background, Publicist Joe Weill.)

aul and Lupita, newlyweds, with Parents Julius and Helene Kohner

Mexican General Cedillo visits the set of *Next Time We Love*, Paul's own production, with Margaret Sullavan and Jimmy Stewart, and Director E. H. Griffith.

William Wyler, Universal director, Carl Laemmle, Jr., and Paul Kohner upon
the latter's return from Europe

At the 75th birthday party for Albert Basserman given by Paul Kohner, from left, standing, Ernst Lubitsch, Fritzi Massary, William Dieterle; seated, Basserman, Charlotte Dieterle

German Star O.W. Fischer arriving in Hollywood, welcomed by Paul, Director Henry Koster, and Star June Allison

Two happy Kohners, Paul and Actress-Daughter Susan

Lupita and Paul with Maurice Chevalier

In production of *Pepe* in Cuernavaca, Mexico: Edward G. Robinson, Lupita Kohner, and Paul

With Ernest "Papa" Hemingway (Papa thought Paul was the money man)

With John Huston and Dino de Laurentiis in Cannes

With Federico Fellini in Rome

With life-long friend William Wyler

Identity crisis solved: The mysterious B. Traven reveals himself to his agent
Paul, shortly before Traven's death

With Superstar Liv Ullmann

Spring in the Eternal City: Paul with Clients and Friends Ingmar Bergman and
Liv Ullmann

Paul makes a point on set of *The Touch* in Stockholm with Client Max vo
Sydow and Ingmar Bergma

n the set of *The White Buffalo* with Producer-Son Pancho Kohner and Star
harles Bronson

Painter Paul Clement with Jill Ireland (Mrs. Charles Bronson) holding Daughter
Zuleika. Painting was a Christmas gift of Paul to the Bronsons.

The three Kohner Brothers: Paul, Fritz, Walter

The Magician in front of his laboratory (197

man—liked this experienced assistant but knew that Paul was reluctant to go to London.

One day at noontime, on his way to luncheon at the commissary, Paul passed by Irving Thalberg. When Thalberg's eyes caught Paul's, he abruptly turned and asked him to come to his office after lunch.

Now what was this? Thalberg was perhaps the least accessible man in Hollywood. Although in charge of all MGM film production, his name never appeared on a credit line. ("If you have the power to put your name on the screen, your name is meaningless," he once said.) But virtually every prestigious picture produced by MGM in the early Thirties had Thalberg's unmistakable "imprint" on it.

Why did Thalberg want to see him right away? Paul wondered. Pleasantly excited, he rushed over to Thalberg's office later on and was immediately admitted.

"No calls," Thalberg instructed his secretary.

Paul and Thalberg, who were about the same age, had only a nodding acquaintance. Thalberg, however, was surely aware that Paul Kohner had often been regarded as his successor at Universal.

"I'm glad that we finally have a chance to sit down and get to know each other," Thalberg started out. "How do you like working here?"

"If I were *working*," Paul said pointedly, "I'd probably like it fine."

"Aren't you with Goetz now?"

"At the moment. But I've decided not to go to England with him."

"Why not?"

"There are many reasons. Mostly personal ones. Above all, though, I hope to produce myself. I don't think I'd make a good assistant."

"You did some fine work for Laemmle in Europe. I also liked the picture you did with Maggie Sullavan and Jimmy Stewart here. What was the title?"

"*Next Time We Love*," Paul supplied, trying not to show his growing excitement. Thalberg did not indulge in aimless small talk. It had been a long time since Paul felt hopeful about his career.

Now Thalberg reclined in his swivel chair. "I've looked into the properties you have suggested since you've been working here. Mr. Mayer didn't like them. Frankly, I didn't either—with one exception." He brought the chair forward with a jerk. "*Victoria*. I like *Victoria*. I read it as a young man, and I just finished reading it again. It would be a wonderful role for Norma, wouldn't it?"

Norma Shearer, Thalberg's wife, had just played Juliet in Metro's production of *Romeo and Juliet*.

"She would be the ideal choice," Paul said, quite honestly.

"Tell me, Kohner," Thalberg probed carefully. "I understand you own the rights to the story. How did you ever get Hamsun to sell them to you? We've tried several times to buy his *Growth of the Soil*. We made him very generous offers. He turned us down."

"I bought the rights to *Victoria* from Knut Hamsun personally."

"And how in hell did you do that?"

"It's a long story," Paul said. And told it to him.

A young Norwegian writer, Erling Bergendahl, had fallen on hard times in Hollywood. Discouraged, virtually starving, he hung around Universal studio, along with so many other unemployed artists. Eventually Paul noticed him and took him to dinner. He offered to read some of his stories. Bergendahl's prose was unremarkable, but his personality appealed to Paul. So he bought a story just to help Bergendahl pay his passage back to Norway. How could he repay such kindness? Bergendahl asked. He might introduce him to Knut Hamsun, Paul suggested. He knew that Bergendahl was a friend and protégé of Hamsun, who was wary of strangers and almost a recluse.

On his next trip to Europe, Paul phoned Bergendahl. "Can you come up immediately?" the Norwegian wanted to know. Paul flew to Oslo, and Bergendahl drove him to a secluded farm in a northern province. There, Hamsun, the Nobel Prize winner, received Paul warmly, impressed to find such a devotee of his work. Paul had indeed read all of Hamsun's books and was especially fond of *Victoria*, which as a boy he knew almost by heart.

Hamsun went to his bookshelf, took out a copy of the book and inscribed it to Paul.

"You have been very kind to my young friend Bergendahl," he said. "If I can do you a favor in return, please tell me."

Paul paused for a moment. "*Victoria* would make a beautiful film. If you would grant me the motion picture rights—"

"They are yours," Hamsun said simply. "But please do not send me any of those middlemen. Just write out a letter now and give me the money you think the story is worth to you."

"Would you accept five thousand dollars?" Paul asked quickly.

"That is a great deal of money," Hamsun said. "Can you afford it?"

Paul thought he could.

"Pay me whenever you can," Hamsun told him. "There is no hurry. As you see, I am not starving. The soil gives me all I need."

So Paul composed a letter of agreement, and Hamsun signed his name to the document.

"Amazing," Thalberg commented after Paul had finished his tale.

He looked at Paul thoughtfully for a while. Then he said, "I will tell you something that is still confidential. I trust you not to talk to anyone about it. I am resigning as head of production at MGM and will form my own production unit. The pictures I produce will be released through MGM— but otherwise I'll be completely independent. My contract with Mayer has one more year to go. Then I'm my own boss. In the meantime I'm preparing my program. And getting ready to recruit and develop my own staff."

Thalberg paused. "I would like to do *Victoria* as my first film, Kohner. And I want *you* to produce it for me. You'll have Norma for the lead and we will get the best possible leading man for Johannes. We'll pick a director we both feel would do justice to the book. Put your price on the property—but don't make it too steep. Meanwhile, get busy. Concentrate on finding a top-notch writer for the screenplay, then come and see me as soon as you have him."

Thalberg got up and held out his hand. "Do we have a deal, Kohner?"

"I would be most happy to work with you," Paul said. They shook hands.

Paul floated back to his own office. Now what would Mannix say? Louis B. Mayer? Laemmle? Everyone who had turned *Victoria* down. And everyone who had failed to value Paul sufficiently.

It would be difficult to keep silent. But he had to tell *someone*. So he told Lupita, of course. Then he placed a long-distance call to Czechoslovakia. Our father had always dreamed of seeing Israel someday, but he could never afford to go. Now Paul told him jubilantly that a check for the trip would be in the mail.

And to celebrate this fabulous new prospect, he took Lupita for the weekend to the nearby mountain resort of Lake Arrowhead. It was September. The leaves were turning. There were long walks and talks with Lupita during which they speculated about the future. All of Paul's hopes and longings—personally, professionally—seemed almost fulfilled.

While they took the long drive home, Paul turned the car radio on. The first item of news made him swerve the car sharply to a stop on the soft shoulder of the highway.

At his home in Santa Monica, thirty-seven-year-old Irving Thalberg had just died after a brief bout with pneumonia.

A Stretch at Columbia

MEANWHILE, I WAS in London, trying to make a living as a screenwriter. I had taken one seemingly preordained route of the refugees from Nazi persecution: first stop France; next England.

Prospects were grim. Writing in a foreign language created an almost insurmountable barrier. I worked occasionally for an "emigré producer," but my scripts had to be translated from the German. None of them ever reached the screen.

No wonder I developed stomach ulcers. Eventually I got so sick I couldn't leave my bed. Every week a little man from the Immigration Bureau paid me a visit. "I trust you'll be better next week," he said, unmoved by my misery. "Don't forget—you can't settle down in this country."

I knew I couldn't. But where could I go, with my wife and young child?

Enter the magician, by way of a telegram:

COLUMBIA PICTURES OFFERING YOU SIX MONTHS CONTRACT
TWO HUNDRED FIFTY PER WEEK WHEN CAN YOU ARRIVE

Two weeks later we left for the States.

This time my arrival on the West Coast seemed more auspicious. I had a contract with a major movie studio. And my brother had rented a small Spanish house, complete with a maid, that was waiting for me and my family.

"How did you manage it?" I asked Paul. "And how will *I* manage—not being able to write in English?"

"They will assign an American writer to work with you. There are many European writers here, and they all work with collaborators."

It sounded simple.

"The six-months contract is just a formality," Paul went on. "As long as I'm at Columbia, you'll have a job there."

That's how I learned that Paul had moved from MGM to Columbia.

But he didn't seem exactly happy. Soon I found out why.

I called the office of the president of Columbia Pictures and asked for an interview.

Next morning I was ushered through a row of antechambers into the presence of my employer. At the far end of a spacious room—behind a circular desk (raised, I guessed, to give the man behind it added power and stature), flanked by a battery of telephones—sat Harry Cohn. And behind him hung a photograph of Mussolini.

He looked up. "You're Kohner?"

I nodded.

"What do you want?"

I was startled. "I want to introduce myself," I said. "And to thank you for bringing me over."

"Thank your brother. He insisted that I hire you. It was part of the deal with him."

I stared past him at the picture of the Italian dictator.

"Anything else?" Harry Cohn snapped.

"No," I said.

The interview had obviously been terminated. Harry Cohn pressed a button on the intercom. "Tell Kahane to come in."

I got up.

"Stay!" he barked. "I want you to meet our business manager, Ben Kahane."

A heavy-set man with a sad face entered.

"This is Paul Kohner's brother," Cohn grunted. "I gave him a six-months contract with options. He'll start at two-fifty a week. If he works out—fine. If not, we'll give him a kick in the pants."

Kahane looked embarrassed.

Incensed, I jumped up and was about to leave the room.

"Hey!" Cohn yelled after me. "Where are you going?"

"I'm leaving," I said. "I'm not going to work here." I was already at the door, trembling. The president of Columbia Pictures came running after me. I felt his meaty hand on my shoulder, pulling me back.

"What the fuck's the matter with you—Herr *Doktor*," he said peevishly. "Sit down, sit down. If you work at my studio, you'd better get used to the way we talk here. Right, Ben?"

"Right, Harry," Kahane echoed, and made an apologetic gesture in my direction. "Mr. Cohn doesn't mean it that way, Mr. Kohner."

"What the hell are you talking about?" Cohn cut in. "I *do* mean it. He who eats my bread sings my song." He returned to his desk. "Ask your brother."

I lost no time in doing that.

Then he told me how he happened to make the deal with Harry Cohn.

After Thalberg's death Paul had again been relegated to oblivion at MGM. His contract still had a few months to go, but he was certain it would not be renewed.

One evening he walked into the Brown Derby. The restaurant was empty, for it was the night of a big fight at the Hollywood Arena. A single customer sat in the far corner of the large room. He waved Paul over. It was Harry Cohn.

"Hello, sucker!" he greeted Paul, then asked him to join him for dinner. "Are they still grooming you for a second Thalberg at MGM?"

"If Irving were alive," Paul replied, "I'd be in production right now." And he told Cohn of the meeting with Thalberg and of his interest in *Victoria.*

"What the fuck is *Victoria?*" Cohn asked amiably.

"It's one of the great love stories in world literature," Paul told him.

"Fuck world literature," Cohn said. "Is there a picture in it?"

"I'm sure of it."

"So why don't you come over to Columbia and do it for us?" Cohn said. "I know what they pay you in Culver City. I'll pay you two-fifty more."

He must have thought highly of Paul's reputation to offer him a producer's job and also raise his salary. Cohn was known to say, "I kiss the feet of talent." That evening he dazzled Paul with visions of grandeur. And even though Paul had heard of Cohn's duplicity, he partially succumbed to his blandishments. He had nothing to lose anyway, he told himself, since he'd be out of a job by the end of the year.

"Got to catch the last fight," Cohn said, dashing away. "Send your agent over to the studio tomorrow."

Next day Frank Orsatti discussed the terms of the deal with Harry Cohn—part of it consisting of a contract for me. Cohn first thought that Paul was looking for a sinecure for his kid brother, but when shown a print of *Burning Secret,* he was impressed. A new screenplay for *Burning Secret* would be my initial assignment at Columbia Pictures, with the well-known playwright Edward Chodorov as my producer.

But after my first meeting with Harry Cohn, it was clear to me that neither Paul nor I would be able to endure him for long. He enjoyed his position of power—amused to see many a good man tumble. He expressed a certain disdain for educated people. Sensitivity he took for weakness and exploited it.

Paul had moved into his new office at Columbia with high hopes, eager to prove himself. The very first day he sent Cohn a copy of *Victoria.* Then he waited for the phone to ring.

It didn't. Eventually Paul called the Front Office to discuss his plans with his new boss. But it would have been easier to get through to Mussolini himself. The silence seemed ominous.

Then Cohn left for Europe. Now there was nothing Paul could do but sit in his well-appointed office, read scripts, go out to lunch, meet with friends and play gin rummy.

One day he got a call to see Bill Perlberg, the studio's second-in-command. When he arrived at his office, the secretary asked him to go right in.

There was no one in the room. On the desk, on top of a stack of scripts, he saw his copy of Hamsun's novel. An interoffice memo was sticking out of the book.

The temptation was strong. Quickly he took the memo and read it.

The studio reader's report unequivocally condemned the novel. When he heard footsteps, he swiftly replaced the paper.

"Sit down, Paul, relax," said Perlberg. A former agent with the William Morris office, he was a dark-haired, thickset man.

Paul sat down—but didn't relax.

"Listen, Paul, about this book. Harry asked me to read it before he left for Europe. I have given it considerable thought, but I'm afraid this is not something we'll want to do. Frankly, it's rather old-fashioned. Too European. I know you have a penchant for this kind of corny story, Paul, but why not pick something meatier? We've got a lot of properties on the shelf. Forget this *Victoria*. I sent Harry my report this morning, and I know he'll agree with me."

"*Your* report—or your *reader's* report?" Paul asked.

"What do you mean?"

"You never read the book, Bill," Paul said as calmly as he could. For he was feeling that same urge he had felt in Carl Laemmle's office: to smash something on the producer's desk.

"What the hell are you insinuating?" Perlberg yelled. His face had turned purple. "That I'm lying?"

"That's exactly what I'm insinuating. You've repeated your reader's words: old-fashioned, too European. You've never read the book, Bill."

"Get the hell out of here!" Perlberg now shouted. The outburst really gave him away. "Go back to your own damn office, and wait till Harry gets here. No one has ever called me a liar and gotten away with it."

"Well, it's about time somebody did." Paul snatched the copy of *Victoria* off the desk and went to the door.

"Wait a minute!" Perlberg loudly commanded. "Give me that slip of paper."

"Gladly." Paul handed him the reader's report.

Back at his office, he called Orsatti and told him what had happened. "I'm quitting, Frank," he said.

"You're nuts," Orsatti cautioned. "You've got an airtight contract that runs a year. You stay put. When Harry comes back, we'll sell him on another property."

"No, I won't wait around," Paul said firmly. "It's *Victoria* or nothing. That's why I came here."

"You walk out on Columbia, and you're dead. No one in town will touch you."

"Sorry, Frank, but my mind is made up."

29

How to Become an Agent

SLEEP THAT NIGHT did not come easily. He worried. He had recently bought an expensive home in Bel Air, and the down payment had depleted his reserves. The prospect of borrowing money to get by for a while distressed him.

But money wasn't the big problem. He felt confident that he could eventually find another job. Idleness was his enemy—and he knew it.

He hadn't told Lupita yet of the Columbia disaster. She was expecting their first child, and he didn't want to upset her. So he got up as usual, ate breakfast and drove away. But instead of going to the studio, he went straight to Orsatti's office.

"Well," Orsatti said when he saw him come in, "you're really quitting?"

"Of course. Are you surprised?"

"I sure am. Can you afford it?"

"No."

"So what do you want me to do for you, Paul?" Orsatti's question was asked cautiously.

"Get me another job."

"You're kidding," the agent said bluntly.

Paul knew that Orsatti was right. He had been blacklisted by MGM, had walked out of Universal—and now Columbia. An obstreperous producer was a hard-to-sell commodity in Hollywood.

"You must be off your rocker, Paul!" Orsatti wailed. "You're making Cohn a gift of about twenty thousand bucks. Go back to your office and sit out your contract. Meanwhile I'll try to dig up something for you."

"I just can't do it, Frank."

An attitude like this was new to Frank Orsatti—and somehow he respected it. Looking at his quixotic client, he said: "I've got an idea, Paul. How about joining my agency?"

Paul was stunned. "What would I do here?"

"Be an agent, of course. Handle the foreign field."

"An *agent*?"

"Why not? I suddenly realized you'd make a damn good one. You have lots of friends in the business, especially abroad. People like you. And you've got something I don't have—" he searched for the right word—"you've got *class*."

Unlike Harry Cohn, Frank Orsatti valued education. Also unlike Cohn, he felt the lack of it. He admired Paul as well as his ideas and achievements. Bringing him into the burgeoning Orsatti organization would be a wise move.

"Thanks, Frank," Paul said. "But I'll have to think it over."

"Sure, sure. No hurry, Paul."

It was a lovely fall day. Paul walked along Sunset Boulevard, which was rapidly becoming the prestigious business center of Hollywood. New buildings were going up, and on many he read the signs of talent agents. He knew most of them. And he knew that an agent was an easy target for ridicule. In books and plays he was caricatured as a cigar-puffing, bald-pated, sweaty man who spoke with a Bronx accent and pretzeled the syntax. A number of them, in reality, eventually became producers. But how many agents had ever been producers? Only a few. Yet agents were essential in the film business. Who else could go between producer and artist, arranging deals that hopefully would benefit both of them, all the while protecting the interests of the creative person, who often was ill-equipped to "sell" himself or herself properly? A hard-working agent surely merited the ten percent he received for services rendered. There was no reason to scorn him. Perhaps it was time to upgrade the whole profession.

The more Paul thought about the possibility of becoming an agent himself, the more attractive he found it. Like a flower bud, it formed, took a definite shape—and then blossomed. Why not? It all made good sense to him.

But one thing became clear. He was too independent to work for Orsatti. He had to cultivate and plant his own garden.

Just then he bumped into a man who was standing in front of a frame building, watching the workmen apply a second coat of paint. It was a lawyer he knew.

Oscar Cummins pointed proudly at the building with its two Doric columns. "How do you like it, Paul?"

"Is it yours?"

"Sure. I'm moving in next week."

"Are you using the whole place?"

"I might rent out an office upstairs."

Paul hesitated for only a moment. "May I see it?"

They walked upstairs. The office was small. Fourteen by fourteen feet. But the window looked out on Sunset Boulevard.

"How much would you take for it, Oscar?"

"I don't know. Maybe forty dollars a month?"

"You've got yourself a tenant," Paul said.

Book II:
The Magician

30

Agent without a Client

IMPROBABLE LINKS IN a life's sequence, in retrospect, often appear to be preordained. What if Paul hadn't gone that morning to Frank Orsatti's office? What if the agent hadn't offered him a position there and set his mind to thinking? And what if he hadn't chanced to meet his lawyer friend in front of his new building?

But these things did happen, in sequence. And on the following Monday Paul bought a desk and a chair for his new office, and ordered a telephone. He was now an agent.

A Hollywood agent—without a single client.

There was something he had not anticipated. That was the terror he felt when he tried to lift the phone and call people to tell them of his new status. A "salesman" instead of a producer-buyer. He sat in his chair and stared out at the busy boulevard. How would he feel when he began to circulate in studios where he had once been a prominent and respected figure and was now just a "flesh-peddler"?

At the time I was—in Hollywood vernacular—"between assignments" and became one of Paul's first visitors. I brought him an original story I had just finished writing and asked whether he would be interested in "handling" it. He read the story, liked it, put it under his arm and drove out to Universal City.

The studio no longer was Carl Laemmle's kingdom. But the guard remembered Paul, greeted him warmly and let him through. Paul headed for the back lot to see his friend Joe Pasternak.

Hungarian-born Pasternak had started his upward climb from busboy in a Long Island movie studio to a place among the well-known, commercial producers of Hollywood. In the early Thirties Laemmle "discovered" him and sent him to Berlin to join Paul's production unit. In this man of small frame burned a fiery ambition. Like Paul, he was in constant motion.

Soon he was producing highly successful musicals in Europe. When he returned to Hollywood from Berlin, he brought an ambitious young director with him. Herman Kosterlitz quickly shortened his name. Koster and Pasternak sold themselves as a team to Universal's new bosses and made the low-budget picture *Three Smart Girls*. Luckily for them, they had picked sixteen-year-old Deanna Durbin as the lead. The film turned out to be a baffling moneymaker—which the company badly needed. Under Pasternak's guidance Deanna Durbin had become the studio's biggest asset.

Paul felt uneasy returning to his Hollywood alma mater in his new role of agent. Nevertheless, he was determined to carry it off in style.

"I've decided to become an agent, Joe. I have a story here that might fit Durbin."

Pasternak showed only mild surprise at this revelation. And he had the kindness of heart not only to congratulate him on this move but also to bolster his morale by telling him that he would make a wonderful agent. In no time, he predicted, Paul would be just as successful as he had been as a producer. Probably even more, in fact. Was there anything he could do for him?

"Yes. Tell me what you need—and I'll get it for you," Paul said.

Joe Pasternak's immediate need was story material for Deanna Durbin. He promised to read my story quickly. And in the meantime, Paul should keep his eyes out for other properties for his star.

He led Paul to the door, inviting him to come and visit him at any time. It would be a pleasure, he said, to help in any way he could.

Feeling greatly encouraged, Paul walked toward his car. It was around noon, and people were on their way to the commissary for lunch. Many of the "leftovers" from Laemmle's time greeted him with deference, perhaps thinking that he had returned to the studio in his former capacity.

He saw writer Konrad Bercovici, whom he slightly knew. Of gypsy stock, Bercovici sold his wit and talent by grinding out hack scripts for a puny salary. Naturally assuming that Paul was still a producer, he felt honored when Paul invited him to lunch.

During the meal Bercovici complained about the assignment he was finishing. He wished he could somehow better himself. Perhaps one day Paul would ask him to do a screenplay for one of the prestigious films he was preparing.

"Tell me, Konrad," Paul asked casually, "would you by chance have a story for Deanna Durbin?"

The big black eyes above the mighty walrus mustache lit up. "Do I have a story for Durbin? I have *the* story for Durbin!"

"Will you tell it to me?"

Bercovici launched headlong into his narration. He told the tale of a gypsy girl (naturally) who through trials and tribulations (naturally) became a celebrated opera star (naturally).

Paul found the story no better or worse than any that had suited

Durbin—but Bercovici's intimate knowledge of gypsy life gave it blood and color.

"I think you could sell that story," Paul said. "How much would you want for it?"

"I'd sell it for five thousand," Bercovici said recklessly, obviously prepared to accept half.

"Have you got an agent?"

"No."

"Good," Paul said. "How about letting me be your agent?"

Bercovici chuckled.

"I'm not joking," Paul said. "I'm an agent now."

"*You—an agent?*"

"Since this morning," Paul said calmly. "And you would be one of my first clients."

Recovering from the shock, Bercovici agreed to accept Paul as his middleman. Immediately Paul left the table and went back to Pasternak's office.

"Joe," he announced triumphantly, "I've got exactly what you're looking for. The story I just heard is *made* for Durbin."

"Go ahead," Pasternak said—and asked his secretary to hold all calls.

Any resemblance between the story Paul now told Pasternak and the one Bercovici had told him was merely coincidental. True, the heroine was still a gypsy girl. But all the rest was improvised. More than once in the past Paul had sold Laemmle the barest skeleton of a story, fleshed out by his own inventiveness. On this first morning as an agent his old skill did not fail him.

Pasternak listened, spellbound. When Paul finished, he jumped up. "Great! Great! When can I have it on paper?"

"Almost as soon as you make me a good offer."

"How much do you want for it?"

"Fifteen thousand dollars for Bercovici's story. Fifteen more for the screenplay."

Pasternak's face froze. But soon it defrosted, taking on an amazed and admiring look. "You're starting off on the right foot, Paul. I won't haggle with you. That story is worth every dollar you're asking for it. Now let me see whether I can put it over with the Front Office."

He got through to Charlie Rogers, the studio head. "Charlie," he said in his husky voice, "I just heard a story for Durbin that is too good to pass up. It's by Konrad Bercovici. You know Bercovici—one of the finest writers we've got here. He's just finishing an assignment and could go to work immediately." And then he told Rogers the terms of the deal.

There were vociferous protests from the other end, demands for a more favorable arrangement. But Pasternak stood his ground. When he gleefully put down the phone, he told the new agent that the deal had been approved.

None of the million-dollar transactions which Paul negotiated in the decades to come would give him quite the same satisfaction as this first sale. It did much to restore his badly damaged self-confidence and provided a good portent for the future in his newly chosen career.

He now wanted the pleasure of giving the news to his client.

Barely one hour had passed since Paul left him, so the writer looked up in surprise when Paul came into his office.

"Now, Konrad," Paul said, first settling down in an easy chair. "How would you like to write a screenplay of the story you told me for—" he paused—"well, let's say for thirty thousand dollars."

Bercovici stared at him. "Please, Mr. Kohner, no practical jokes."

"It's no joke, Konrad. I have just closed a deal for you. Fifteen thousand for your story, fifteen for the screenplay. Of course, if you feel it's not enough, I can go back and try to improve the terms."

Bercovici—a gifted but impecunious toiler—sat petrified. He had the unbelieving look in his eyes of those to whom success comes unexpectedly: a fearful expression, as though the dream was still in process, and moving or speaking might shatter it. Tears came to his eyes and ran down his cheeks into the thicket of his gypsy mustache.

The Reinhardt Touch

NOW HE WAS an agent.

The Hollywood Reporter and *Variety* carried the story prominently on their front pages.

News of the fabulous deal he had closed for Bercovici made the rounds. His phone began ringing.

People called to wish him well. He had always been generous in many ways, and it was well remembered. Actors remembered the producer who at all times had words of cheer and encouragement—even if he didn't have a role to offer them. Directors who had worked for him remembered his enthusiasm and his loyalty. Writers remembered the respect and admiration he had for the written word.

One of the first "name" clients to sign a contract with Paul was John Huston. He had started out as a writer, and had written a script for Paul at Universal. Now he had just been offered a writer-director deal by MGM and felt confident that Paul could negotiate the best possible terms. Huston still had a year on his contract with another agent, but he didn't mind paying two agents' commissions to show his faith in Paul.

When Paul walked into MGM, however, an unpleasant surprise awaited him. "Sorry, Mr. Kohner," the receptionist at the entrance to the Thalberg building said, "but we haven't got a pass for you. Maybe you'd like to talk to Mr. Mannix's office?"

No, he wouldn't like to. The message was clear enough. He was banned from the studio: a persona non grata. Mannix had neither forgotten nor forgiven.

But Paul still had friends there at the studio. One of them was Gottfried Reinhardt.

Gottfried was the son of the famous German stage director and producer, Max Reinhardt. Born in Berlin, he had arrived in the States for a visit at the age of nineteen. Ernst Lubitsch had worked for Max Reinhardt in Europe, and offered Gottfried a position as assistant director. Something of a *Wunderkind,* he had advanced rapidly, and was now a producer at MGM. While Paul was working at the studio, the two became close friends. Every day after lunch, a group of gin rummy and chess aficionados repaired to Gottfried's office for fun and games.

So that morning when Paul found MGM closed to him, he quickly called Gottfried, who came out to escort him to his office. He knew, of course, of Paul's switch of professions, and asked what he could do for him.

"I've just learned that I'm barred from the lot," Paul told him. "Which means I can't sell any clients to MGM. Which means—well, I don't have to tell you, Gottfried. At the moment John Huston is up for a big job here, and if I can't negotiate for him, he'll probably take his business elsewhere."

Reinhardt flopped back in his huge swivel chair, took a few puffs from his cigar, then chewed it around to a corner of his mouth. His narrow forehead wrinkled. "There is only one way to make the studio change its policy," he said dryly. "You've got to talk to Mayer."

"You know he won't see me."

"Oh, yes, he will. You tell the secretary that you *have* to see him, that it's a matter of life or death."

Paul twirled the long gold chain around his index finger. "You're right, Gottfried. It *is* a matter of life or death."

"So—pick up the phone and call Mayer's office."

"Okay. What next? When I get there, what do I tell him?"

Reinhardt narrowed his eyes. A long strand of hair fell over his right eye. He leaned back in his chair and brooded. Then he jumped up.

"Mr. Mayer—" he said. Suddenly he was Paul Kohner. "I am grateful to you for seeing me. Ever since the day I drove with you to the station I have been a haunted man. I told you a lie, and God has punished me. I haven't had a good night's sleep since. You were kind to me, and I betrayed your confidence. I've suffered for two years, and I'm at the breaking point. I came to ask your forgiveness. Please, Mr. Mayer, forgive me. I beg you, give me back my peace of mind, and I'll be forever grateful."

Gottfried looked triumphantly at Paul. "You tell him that, and you're back in business."

Paul stopped his chain-twirling and stared at Reinhardt. "Ridiculous!"

"No, seriously. I know L. B. It'll go over big with him. Of course, if you could manage to go down on your knees, it would be even more effective—"

"You must be kidding, Gottfried," Paul said. "You know damn well I couldn't do a thing like that. Not for the biggest commission in the world."

"To be prevented from making a deal at MGM—not just this deal, but *any* deal—could very well break you, Paul," Reinhardt said matter-of-factly. "That's the best advice I can give you."

"Impossible! Absolutely impossible, Gottfried! I cannot humiliate myself in front of Mayer—never. *Never!*"

He thanked Gottfried just the same, and left.

A couple of days later Reinhardt called Paul to find out if he had changed his mind. Thinking it over, he still thought it was an excellent ploy.

"Forget it, Gottfried," Paul said. "I've got to find some other way."

"There *is* no other way," Reinhardt said.

A week or so later Reinhardt had to see the MGM boss on some production matter. The meeting was over, and Gottfried was already on his way out when Mayer stopped him at the door.

"Aren't you a friend of Paul Kohner's?"

"Yes, Mr. Mayer."

"I want to tell you a story about your *friend,*" Mr. Mayer said with relish. "He is one of the most objectionable characters I have ever met. You know what that man did? He lied to me. Lied to my face in the most brazen way. But he didn't get away with it. I got his number." He paced up and down, stopped, shook a stubby finger at Reinhardt with a fierce defiance.

Then he moved closer, and his face softened perceptibly. "But something quite amazing happened—something I never expected. Yesterday morning he called and said he had to see me. Said it was a matter of life or death. So I told him to come right away. He looked like a ghost. I felt sorry for the son-of-a-bitch, believe me. And you know what he said?" He paused dramatically. " 'Mr. Mayer,' he said, 'I've suffered for two years. You were kind to me, and I betrayed your confidence. I haven't had a good night's sleep since I told you that lie. Now I've come to ask your forgiveness. Say that you'll forgive me, Mr. Mayer, and I'll be grateful to you for the rest of my life.' "

Mayer's face began to twitch. His eyes were watering. "I'll tell you something, Reinhardt." He lowered his voice to a whisper. "If a man comes to me and unburdens his heart—if he begs my forgiveness—I can't turn him away." He drew his handkerchief from his breast and wiped away some tears. "Not one good night of sleep—for two years!" he suddenly hollered. "That's enough punishment, don't you think so?"

"Certainly, Mr. Mayer," Reinhardt said deferentially.

"So this morning," Mayer went on, "I called in everybody—Mannix, Rubin, Thau, MacKenna. And you know what I told them, Reinhardt?" There was another pause. "'The boycott on Kohner is lifted as of this moment,' I told them. I didn't tell them about your friend's visit. I don't like to humiliate a man. I just said we're going to do business with him the way we do business with everyone else. With every one of those goddam flesh-peddlers and cut-throats."

"That was most gracious of you, Mr. Mayer," Gottfried said.

"Did you expect anything else?" Mayer bellowed. "I am not a monster. I'm a good Christian." And with an imperious wave of the hand he dismissed Reinhardt.

A few days later, Paul and Gottfried met in a corridor of the studio. Gottfried was deep in conversation with a writer, and Paul had John Huston in tow. The two friends exchanged brief, conspiratorial smiles, winked at each other and went on their separate ways.

How to Win an Oscar

H E MADE THE deal for John Huston. And for me and other writers. It was a good beginning.

Writers flocked to him. At first the core of his clients consisted of writers. There is in all of us a "poet whom the man survives." The poet in my brother Paul was very much in evidence at the start of his agency career. He had a boyish veneration for writers. He understood their multifold difficulties, easily punctured egos, economic insecurities, cravings for praise, writing "blocks," laziness, terrors of failure.

Writers came to Paul not merely in search of jobs, but to test ideas for stories, detail their domestic problems, discuss their creative hang-ups and recount sundry woeful tales of impecunity. Many European writers, displaced by the political upheavals of the Thirties, sooner or later landed at the Paul Kohner Agency.

George Froeschel was one of them. They had known each other in Berlin, when Froeschel was editor of the *Berliner Illustrierte*, Germany's most influential and prestigious weekly magazine. Jewish, he left Germany after Hitler's takeover. Before coming to the West Coast, he had held a position for a time with *Esquire* in Chicago, but the English language proved too hard to perfect swiftly. As a young man he had been a story editor at UFA in Berlin. He now hoped to find employment in the Hollywood movie industry.

On his own, he told Paul, he had tried to get work. But the studio executives couldn't have cared less about the lyrical introductions from prominent people that he produced from his briefcase, nor were impressed with the work he had done for UFA, nor even wished to consider the many excellent novels he had published in Germany.

Paul was touched by his predicament. He felt none too optimistic about placing him as a screenwriter, but he promised to try.

Froeschel sat in his depressingly tawdry, furnished apartment, waiting for the phone to ring. That he shared this melancholy pastime with a few hundred other indigent emigrants in Hollywood was small solace for the frustrated novelist.

One day Paul received a call from Mrs. Froeschel, who spoke from a telephone booth. Her husband was becoming extremely despondent, she said. And unless Paul could soon find him employment, she feared for George's life.

Paul had just read an item in the trade papers about a literary property MGM had acquired: *Mortal Storm*, a novel by Phyllis Bottome, which dealt with the plight of Jewish refugees forced by the Nazis to leave Germany. Sidney Franklin was assigned to produce the film.

Franklin, the producer of *The Barretts of Wimpole Street* and *The Good Earth*, was an intelligent and sensitive man. One of the few filmmakers convinced that ninety percent of a movie's success lay in the choice of a scriptwriter, he hired only the finest craftsmen and kept absolute control over their written work. An assignment from Franklin was no easy task, but it almost guaranteed the holder a long run.

Before trying to see the producer, Paul went to the story department at MGM and asked the editor for a copy of *Mortal Storm*. Of course he could have just read the synopsis. But as a former producer, he knew how fraudulent a synopsis could be. So he sat down in the anteroom and immediately read the book. When he finished, he was convinced that Froeschel would be the perfect man to do the adaptation.

Then he set out to convince Franklin himself.

"Well, I think I have the right man to adapt *Mortal Storm*," Paul said.

"You might have," Franklin said, aware that Paul represented some important European writers. "Who is it?"

"George Froeschel."

"Never heard of him."

Paul told him who Froeschel was and why he would be a good choice. Not for the screenplay itself, to be sure, because his English was—well, minimal might be the word. But he was brilliant, experienced, hard-working and—above all—thoroughly familiar with the Nazi scene in Germany.

"Bring him around," Franklin said warily.

Now Paul called Froeschel. In his mind, the deal was already closed. "I'm sending you a copy of a book, George. Read it tonight and prepare yourself for an interview. Be at my office at eleven. I'll drive you out to MGM."

This was not routine procedure with him. But then this was no routine situation.

Driving out to Culver City the following day, he listened to Froeschel's analysis and evaluation of the book. He had sound ideas on how to improve the characters and the story line for the film's purposes.

"Excellent, George," Paul interjected here and there. "Very good." The one thing that worried him, though he couldn't say so, was Froeschel's English. It was minimal, all right. "If I could advise you, George," he said, "don't talk too much. Franklin likes a good listener. And since I know your ideas, let *me* do the telling."

They had to wait for a while in Franklin's outer office. Although the place was air-conditioned, beads of sweat appeared on the writer's forehead.

Finally they were ushered in. George Froeschel—a gentleman of the old Austrian school—made a bow from the waist down.

Franklin offered him a limp hand. "Have you read the book?"

"Yes, Mr. Franklin." Froeschel looked at him, fearful.

"Sit down, George," Franklin said. "Relax."

Everyone settled down. Pause. Sunlight flooded the room. It seemed to bother Franklin, for he went to the window and fussed around with the shutters. Then he gazed at Froeschel.

"George thinks it's a beautiful story," Paul started out, "and he has some excellent ideas—"

"I'd like to hear them from Mr. Froeschel," said Franklin, cutting him off.

Froeschel paled. He opened his mouth. No words issued. He cleared his throat.

"What are *your* ideas, Mr. Froeschel?" Sidney Franklin asked pleasantly.

Froeschel looked like a child about to break into tears. He launched himself desperately on his analysis of the book, frantically veering from English to German, and back again. He used pantomime where words failed. Finally he abandoned English altogether.

Good God, Paul thought. There went the job. "Maybe if George would put some of his suggestions on paper—" he offered.

"Yes. That might be a good idea. And in English," Franklin said directly to Froeschel, terminating his ordeal.

"I'll talk to you later," he told Paul with a wan smile.

The interview was over. Silently they drove toward Hollywood. "If it doesn't work out," Paul ventured soberly, "we'll find something else for you, George. And listen, why don't you go to night school? English. Quite important."

To Paul's surprise, Franklin called the following morning.

"About that writer with the sad eyes—" Franklin began —"what's his name?"

"George Froeschel," Paul supplied.

"Oh, yes." Pause. "Well, I thought it couldn't possibly work out, Paul. And I still don't think so. But then I had a dream last night—a weird dream. I don't remember the details—except there were those sad, sad eyes haunting me, trying to give me some message. I haven't been able to shake them off ever since. So I guess I'll have to give him a job. I can't pay much because there'll be another writer with him on the assignment. A hundred and fifty a week. That's all I can offer. I consider it more of a charity case—you understand, Paul."

"I have to disagree with you," Paul said. "You're getting the best man for the job. You'll thank me one day."

And Sidney Franklin did. For twenty years, George Froeschel worked exclusively as a screenwriter for him. During his long tenure at MGM, Froeschel collaborated on some of the most successful films that Franklin produced—and received an Oscar for his brilliant screenplay for *Mrs. Miniver.*

33

Life Saver

As WORLD WAR II drew ever closer, more and more European writers sought places of refuge. Many who had left Germany and Austria for a time found safety in France, Switzerland, Spain—even Italy. But in the first days of September, 1939—when war *did* break out as Hitler's tanks steamrolled over Poland—frantic calls for help reached Hollywood.

Many requests for aid came to Paul, because he was the one European in America who was known by them to be approachable. During his working years in Berlin and Vienna, he had made the personal acquaintance of many writers—who now implored him to save their lives.

Sending affidavits to a few stranded men might help them to escape, as indeed it had in the past. One had to pledge that none of the refugees would become an economic liability to the United States by guaranteeing the livelihood of the emigrants and their families.

But there were only so many affidavits a single man could furnish. Paul had sent affidavits already to a number of family members and friends. And now he feared that, apart from heavy personal financial commitments, the State Department would surely question the validity of more affidavits from him.

Paul worried. He had never yet left a plea unanswered. He wanted to help all of the petitioners.

He called Ernst Lubitsch and explained the urgency of the situation. Could he sponsor an emergency meeting to which all prominent members of the European film colony would be invited? The director agreed, offering his own home as the meeting place.

A summons from Lubitsch was like a summons from the king. Everyone in the large, affluent group of filmmakers and artists rallied. Wilhelm Dieterle and his wife Charlotte. Bruno and Liesl Frank. Fritzi Massary. Eric Charell. Joe and Mia May. Berthold and Salka Viertel. Gottfried and Wolfgang Reinhardt. William and Robert Wyler. Billy Wilder. Walter Reisch. Henry Blanke. Joe Pasternak. And many others.

Lubitsch welcomed his guests and then turned the meeting over to Paul, who began to discuss the problem of the stranded writers. He had found a way, he thought, not only to rescue them, but also to give them the chance to lead lives of dignity and self-respect while in exile.

Paul's plan was simple. The most influential personality in the European colony should approach the head of each major studio and make a plea for the refugee writers. A plea—along with a constructive proposal to hire them for the minimum salary. Granted, they might have little to contribute directly at first to the making of motion pictures. But certainly they would all have fertile ideas which could be turned into films by other script writers. Most importantly, the promise of a work contract would guarantee their entry into the country.

Almost everyone backed Paul's idea. But who would be the best person to plead the cause?

Ernst Lubitsch was the obvious choice. As the most respected European filmmaker in Hollywood, his intercession would assure success. Lubitsch was a man of many and curious whims—but championing a cause was not one of them. He flatly stated he would feel out of character as a spokesman. "However," he said, "you can count on my cooperation. I think Paul is really the man for the job. After all, he's an agent. And what we need here is a good salesman. One who can convince the studio heads that this is not just charity, but good business too. A good story from each of the writers could recoup the whole outlay."

For once all the European colonists agreed on something. The appointment went to Paul Kohner.

He faced the challenge head-on. The next morning he arranged for an interview with Jack Warner and asked Henry Blanke to come along. Blanke, the most aggressive young producer on the lot, was well liked by the Front Office.

Warner listened to their appeal. Paul emphasized the fact that most of the stranded writers were Jewish. The Jew in Jack Warner was very much alive. Unhesitatingly, he agreed to take four of them under contract.

That made a fine start.

Confident now that he had been successful with Warner, Paul drove out to MGM. To get through to L. B. Mayer he roped in Gottfried Reinhardt, the proven expert. Reinhardt felt that his boss would have to be approached in a more subtle fashion. He reminded Paul that one of L. B.'s salient traits was the impulse to aggrandize himself by being charitable—on the lowest possible budget. Especially if he could outdo his friend Jack Warner.

Which was precisely what happened. When Mayer heard that Warner had consented to take four writers, he quickly opted for six.

The toughest assignment awaited Paul at Columbia.

"How much would I have to fork out?" was Cohn's first question.

"A hundred a week."

"And you get ten percent?"

"Certainly not."

"Okay," Cohn said with surprising alacrity. "What Jack and L. B. can do, I can do better. I'll take ten of those scribblers."

Contracts were dispatched to the ports of Europe—Marseilles, Toulon, Cannes, Casablanca—where most of the writers had taken refuge. Now that they held studio contracts in their hands, they found sudden welcome in the American consulates.

In Hollywood the newcomers moved into small bungalows or apartments. Displaced persons, they drifted into Paul's office. Waiting around in their heavy suits, starched shirt collars and durable shoes, they expressed their gratitude to him. They now wanted the chance to prove to the studios that they could do something in return for the generous contracts. Though the medium of film was alien to most of them, they were, after all, practiced storytellers. Certainly the American movie industry must be in need of stories. So when could they start to work?

Soon, Paul reassured them. He would see that they were assigned jobs that would make them again part of the writing fraternity.

The story editors, however, wouldn't consider using the refugee writers. They had set little speeches. We must give these people time to get acclimatized. Learn the language. Put down roots.

In vain Paul reminded them of the presence in their midst of the elite of European letters, who had gotten affidavits by other means and were already settled in southern California. Thomas and Heinrich Mann. Franz Werfel. Vicki Baum. Carl Zuchmayer. Erich Maria Remarque. Jules Romain. Ernst Toller. Alfred Doeblin. Alfred Neuman. Gina Kaus.

Hollywood's filmmakers, though, seemed little impressed with the past accomplishments and future potentials in European writers, however exalted their reputations.

Weeks went by. Paul's refugee writers reported every morning to the studios. They sat in their offices and waited to be called to do something. Every Thursday their weekly salary check was slipped under the door. They felt they had not earned it.

Again they headed for the Kohner office. Listening to their grievances, Paul had a thought. He suggested that the studios assign each of the European writers to work as an apprentice to established practitioners so they could learn the techniques of screenwriting. It was tried. It usually failed. The newcomers seemed hopelessly lost in this new world of film imagery.

For instance, the German novelist Doeblin was asked to write a sequence for the film *Mrs. Miniver:* the rescue operation of Dunkirk. He wrote it, in German. His description was brilliant. The dramatic build-up breathtaking. The style poetic. It was truly the work of a master. Published, it would have been worthy of a literary prize. But it was hardly what was needed for a screenplay.

Uprooted, bewildered, alienated, the refugees were rarely able to make satisfactory contact with their American colleagues. They never became part of any group—except their own. At lunch they sat together and spoke German. Evenings they met at someone's place, in a nondescript living room, and commiserated about the fate of Europe. After a year of the *Sitzkrieg*, the war was now on in earnest. Meanwhile, America—at least outwardly—still held strict neutrality.

Foreseeing the difficulties that would confront his charges once their contracts were terminated, Paul again called the rescue committee together.

He felt that the many Europeans who held prominent positions in the studios should pledge themselves to pay a monthly contribution. The money could be distributed fairly to those in need. And by incorporating the fund, contributions could be made "tax-deductible"—a most tempting bait for executives and artists in the high-income bracket. It seemed a workable plan, and the committee endorsed the idea. Charlotte Dieterle and Liesl Frank volunteered their services as fund-raisers and administrators.

Thus the European Film Fund was founded. Ernst Lubitsch became the nominal president, while Paul was in charge of distributing the contributions.

The "Fund" was a vital, benevolent and successful undertaking. Throughout the years it supported indigent artists and their families in the European colony who were unable to earn a living.

On a minuscule scale the "Fund" is still operating today.

34

Mama

THE TIME HAD come to get our mother out of Europe.

Our father passed away in 1936, before Hitler had raped Czechoslovakia. When the Nazis moved into the Sudetenland, where our hometown was situated, most of the Jews in the community had fled to Prague (still in Czech hands) or had been able to go abroad. Our brother Walter gave up a promising acting career and came over to join us in California.

But our mother wouldn't come. Stubbornly, she had decided to stay in Teplitz, in the old house she had lived in all her life, and where everyone knew her as the widow of the "Kino-Kohner."

Paul long before had sent the requisite affidavit and money for her passage to America. He warned her repeatedly and urgently to leave—to no avail. Naively, she thought that nothing would happen to her as long as she stayed within her own home. Among her heirlooms and flowers, visiting with her friends.

Until it was too late.

In the fall of 1939 Paul knew he must make one more effort to get her to leave. When he tried to telephone her, he found out that the telephone had been removed from our house. Our mother would have to take the long-distance call at the post office.

Two days later he managed to contact her. Her voice came over, trembling and fearful. (We learned later that the call was being supervised by the local Nazi commissar.) Yes, she said, she would love to come to America if "they" would let her go. Paul instructed her to travel through Austria to Italy. He would arrange for passage from an Italian port.

Suddenly he was cut off. He tried to phone back, but was told that the connection with the "German Protectorate of Bohemia" (as the Sudentenland was now called) had been permanently severed.

Through underground channels we had heard of the Terezin concentration camp, only one hour away from Teplitz. At any moment our mother might be taken from her house and "removed" to the camp.

In desperation, Paul turned to the one man in Hollywood who might be able to help: James Roosevelt. The President's son had taken a fling at producing motion pictures, and Paul had once met him at the home of William Wyler.

He now went to see him at his office. Roosevelt listened with sympathy and concern to Paul's story of our mother's plight. He then wanted to know what he could do to aid him.

"She has an emigration visa to America," Paul said, "but I'm sure the Nazis won't let her leave the country. I am unable to communicate with her any longer. However, the United States still has a consular office in Prague. Maybe if the State Department—"

"What is the name of your hometown?"

Paul gave him all the details. F.D.R.'s son jotted them down on a memo pad.

"You'll hear from me," he promised Paul.

In Hollywood lingo, this of course could mean a polite note of regret—or no reply whatsoever.

But James Roosevelt, like his father, was an active humanitarian. Twenty-four hours later he called Paul.

"I've spoken to my father," he said. "He has given orders to the State Department to get your mother out of Czechoslovakia and guarantee her safe conduct across the border."

The script of the miracle that now unfolded went like this: On orders from the President of the United States, an official of the American Consulate in Prague appeared in Teplitz. Outfitted with the proper credentials, he presented himself to the *Ortsgruppenleiter* (the local Nazi commissar)—who happened to be a movie projectionist and a former employee of our father.

Our mother's Czechoslovakian passport was in order. She also had the entry visa to the United States. All that she needed now was the exit permit from the local authorities. This was given, albeit reluctantly, by the Ortsgruppenleiter, who since his new promotion had looked the other way whenever he met our mother on the streets of the town.

There was just one condition: she could take with her only what she wore. Everything else she had to relinquish to the Nazis. Important as her possessions were to her, they weren't as valuable as her life. Escorted by the consular official, she paid a last visit to the cemetery, filling a small leather pouch with soil from her husband's grave.

A stalwart American escort accompanied her across the border into Italy and left her side only after he had taken her safely aboard the *Conte Savoia*, which was sailing to New York from Genoa.

Though it was a cold and grey November day, we three brothers were elated to see our mother step off the train that had brought her to us from New York.

Many messages of welcome awaited her. One from the writer Mary McCarthy, a client of Paul's, said:

WELCOME HOME HELENE KOHNER FOR AMERICA WAS YOUR HOME IN SPIRIT LONG BEFORE YOU CAME HERE HOW GLAD YOU MUST BE TO SEE YOUR THREE SONS HOW GLAD THEY MUST BE TO HAVE THEIR MOTHER HOW HAPPY WE ALL ARE THAT YOU HAVE ARRIVED SAFELY MAZELTOF AND GOD BLESS YOU.

We ourselves blessed James Roosevelt, for had he not acted swiftly, our mother would surely have ended her life in Hitler's incinerators—as happened with relatives who had to stay behind.

But our mother's American life went differently than we had anticipated. Although her children had found, or made, places for themselves in the New World, and were able to fit in and move with the times, our mother never did. Never really could. For, whether waking or sleeping, she was still living emotionally in Teplitz.

All her life she had been firmly, unabashedly, familial and tribal. We, her sons, made an effort to simulate the kind of intensely involved family life we had experienced when growing up at home. But it just didn't come off, not really. She detected this, of course, and felt dislocated, lost—remembering all too well what she had left back at home or preserved in her memories of the past.

For a time she lived with Walter and his wife Hanna, then with an elderly lady—one of the thousands of refugees from the Old World still dear to her heart. Eventually she resided in a *pension* with a whole group of displaced Europeans. And every Sunday she went to one of her three sons' homes, to eat her meal mostly in silence. Her life and ours barely connected. Spasmodically she would bravely try to communicate with her grandchildren in her broken—and to the children "funny"—English. And that often failed.

One late afternoon, as I was driving homewards from a studio job, I noticed an old woman standing at a street-corner. She was waving her hand, awkwardly begging for a ride.

It was my mother. I stopped. When she recognized me, her face turned red. She looked as embarrassed as a child caught committing some misdeed.

"You shouldn't hitchhike, Mama," I scolded her when she got in. "It's dangerous. You don't know what might happen to you. Why didn't you take a cab?"

"But in a cab I'm all alone," she said. And she now confessed that hitchhiking had become a regular habit of hers. She enjoyed standing at street-corners and being picked up by friendly people. She had discovered that there were Americans generous with their time and interest, who were willing, even eager, to listen to her tell about life in Teplitz and of her displacement to America or to hear details about her sons' successes here. These people really *cared*, she said—clearly implying that she knew our attentions had strayed far from her domain of domestic concerns and dramas. Some of these strangers did indeed become her friends, inviting her into their homes and lives.

Obviously, then, she had to find sympathetic audiences elsewhere. So sometimes she rode around on city busses—not going anyplace in particular, just searching for someone to talk to. And now and then she came into Paul's office and sat for hours in the foyer, bending the ears of any courteous clients who had paid her the slightest heed.

But there was no sending her back to Teplitz when the war ended. The town she had known and loved no longer existed. Physically, yes. Spiritually, culturally and socially—an emphatic no. Both Walter and I saw it for ourselves. What the Nazis had not earlier destroyed or removed—our mother's relatives and friends, her cherished possessions, the synagogue, the very atmosphere itself—the Communists moved in afterwards to wholly alter. The new occupants of Teplitz were strangers. Cows wandered up and down the promenades of the once-elegant spa. And our spacious home was now occupied by several dozen people. Individuals and families were crowded into compartmentalized living quarters that had once echoed the sounds of our laughter, our mother's piano playing, our father's booming voice.

On a December night in 1952, in her small boardinghouse room, our mother died as quietly and unassumingly as she had lived—surrounded by a gallery of photographs of her family. She had given up reaching out further for her Americanized sons, who had been patient, tolerant—and dutiful.

Dutifully, we buried her and then poured the contents of that small leather pouch—the soil she had taken from her husband's graveside in Teplitz—onto the ground above her.

Doubtless our mother possessed charms and a colorful character that we, her children—who took her presence for granted and had much earlier seen her always in our father's shadow—failed to perceive or acknowledge. Or perhaps she did not show that self to us. After we grew up, most of our encounters with her had been awkward to us and disappointing to her. Yet for a quarter-century now, one of Helene Kohner's "new friends" in America goes faithfully to visit her every year on her birthday, placing flowers on the near-forgotten headstone in the Hollywood cemetery.

And thus America did become her final home, after all.

35

Bassermann

HOLLYWOOD DURING THE war years was a lively place. Studios operated profitably and at full capacity. There were no "run-away" productions then, for there was no place to run to. If Hollywood couldn't provide the right locale, they simply constructed it on the spot. Old stars and new were paid extravagant sums. In this pre-smog era the sun still shone lavishly. The estates in Beverly Hills abounded with butlers. Even after sundown, the streets were safe and accessible.

Accessible for most of the inhabitants. But not for the German-speaking refugees, who were unjustly labeled "enemy aliens." Though the earliest and most vocal adversaries of the Nazi regime, whether Jewish or Aryan, they were subjected to a humiliating curfew that confined them to their homes after eight P.M. Most of them accepted the ordinance without protest. Writers devoted their evening hours to writing. Musicians made music. Composers composed. Painters painted.

Yet what about the actors? Among them were some of the noblest figures of the German and Austrian stage. Had they been able to land even small roles in films, they could have used their long, quiet nights to study roles. But try as he did, Paul was unable to secure even walk-on parts for them at first. In Hollywood they were forgotten men, if not pariahs.

The rich traditions of the European theatre and the high accomplishments of its cinema held no fascination for most California producers. The names of famous and fabled talents which Paul recited to them fell on deaf ears. Ah yes, they had heard of Max Reinhardt—because most of the pashas had been to the Salzburg Festivals, so his name could hardly have escaped them. But that was about it.

Thus when Paul made the rounds of the studios to announce triumphantly that Albert Bassermann had arrived in town, casting directors and producers looked at him blankly.

Albert Bassermann had been no less than the giant of the German stage. The actor's voice and mannerisms had affected a whole generation. It was said that Hitler had sent Goebbels personally to the actor's home to beg him to remain in Germany and to convey the Fuehrer's promise that Bassermann's wife Else, of Jewish extraction—a fine actress in her own right—could stay there in safety. The story that Albert Bassermann sent the club-footed propaganda minister scurrying back to Hitler with the famous quote from Goethe's *Goetz von Berlichingen*—"Tell your master he can kiss my arse"—may well be apocryphal. But unquestionably he was a man of rare honor and courage, who found the Nazi regime intolerable and said so, sacrificing his highly successful career by moving to America. Indisputably too, he possessed a gift for acting that appears perhaps only once in a generation.

Like most Europeans in the performing arts exiled to California, Bassermann eventually ended up in Paul Kohner's office.

"Mr. Kohner," he said in his rasping Mannheim dialect, "I am willing to accept a part in a film. It must be the leading role, of course. And my wife must also have a part in the same film. Can you secure such an arrangement quickly for me? My reserves are dwindling away at an alarmingly fast pace."

"It will be an honor for me to represent you, Mr. Bassermann," Paul said. "How is your English? Passable, I trust."

"Passable? Nonsense! I don't speak a word of that atrocious language." He firmly believed that the "Thousand Year Reich" would not endure for long and that soon he would be back on the German stage.

It posed quite a problem.

After unsuccessfully trying a few studios, Paul approached director William Dieterle, who was preparing for Warner Brothers a picture on the life of Dr. Paul Ehrlich. Dieterle himself had once been a prominent actor in Germany, so he said that nothing would please him more than to have his great colleague appear in the new film. Although there wasn't a part for him in it now, Dieterle would simply have one written into the film.

Paul cunningly withheld from the director Bassermann's deficiency in English.

A few weeks later the first pages of the revised script for *Dr. Ehrlich's Magic Bullet* came through. Paul rushed them to the actor. He hired a speech expert. Bassermann learned his lines by rote, rehearsing phonetically. The contents had been translated into German for him so that at least he would know what he was saying.

On the day Bassermann was to do his first scene, Paul picked him up and drove him to Warner Brothers. He hung around for the actor's first take. He was nervous. So were Dieterle and Blanke, the producer. To add to the tension, Jack Warner, who rarely showed up during shooting, made an appearance.

The scene with Bassermann was set up. He had to open a door, enter a laboratory and address himself to Dr. Ehrlich, played by Edward G. Robinson.

Bassermann wore a white doctor's coat. An aura of human dignity always surrounded the actor. And now, despite the heavy makeup, it was intact—shining out from his remarkable face.

He delivered his lines faultlessly. His peculiar Mannheim inflection had been incorporated into the role itself. He was a German scientist speaking English.

Bassermann's untried audience seemed spellbound. Robinson forgot his cue. Dieterle had a grin of pride on his face. Blanke stared in amazement. Even Warner sat mesmerized. And when Bassermann had finished his rather lengthy speech, something quite extraordinary happened. Hands started to clap in approval. The applause was coming from the toughest audience imaginable: from the grips up on the rafters—the most cynical, hard-boiled workmen among the ranks of studio employees. They certainly had never heard of Albert Bassermann before, but instinctively they knew that they had just witnessed a master's performance. They recognized the actor's powerful ability to be more human than humanity, more regal than royalty, more truthful than gospel.

The applause was picked up by everyone on the set—the camera crew, the make-up people, the assistants, the script girls. And finally the director, producer, agent and even Jack Warner joined in.

The audience response generated by the presence of a great performer is seemingly universal. Whether he stands within the proscenium of a theatre, speaking his mother tongue, or on a sound stage of a movie set, reciting a language foreign to him, he somehow conveys the very essence of high drama.

And how did Bassermann accept this rare homage? Only with an oblique smile on his craggy face. After all, it was his just due.

From that day on, the dearth of assignments ended for Bassermann. Because he couldn't carry off long roles in English, at first he was given only minor parts. But each one he imbued with the Bassermann charisma.

He even began to learn English on his own, if only for practical survival purposes.

And then he got his big chance. Walter Wanger offered him the part of a Dutch statesman kidnaped by Nazi agents, in the production of *Foreign Correspondent*. Bassermann was to receive a salary—most impressive at that time—of fifty thousand dollars.

However, there was a problem. He had contracted to appear in a small role in a film for Columbia Pictures. The shooting schedules of the two films conflicted. A postponement of either picture to accommodate Bassermann was out of the question.

Paul offered to reimburse Columbia for employing an actor of equal stature as a replacement. But he hadn't figured on the long, vindictive memory of Harry Cohn. "You deliver the man for that picture," Cohn yelled, "or I'll sue the s.o.b. for breach of contract—and you too." Coming from Cohn, this was no empty threat.

A gloomy meeting took place at the Bassermann bungalow.

"Maybe," the German actor suggested, "I could make a personal appeal to Mr. Cohn."

Why not? The idea seemed worth a try, anyway, to Paul. He called Cohn the next day.

"Mr. Bassermann would like to have a meeting with you, Harry."

"What for?" Cohn asked suspiciously.

"I don't know."

"Who in hell should know if you don't?"

"Well, let's just say it's a courtesy call. Don't forget, he's the greatest living German actor, and I think you owe it to him to—"

"I don't owe anybody a fart," Cohn bellowed. Then he softened. "Okay, tell that character to be here tomorrow at eleven."

Five minutes before the appointed time, agent and actor met in the studio lobby. Bassermann's appearance was startling. The usually dapper gentleman, who always dressed impeccably from his polished shoes to his starched collar, now wore a moth-eaten raglan that looked like a rental from Western Costumes. His shoes were scuffed and had holes. He was unshaven. His face looked grey and haggard.

Disregarding Paul's obvious consternation, Bassermann imperiously strode down the studio corridor. As they waited for a few minutes in the outer office, Cohn's two secretaries threw bewildered side glances at the weird-looking visitor.

Then the buzzer sounded and the door opened. Harry Cohn sat behind his large circular desk.

"This is Albert Bassermann," Paul said.

Bassermann walked slowly up to the desk. His gait was wobbly, his breathing labored. He was withering away before Paul's very eyes.

Cohn stared dumbly at this apparition.

"Mr. Cohn—" Bassermann began in a high-pitched, whining voice—"it is a great honor to meet you. You have saved the lives of many poor refugees, and the good Lord will bless you for it. And now you have an opportunity to bring more of God's blessings upon yourself and your family."

Cohn's eyes darted almost pleadingly from Bassermann to Paul.

"You are one of the chosen, Mr. Cohn," Bassermann went on, "a credit to your people. I, on the other hand, am one of the condemned. I had to leave my homeland, where I possessed everything you have—and more. Here in America I am a pauper. Destitute. I live in a single room with my wife and daughter. Mr. Cohn, think for a moment of how it would be to be old and penniless like me. Not to be able to provide for your family. Worrying day and night what will happen to them when you are not here any more.... But suddenly—thanks to my agent here—an important part has been offered to me, an old man on the edge of the grave. This part, Mr. Cohn, would not only give me and my family financial security. It offers me the chance to be a real actor again. That has been my whole life—being an actor who stands in front of an audience. With this part there would be a whole new audience to see me. Millions, Mr. Cohn—millions of those wonderful Americans who have been so kind to me and my family and given us refuge here."

He started toward Cohn. Tears rolled down his face. "Mr. Cohn," he sobbed, "do you find it in your heart to deprive me of that opportunity? You're a good man. You will let me out of that contract with your studio. I know you will. Let me kiss your hand, Mr. Cohn—" he wailed as he knelt to grab Harry Cohn's hand.

Cohn sprang from his chair as if stung. All color was drained from his face. "Get up! Get up!" he screamed.

Slowly Albert Bassermann got to his feet. But his eyes would not let go of Harry Cohn. The two men stared at each other.

And then Cohn did something totally uncharacteristic. He turned to Paul. "You can tear up that contract with us," he said gruffly. Then he spoke to Bassermann. "When you're finished with Wanger, you can come here. We'll find a part for you, Mr. Bassermann."

The actor straightened up. "Thank you, Mr. Cohn," he muttered. And to himself, yet audibly, he whispered, "A noble man. A *noble* man."

Slowly he walked the length of the room toward the door—every inch now the great Bassermann making a majestic exit.

Paul rushed to the door and held it open. As Bassermann passed him, he winked.

Paul, who had seen the actor in most of his famous parts, from King Lear to Peer Gynt, felt he had just witnessed the master's finest performance.

The German Invasion and Retreat

VEN THOUGH PAUL utterly abhorred the Nazi regime, he always had a natural affinity for Germany itself. German was his mother tongue. Germany was the scene of his earliest professional successes. And he had some good friends among the Germans.

In the Twenties as a producer Paul had opened the doors for German actors and directors. In the Thirties he was the first to import a German repertory group to Hollywood. Later he brought directors like Luis Trenker and Arnold Fanck to the West Coast. During World War II no one looked after the welfare of the exiled German-speaking artists, whether Jewish or Aryan, as vigorously as Paul did.

In fact, he reveled in the role of Patron Saint to the European refugee colony in Hollywood. He was not merely head of an employment agency who canvassed the studios in search of assignments for them. He became a friend to his charges and spent as much time in nursing them out of their near-breakdowns as in looking for work for them. He kept their hopes up, encouraged them, restored their egos. Every Sunday they gathered in his home in Bel Air, where they were treated with respect, sympathy and *Gugelhupf.* And in extremis they could always call on the Fund, which he administered.

Paul knew that their time would come. And it did come, sooner than he had anticipated, with the flood of anti-Nazi pictures swiftly prepared after the United States entered the war. Suddenly the industry needed Prussian generals, bullnecked S.S. officers, Fuehrers, Stuka fliers, Austrian zither players, Jewish scientists, U-boat captains, revolutionaries, spies and counterspies. Paul supplied them all. Actor Fritz Kortner went to work, as did Ernst Deutsch, Alexander Granach, Carl Esmond, Felix Bressart, Curt Bois, Sigi Arno, Ludwig Stoessel.

Continental directors like Robert Siodmak, Max Ophuls, Joe May, Otto Preminger, John Brahm, Curtis Bernhardt, Richard Oswald, Max Nossek, William Thiele, Hanns Schwartz were suddenly in demand. Composers hitherto neglected were hired to write film scores: Igor Stravinsky, Oskar Straus, Carol Rathaus, Hanns Eisler, Franz Waxman, Erich Korngold, Dimitri Tiomkin, Bronislau Kaper. And the brilliant pianist Jakob Gimpel found employment at MGM.

At the end of the European war, when Paul learned the extent of the horrible crimes committed by Germans, especially toward the Jews, he was revolted. For a long time he felt unable to cross the German border on his postwar trips to Europe. But after most of his exiled clients returned to Germany, he gradually eased his attitude about "collective guilt." When he visited Berlin and Munich, many of his former friends and associates rushed to greet him. They assured him of their innocence, documented help they had extended to the persecuted, gave an account of courageous deeds performed. No one, of course, ever admitted to having been a Nazi or Nazi sympathizer.

In many of the films produced in postwar Germany, Paul saw a new spirit emerging from a new generation. Always keeping a sharp lookout for fresh talent, he signed some of the actors to agency contracts. He was aware that the climate for the former enemy's entry into Hollywood was not yet favorable, but he knew that weather can change quickly. And it did.

Most of the German actors who had emigrated to Hollywood during the Thirties and early Forties returned to Europe. After Kortner, Deutsch, Bassermann and Boise had all left, Paul's "German stable" was nearly empty for a while. But soon the Kohner Agency began to fill up again. Lilo Pulver—one of Germany's newest, brightest faces—came to town. By and by others followed: Marianne Koch, Annemarie Dueringer, Senta Berger, Horst Buchholtz, Oscar Werner, Heinz Ruehmann, Helmuth Kaeutner, Bernhard Wicky. When Paul ardently started to beat the drum for his clients, it took time and effort to overcome Hollywood's ready reply: Lilo *who?* Horst *who?* That their names were "household words" abroad hardly impressed the studio bosses.

By the Fifties, though, the resistance seemed broken, and German actors were cast in leading roles that permitted them to speak their lines with a foreign accent. These "New Germans" acquitted themselves well, and their American colleagues treated them with kindness and respect.

Yet *real* success—success in Hollywood terms—somehow evaded these newcomers. In America they were just plain actors or directors doing a "job." Feeling dislocated and depressed, they soon abandoned their dreams of Hollywood fame and fortune and retreated to their homeland. In Germany the "star cult" flourished, and there they were celebrities. In fact, no other country worshiped film personalities as much as Germany did in the postwar period. Their faces appeared constantly on the front pages of glossy magazines and were familiar to every schoolchild. Revered like deities, no wonder some of them behaved like demi-gods.

O. W. Fischer was one of these half-gods. Starting out as a stage actor, he eventually achieved a popular appeal in German films that could be compared to Valentino's or Gable's here. He was a fine actor—full of good looks, strut and oratory, a master of vocal tricks and mannerisms. At the same time, he also possessed an inordinate vanity. Yet except for a few Europeans like Paul who kept in touch with the German cinema, no one in America knew of O. W. Fischer at all.

Fischer had agreed to sign an agency contract with Paul if an important enough part could be found for him in Hollywood. Paul spotted an opportunity when Universal began to search for an actor to portray the famous butler in Erich Hatsch's *My Man Godfrey.* In order to place his illustrious client, Paul suggested that the producer change the protagonist's nationality. Why not transform the former stockbroker into a destitute Austrian nobleman? A studio executive, Al Daff, in Europe at the time, made a side trip to Munich to interview Fischer. Sufficiently impressed, he signed him for the leading role.

Paul arranged for Fischer to be given the "Hollywood treatment" at his arrival. The reporters and photographers were at the airport to greet him—and so were the film's director, Henry Koster, and its female star, June Allyson.

Fischer was a cat fancier. His country home in Germany, the "Cat Castle," swarmed with more cats than personnel. Paul had spent a full day finding the most attractive—and expensive—Siamese cat to make Fischer feel thoroughly at home. It was waiting at his hotel suite when he arrived.

The surprise fell flat. Spotting the animal, Fischer reeled. "Out with it!" he screamed.

Paul was baffled.

"You expect me to give my affection to a *strange* cat?" Fischer asked him sternly. "You want me to be unfaithful to my cats at home?"

Not an auspicious start.

Soon Paul learned that Fischer had rewritten part of the screenplay which the studio had sent him to read and study. Informed by Koster that this procedure was unacceptable, Fischer asserted that he could portray the character only according to his own feelings and concepts, not somebody else's.

Paul was summoned. Diplomatically, he tried to reason with his star. But Fischer remained adamant.

Shooting began in an atmosphere of high tension. Fischer opted a stance of passive resistance. He scowled at the dialogue, shuddered at jokes, delivered his lines woodenly. He wholly antagonized the director and co-star who had welcomed him to America with such special courtesy and *esprit de corps.*

After a few days Paul was called into the Front Office. In unmistakable terms he was told that unless Fischer conformed, he would be taken off the film and sued. Getting quite perturbed, he worked hard to persuade his client to cooperate. Spoiled by the veneration he enjoyed in Germany and considering himself infallible, Fischer turned a deaf ear. He couldn't believe that a studio would dare to fire him. The director, yes—he could be removed. But not O. W. Fischer.

Two days later he was informed that his presence was no longer wanted on the set. Shooting closed down. An actor to replace Fischer then turned up—in the person of David Niven. And Paul was served with a lawsuit on behalf of his difficult client.

O. W. Fischer returned unceremoniously to Germany.

This case, however, is hardly typical of Paul's German "imports." All of the others adjusted well to Hollywood's working methods. But none of them ever felt like making their stay permanent here. One after another they drifted away, returning only occasionally when suitable parts came up for them.

Today, German actors and directors form only a small part of the international creative talent represented by the Paul Kohner Agency. But he still manages the American interests of such film stars as Ursula Andress, Senta Berger, Curt Juergens and Gert Froebe. And he's always willing to take on others who are good too—if they wish to come over and try Hollywood for size.

Paul felt both pleased and proud when he was awarded the Cross of Merit in March of 1976 at West Germany's Consulate-General in Los Angeles. The federal republic wished to honor him by acknowledging his many services to Germans throughout the years: first as a producer employing German artists in both Hollywood and Berlin, then as the primary caretaker of the refugees during the wartime, and finally in helping to heal relations between the two countries' film industries during the postwar period.

Personality and Personalities

EVERY SO OFTEN through the years I have tried to figure out why my brother has been so successful as an agent.

Once up in the High Sierras on a skiing trip, I came across a rather worn copy of *Poor Richard's Almanac*. Among the many edifying stories I spotted one that seemed to provide an answer.

The tale went something like this:

Two boys, John and Larry, are fishing out on a lake. They stand in a rowboat and cast their lines. Every time John hauls in his line, there is a fish on the hook. Larry catches nothing. Naturally this is quite upsetting to him, and he suggests that they change places. But even with their switched positions, John still brings in fish after fish, while Larry doesn't even get a bite. Finally, in disgust, he throws the rod away and turns to John. "Hey, man, what's your secret?" John grins. "Personality, kid. Personality."

And that may sum up Paul's own secret of success rather neatly. Through the years many talented and illustrious people have been attracted to Paul enough to entrust their careers to him. Sometimes they slipped off the contract "hook" because of circumstances beyond his control. But most of the time he landed them—sometimes even without a hook on his line.

Consider the case of Walter Huston, one of the truly great character actors of his generation on both stage and screen. One morning back in 1938, when Paul was still conducting his agency business in a cubbyhole office, Walter Huston walked in. Paul was stumped and became quite flustered. His visitor settled down in the easy chair, lit a dainty cigar and came right to the point. "My son John is very fond of you, Paul. I see you're doing very nicely for him. So I thought it might be a good idea if father and son were represented by the same agent. How does that strike you?"

It struck him. To become Walter Huston's manager would lift Paul instantly to the heights of his newly acquired profession.

"But don't you have an agent already?"

"Of course I have an agent, my boy. I have the most powerful agent in town. My contract with him still has two years to run. But this shouldn't bother you. I will pay him his pound of flesh for every deal you're going to make for me. But I want *you* to be my manager from this moment on."

Paul could hardly control his excitement. Could he be imagining this whole thing? Just to make certain that it was real, he opened a desk drawer where a stack of neatly printed, standard agency-client contracts lay. He handed Huston a form across the desk.

Walter Huston smiled. "With me you do not need a contract, Paul. I came here because my son likes you. If I am satisfied with your services, I will stay with you. On the other hand, if I am dissatisfied, no contract will make a difference. Here—" he stretched out his hand—"this is all that's necessary between us."

That was Walter Huston. One might search in vain for his like today. He had come to see Paul face to face and had sized him up. Then he made up his mind. And that was the end of it. Throughout his lifetime he was a Paul Kohner client.

He also taught Paul a lesson—or Paul thought he had, anyway. That a gentleman's agreement was as good as a signature on the dotted line.

But it didn't always work that way. Take the instance later on with Curt Goetz, the renowned Swiss-German playwright and actor. When he and his actress wife, Valerie von Martens, moved to Hollywood during the Second World War, naturally he wound up at Paul's office—like so many other Europeans.

Few people knew the work and worth of Goetz as well as Paul. Seeing the possibility of placing him with MGM studios, Paul consented to act as his representative. As a matter of routine he called his secretary to bring in a contract form.

"Mr. Kohner," the suave author said, "why do we have to have a contract? You know I respect you. My word is as good as my signature."

Remembering the Walter Huston incident, Paul dismissed the secretary. Goetz and Paul shook hands. Immediately, Paul called the story department at MGM and made a date to discuss his newly acquired client.

A couple of days later he had some business negotiations in another agent's office. Their dialogue was interrupted by a phone call. The agent advised his secretary, "Tell Mr. Goetz I cannot talk to him now. But I'll have lunch with him at Chasen's at one and then take him out to the studio."

"Did you say Goetz—Curt Goetz?" Paul asked after the agent had hung up.

"Yes. You know him?"

"Of course."

"I hear he's a fine writer," the agent said. "I have just closed a long-term deal for him."

"*You* did? But *I* happen to be his agent!"

"Since when?"

"Since Wednesday."

The agent gave a very loud guffaw, flipped the switch on his intercom and asked his secretary to produce the Curt Goetz contract.

There was the usual form—signed by Curt Goetz only the day before.

When Paul came home, a delivery truck from one of the posh Beverly Hills hostelries had just driven up to his front door. The driver was unloading a case of champagne. It came from Curt Goetz.

Paul told the driver to return the gift to the sender.

Sometimes clients insist on signing a contract even under curious conditions.

Like Marcel Pagnol, the brilliant French playwright who wrote *Fanny* and *The Baker's Wife*.

Pagnol was sitting in the diner of an express train going from Paris to Berlin when Paul happened to recognize him. During Paul's tenure at Universal he had come across an old play by Pagnol that he liked, and had corresponded with him.

Paul introduced himself now, and Pagnol invited him to his table.

Over a bottle of Bordeaux, the two talked about this and that for a while. Eventually Paul got around to telling the writer that he was no longer a producer, that he had become an agent.

"Wonderful," said Pagnol, who had taken a quick liking to Paul. "I've been looking for someone to represent my plays in Hollywood."

"I would be delighted to see what I can do for you," Paul said.

Pagnol ordered another bottle of wine. "You must come to visit me in Marseilles. Come in fall when we harvest. There you'll get a grape, *mon vieux!*" Real human warmth flowed back and forth across the table.

Paul told Pagnol he would love to see him on his next trip.

Before the two parted, Pagnol said, "Just a minute, *mon ami*. Do I not have to sign a contract with you?"

"I'll send you a contract when I get back to California."

"Oh, no. We will sign a contract right now," Pagnol insisted. He sat down again and wrote a short agreement stating that Paul Kohner was his sole and exclusive agent for motion pictures in America. The "contract" was on a big white paper napkin.

However, not all of Paul's contacts proceeded from chance happenings like this one. To be able to represent someone like Greta Garbo takes years of building a solid reputation.

After about a decade in the agency business, Paul was so highly respected that Salka Viertel, Garbo's closest friend and special script writer, came to see him. She told Paul that she had written an original screenplay, *Iceland*, with a leading role designed for Greta Garbo. Garbo had read the script and liked it. And then consented, after many years of self-enforced retirement, to appear in it.

After Paul read the script, he called Salka Viertel and said that he could, without doubt, come up with a major studio offer. Garbo's name still rated supremely high.

And then he was invited to dine with the actress at Salka Viertel's home. They already knew each other socially, having met during the early days of the European movie colony in Beverly Hills. But Paul hadn't seen her for some while and feared that the years might have been unkind to the actress. His apprehension was quickly alleviated. Garbo still possessed in full measure those attributes that made her the most beautiful woman of her time. That evening, perfect understanding of everyone's intentions regarding the film project was established.

Within a short time Paul relayed to Garbo a most tempting offer from the powerful RKO Pictures. Garbo accepted. RKO bought Salka Viertel's script and hired the writer to make changes in it.

Consummation of the deal was highly publicized. The usual battery of legal men went to work drawing up Garbo's contract with the studio— which of course included options for her future service.

When the contract came through, Paul and his lawyers studied it and found it in order. Only his client's signature was needed now.

Greta Garbo made one of her rare appearances in Paul's office. "There is only a very minor detail, Paul," the actress said. "I would like to insert a paragraph into the contract."

"Yes?" Paul said, alarmed.

"I do not like to work till six in the evening, Paul. I will stop at five."

Paul felt a marked relief, certain that the studio would agree to this small request. "Of course, Greta. No problem."

He was wrong.

It wasn't so much the one hour of "shooting time" that RKO insisted upon keeping. The studio foresaw other whims and peccadillos by the actress. It became a contest of two giants: the studio establishment versus the artist. The contract never got Garbo's signature. This was her last known willingness to try what is euphemistically called a "comeback." And so one more promising Hollywood project failed to reach the screen.

The divine Garbo had never signed an agency contract with Paul. Neither had another, less divine but more earthy star—the Viennese comedienne, Gisela Werbezirk.

She has been dead for quite a while now, but her stories and bon mots live on. She was devoted to Paul. Her loyalty and confidence were so strong that when another agency tried to lure her away with a tempting offer for a year's studio contract, she sent the emissary on his way with the classic line, "I'd rather have no job through Paul Kohner than a fat contract through William Morris."

Personality, kid. Personality!

A Sampling of Clients

B Y NOW PAUL has worked in Hollywood long enough to have watched the comings and goings of practically everybody. As an agent he has represented such diverse actresses as Pola Negri, Luise Rainer, Myrna Loy, Greta Garbo, Dolores del Rio, Rita Hayworth, Lana Turner and Jeanne Moreau. Actor-clients on his roster have included Walter Huston, Robert Taylor, Eric von Stroheim, David Niven, Max von Sydow, Henry Fonda and Charles Bronson. And in recent years he has guided the international careers of performers like Liv Ullmann, Mia Farrow, Geraldine

Chaplin, Isabelle Adjani, Maria Schneider, Peter O'Toole, Mick Jagger, Martin Sheen, Charlotte Rampling.

And then there is John Huston—director, writer, actor—who has stuck with Paul from the very start of his agency. But there's only *one* John Huston.

What is an agent? According to Noah Webster: "One who acts for or in the place of another, by authority from him." An agent is also an active element that makes things happen. Either definition applies to Paul. The first role is embodied in the "agency contract"— or a Theatrical Motion Picture Artists' Manager Contract, in a predetermined, standardized but nonetheless alterable form. The second is derived from the special ingredients in Paul's personality that make him a talent agent par excellence. He is a superb meeter and greeter, an imaginative energizer—and, above all, a *doer.*

What is a client? If you want to go along with Webster again, it is "a person depending on another for protection or patronage." But if you listen to Paul sometimes, you might think that a client is someone in dire and perpetual need of psychotherapy.

The clients of talent agents are usually fascinating people whose virtues have been well-publicized. But at times they can also be irritating, demanding, insecure, pompous, unpredictable, vainglorious, jealous, greedy, bitter, megalomanic, cowardly, hysterical. Nine out of ten at one time or another hate their agent. When he does well by them, they may show little or no gratitude. When he performs poorly—or when he fails to fulfill their own expectations—they walk out on him. Clients who continuously keep faith with their agents are exceptional. The majority flit from agent to agent, always in the hope that a new one, like a new doctor, will find the cure for whatever ails their careers—or themselves, really. And they frequently return at long last to their first agent, probably because a healthy animosity can make for a very viable relationship between two people.

A successful agent has a twenty-four-hours-a-day, seven-days-a-week job. He is literally "on call" at all times, ready and willing to listen and advise about a wide variety of matters both professional and personal. One's own private life gets frequently interrupted. Because of the close-working interdependency of agent and clients, an agent may find that his own mood swings hinge on the successes or disappointments of a few key people whom he represents.

Somehow, though, the drawbacks in an agent's career have not unsettled Paul. Agenting has provided the challenges of high adventure. And he is particularly pleased when he makes a "discovery." He has a singular gift for spotting potential talent—and an equal gift for persuading others to trust his intuitions.

For instance, one morning some years ago he got a call from Walter Wanger, who was looking for a leading lady for an offbeat Western, *Salome,*

Where She Danced. A publicity campaign had already been launched to locate "the most beautiful girl in the world."

"I thought you might have somebody on your list who could qualify," Wanger said.

"Of course I have," Paul said promptly. "She is sitting right here in my office."

"Send her over to the studio tomorrow."

Paul did not believe in putting things off. "I'll bring her right now," he said.

"No," Wanger cut him short, "I'm busy. Make it tomorrow noon."

"You have to see her *now*," Paul insisted. "I'm supposed to take her out to Paramount tomorrow. They want to put her under contract."

Normally producers refuse to be high-pressured, but Wanger reluctantly gave in. "Okay," he said. "Have her here in fifteen minutes."

Waiting in Paul's foyer was a young Canadian actress named Peggy Middleton. Young, fresh and unusually attractive, she had drifted into the agency by chance.

"I thought you were taking me to Paramount," she said when she noticed that Paul was driving out to North Hollywood.

"We're going to see Walter Wanger at Universal," Paul told her. "He's looking for the most beautiful girl in the world."

Smiling bravely, Peggy dabbed self-consciously at her face.

As they waited in Wanger's outer office, Paul eyed Peggy Middleton speculatively. "Maybe you could use another name. Something a little more glamorous than Middleton."

He paced the room, concentrating fiercely. And then, out of the magician's hat, popped the rabbit.

"How about 'de Carlo'?"

There was no time for Peggy Middleton to cast her vote. Walter Wanger had opened the door.

"This is Yvonne de Carlo," Paul said as he introduced his new client to the producer.

Afterwards, Paul couldn't account at all for the sudden appearance of that particular rabbit.

But Yvonne de Carlo she was from this moment on.

Another ingenue who achieved stardom came to Paul's attention through a photo. One of his wartime assistants was Ernst Haeusserman, an Austrian refugee (who later became general manager of the Viennese Burg Theatre). He had struck up an acquaintance with a Marine, who showed him a photo of his sweetheart. Finding her particularly appealing, he asked to have the picture so he could show it to his boss.

Paul was intrigued by her beauty and wanted to meet the girl. But Haeusserman's Marine friend had vanished. The only clue to the girl's identity was the photographer's name and address printed on the back of the picture.

Paul drove down to the small beach community of Laguna. After locating the photographer, he searched through hundreds of negatives at the studio. Finally he found the one that matched the photo. The photographer had her name on file.

Paul persuaded the girl to let him take her up to Hollywood. He introduced her to Darryl Zanuck at Twentieth-Century-Fox.

And this time he didn't even change the name. Jeanne Crain.

Then there was the time when Paul went to the rehearsal of a stage play, *The Girl in the Via Flaminia*. A client of his was testing for a part—and he took his fourteen-year-old daughter Susan along. During a break, the director came over and asked Susan if she had done any acting. Yes, she said; in school plays. Would she like to try out for a small part in this play—an Italian servant girl? Flustered, Susan turned to her father. "Why not?" he said, rather hesitantly.

She got the role. And later, when Paul and Lupita saw her in the small theatre, they were stunned. Susan had a genuine talent. And besides, she was beautiful.

Now that her father had discovered her as an actress, he promoted this new client enthusiastically. He followed her developing career with happy attention, helped Lupita guide her from school to school and from role to role—sometimes galloping off with her across the world.

Unlike many other show-business families, the Kohners were remarkably close and trouble-free—and have remained so through the years. Both Susan and her younger brother Pancho may have been indulged by their loving and generous parents. But they were never "spoiled," managing to stay pleasant, unaffected and diligent.

Susan commenced a busy career as an actress. She played a variety of parts—mostly shy, brooding girls who were subtly sensuous. After she received an Oscar nomination for her role in *Imitation of Life*, opposite Lana Turner, she was swamped with offers. The one she accepted eagerly was a leading role in the stage play *A Quiet Place*, starring Tyrone Power. Subsequently she appeared on Broadway in *Love Me Little* to critical accolades.

One night in Florida, where she was playing the lead in *Bus Stop*, a dashing man came backstage and asked her out for dinner. He was a well-known New York fashion designer.

They fell very much in love—I guess there is no simpler way of saying it. When they married, Susan Kohner renounced her acting career forever.

Mrs. John Weitz is the part she plays now. And looking in from the outside, the casting seems perfect.

Once in a while a performer somehow will "discover" Paul and his agency instead of the other way around. Like the quite recent story of "The Girl from the Street."

The most pathetic place to see an actor is in the antechamber of an agent's office. At any time of the day, Paul's emporium contains boys and girls with eager faces, bivouacked with their glossy photographs and imitation-leather scrapbooks clutched to their bosoms, trying to catch the attention of one of the agents. Generally they are sent on their way with some polite words of regret.

There is something admirable about the foolhardy courage of these neophytes, who maybe appeared as the leads in high-school plays and were assured by a few dazzled advisers that they were indeed "Hollywood material." Somehow they have made it now to the fabled town. Along glamor-pulsating Sunset Strip they strive to get their first foot in. In where? Into a middleman's office, naturally.

My brother Walter, for long an associate in Paul's agency, has always felt great compassion for the young, the innocent and the ambitious, for he was an actor himself and still treasures memories of moments of triumph which success brought him. But that was long ago. Nowadays he tries to protect his thin skin from the onslaught of eager ingenues by delegating his secretary to fend off the intrepid unknowns. Yet even she at times is outwitted. A short while ago she was overrun by a weird-looking young woman in tight jeans, with long tangled hair and the inevitable enormous dark glasses, who got past her and charged into Walter's office.

"Are you Mr. Kohner?"

"I am Walter Kohner," he said cautiously. "What do you want?"

"An agent."

"I see," Walter said wearily. And then with the politeness that is his trademark, "Will you please sit down?"

She sat down and crossed her legs. Shapely legs.

"Are you an actress?" he asked.

"I certainly hope so," she replied.

"French?" Walter is an expert at spotting proper accents.

"Yes. French."

"Do you have any acting experience?"

"Well, yes," she said casually. "I was in a film with Marlon Brando."

"Oh?"

"You know. That porno thing. *Last Tango in Paris.*"

This elicited a smile from Walter. "Anything else?"

A pause. "One with Jack Nicholson. Have you heard of him?"

Walter nodded, trying to show no expression at all. "What's the title?"

It seemed to take her a while to remember. *"The Passenger,"* she said.

Now what on earth was he supposed to do with this one? She was either a fraud—or had flipped. Still, Walter has manners. "Why have you come to our office?" he asked.

"I saw the name Paul Kohner on the building. It is well-known in France. In the movie business."

So she had come in to see Paul. Then let Paul handle her! Walter did not wish to dismiss her himself. Let "Big White Brother" do it!

"Please wait a moment," he told her. "I'll see whether Paul is in."

He walked out of the room and straight into Paul's office. "There's a strange girl with a French accent in my office. She says she's come to see you. She sounds nuts to me. But she says she has been in two pictures— with Brando and Nicholson."

"What does she look like?"

"Freaked out."

Paul perked up. "Has she got long black hair—sort of messy?"

"Yes, sure."

"Huge sunglasses? Pants?"

"Yes," Walter said, puzzled.

Paul jumped up. "That must be Maria Schneider!" he cried, dashing out of the room.

For a moment Walter stood stunned. Was it possible? The world-famous Maria Schneider coming in off the street, walking into his office, wanting a job? He ran after Paul and got there just in time to see him planting one of his most elegant Continental kisses on the girl's hand.

Then Paul ushered her into his own office. A short while later he had the French star's signature upon his agency contract.

To tell the stories of a few of Paul's contacts with clients takes more than several paragraphs or a page or two. Since Paul's own history is often entwined at some points with other people, I shall now present chapter-length sketches of some personal and business relationships of his, gathered loosely together as a sort of "Cast of Characters."

B. Traven

TRAVEN, AN EMINENT twentieth-century storyteller, was barely noticed in the United States during his lifetime. Only now is his work gaining a deserved critical and popular recognition.

For reasons known only to Traven, he went to elaborate lengths to guard his privacy. For forty years the legends this resident of Mexico built as protections around himself led to wild speculations among people interested in the writer and his stories. He was Jack London reincarnated, a refugee Bavarian socialist, a derelict Hohenzollern prince, a fugitive Austrian archduke, a leper, a Negro fleeing from American injustice, an Arctic explorer, a deported "Wobbly" (member of the old communistic Industrial Workers of the World), the illegitimate son of either Kaiser Wilhelm of Germany, President Lopez-Mateos of Mexico or—as the *New York Times* once reported—none other than his agent Paul Kohner.

Whoever he was or had been, Traven's identity remained a confounding and closely kept secret while he lived. Only after his death in 1969 was the real and conclusive information about him made public. The mysteries he promoted were strange and intricate enough to give a generation of Ph.D. candidates material for dozens of speculative dissertations.

Paul first contacted Traven in 1932, when as a producer he wanted to acquire the motion picture rights to his novel *The Death Ship*. Since he didn't know the writer's whereabouts, he started negotiations through the German book club Bücher Gilde. Subsequently he exchanged a series of letters with Traven through a third party named Martinez, who lived in Mexico City. Nothing came of that project. But after Paul opened his agency business, he again wrote to Traven, c/o Martinez. He told him that since he had always admired his work, he would feel honored to represent his books for movie sales.

A voluminous correspondence between them began. An oddly piquant element entered into the client-agent relationship when Traven also started writing letters to Paul's wife Lupita, who had become a movie star in Mexico.

Traven said he had long admired her as an actress. However, he deplored the roles assigned to her. And there were so many beautiful stories with parts ideally suited to her! He saw every film Lupita ever appeared in—not once, but again and again. He would comment on every scene, writing pages and pages of analysis that made profundities out of trivia. He sent miscellaneous clippings from provincial Mexican papers, reviews of her films, advertisements, photos. He also wrote long letters to Paul telling him of his wife's unique qualities as an actress and asking why he didn't manage her career better.

Paul was intrigued—but not entirely at ease. Once he suggested that surely Traven had a story that would give Lupita the kind of role that the writer visualized for her. Traven answered promptly: he would go to work immediately on a script. A few weeks later a weighty package arrived, containing some five hundred pages of a "screenplay"—a good story but totally disregarding the cinematic format.

The next time Lupita visited her family in Mexico City, Traven sent her a note saying that he wanted to meet her. But not in the city. He was scared of the city. Could she possibly come to Acapulco? He lived nearby. She called Paul to get his advice. Reluctantly, he told her to go ahead—but not unchaperoned.

She drove to the resort town, sent a message to Traven's postal-box address, then waited to hear from him. The next day a letter arrived. He enclosed a map of the coastline along with detailed instructions on how to proceed to an isolated spot marked on the map. She must come at six in the evening. Alone.

At the appointed time Lupita drove to the rendezvous. Her companion stayed in the car while she walked by herself to the designated promontory.

It was the end of September. The sun was setting. The place Traven had chosen for their meeting was deserted—and extremely romantic.

Lupita sat down. While she looked for a legend to materialize in human form, the sky and sea began to darken. Once during the half-hour she waited she thought she saw a figure in the distance. Traven? She would never know.

That evening another letter came—in which he berated her. She hadn't observed the terms of the deal. She had brought someone along in the car. He had said *alone*.

This episode was just one of many exchanges through the years that indicated a disturbed personality. Once Traven wrote in great detail about a dream in which he saw Paul lying dead in a hotel room in Mexico City. Bruises all over his body. Obviously murdered. Lupita begged Traven to help her carry the body out of the room. He knew that the cause of the murder was jealousy. It was unclear, however, who was jealous of whom. Nor was it clear whether Lupita had done something which Paul resented. Yet Lupita *knew* the murderer. It even seemed she might have been an accomplice—and so on.

After the long, confused narrative Traven came to the conclusion: the dream was an omen. His conscience urged him to warn Paul. That was all—for a while.

"Certainly you remember the dream I told you about several months ago," he suddenly wrote to Paul half a year later, "and that the lamentable happening had been caused by a personal relation. Now I know who it is, or better, who it was in the dream. For your own sake, I advise you to avoid being anywhere in Mexico when for one reason or another F. K. should also happen to be around. Sorry, Paul, I surely don't wish to tell you, but it's *him*. You'd better be very careful."

No, *I* was not the "F. K." whose treacherous image had loomed in Traven's unconscious mind, a projection of his own jealous fantasies. These were also the initials of a gentleman employee in Paul's agency, who handled various financial transactions and signed Traven's royalty checks. An austere looking, upright-living, middle-aged man, he would have been most amazed to hear of his role as the murderous rake in Traven's demented dream world.

Another time, when Paul was visiting Mexico, Traven promised to meet him at the Hotel Reforma at seven P.M. Paul believed that this time his elusive (and illusive) client might actually reveal himself. The film sale of Traven's book *The Treasure of the Sierra Madre* was to be concluded, needing only the author's signature before Paul would hand over the sizable check.

Exactly at seven o'clock a letter was delivered to Paul. Traven scribbled that he had suddenly been taken terribly ill. He was at a hospital, where doctors "had pumped a quart of blood out of him and had pumped a quart of some jelly *into* him." The nurses had prevented him from calling the hotel. The note went on to say that he was not at all interested in any business proposition but had wanted solely to meet Lupita and bring her a "carload of orchids and a five-pound box of Lady Baltimore Chocolates." Moreover, this was his second letter, he said, for the first one had been destroyed by the nurse because it divulged the name of the hospital. "Another thing I must tell you is—" End of note.

Paul suspected that he actually met Traven once. After the deal for the film version of *The Treasure of the Sierra Madre* was closed, the author expressed the wish for a trusted friend to serve as consultant while the picture was being made in Mexico. The proposal was readily accepted.

One day a man introducing himself as Hal Croves called on director John Huston in his Mexico City hotel. He said he was Traven's cousin and had been delegated to assist the director in the sequence to be filmed in the interior of the country.

From the beginning, Huston felt certain that Hal Croves was none other than B. Traven himself. And when Paul came to visit the set and was introduced to Croves, they looked into each other's eyes. Croves smiled. Paul smiled. They shook hands. Croves continued to hold Paul's hand for a few moments—as if this were more to him than a perfunctory meeting. Then he walked off the set.

Paul evolved two theories based on his strange and sundry dealings with Traven. Either the writer had a shrewd and perhaps mischievous desire to construct a mysterious mythology around himself, or else he was a bona fide, eccentric recluse who harbored paranoid delusions.

The second theory was borne out by a letter Traven wrote to Paul in 1950, in which he unjustly accused his agent of malfeasance in the most vituperous language. "I have never looked into this so-called representation closely enough," he said, "because I seem to have trusted you more than the law should allow an author who is too much absorbed in his work to watch out for the material side of his life."

For fifteen years Paul had tried to sell Traven's books for motion pictures and sometimes had been quite successful. Now he gave way to anger. He advised his client to go to see a psychiatrist. Otherwise, he told Traven, he would have to send his regular gift packages—mostly cases of whisky—to him at "La Castañeda," the Mexican state hospital for the mentally sick.

Traven must have been deeply wounded. Pretending never to have read the registered letter, he returned it. But obviously the envelope had been opened.

So their correspondence ceased. And so did their business connection. Paul regretted his intemperate letter and wished he had shown more restraint. During the Fifties he made a few attempts at reconciliation. But the apologetic letters he sent to Traven, as before c/o Martinez, were always returned—unopened.

In the late Sixties, on one of their frequent visits to the Mexican capital, Paul and Lupita were invited to a party for President Diaz Ortez. At the formal dinner which followed the reception, an attractive lady sat to the right of Paul. Her place card read "Rosa Elena Lujan." With a vaguely amused expression, she studied Paul's face.

"Do we know each other?" he asked.

"Indirectly," she said. "You see, I also have another name. I am Mrs. Hal Croves."

It took Paul a few moments to collect his wits. "You mean—you are Mrs. Traven!"

Mrs. Lujan-Croves smiled. "No," she said. "I am Mrs. Croves. Mr. Croves is not Mr. Traven. He is his cousin."

But Paul knew better. He quickly decided that she must have arranged the seating order for some reason. So acting on this suspicion, he pressed his advantage. He told her how badly he had felt all these years after alienating his old friend Traven. Could Señora Lujan possibly arrange for him to meet with this "cousin"?

She promised to make an effort. She would send him a message.

Next day Paul found a note at his hotel. "Perhaps next year—when you come again to our city."

The following autumn Paul returned. He announced his presence to Señora Lujan. He and Lupita received an invitation for tea.

They were led to an upstairs room in a patrician Mexican home. Traven himself—whom indeed Paul had met years before as Hal Croves—stood in his studio. He was an old man now. Greatly moved, he stretched out his arms in a welcoming gesture. Paul and Traven embraced. When Traven kissed Lupita, there were tears in his eyes.

"What a pity," he said, "that it took so long!"

He died a year later.

His will confirmed what many Traven sleuths had long suspected: he was actually an American citizen. Born in Chicago to German parents and given the name of Traven Torsvan Croves, he spent his youth in Germany, where he became an itinerant actor and later a revolutionary journalist.

In the political upheaval following World War I, Traven was a leader in the abortive Bavarian revolution. As a staunch supporter of the German left—at the same time keeping a cautious distance from the Communists—he helped to uncover the secret exploits of the infamous pre-Nazi FEME, which had plotted the murders of Erzberger and Walter Rathenau, the great statesmen of the Weimar Republic. Apprehended, he escaped by becoming a seaman on a tramp steamer and then jumped ship in Tampico, Mexico. Knowing the long, ugly hand of the FEME murderers, for the purpose of personal safety he chose to remain anonymous when he set up residence in Mexico. And when he began to sell his stories abroad, he apparently realized that anonymity could eventually make for a tantalizing legend that could work to his advantage as a writer. He played the name game successfully for a half-century.

40

Chevalier

A MAN STOOD ON the shores of the Mediterranean on a windy morning in May in the early Fifties. His collar was up, the checkered cap pulled far down over the face.

Paul, out for a morning walk, saw him and stopped. The man's lower lip seemed familiar.

"Maurice?"

The man with the most famous protruding lower lip in the world looked back at him. "Paul Kohner?"

Paul nodded. Maurice Chevalier's face brightened for a moment as they shook hands.

"What are you doing at Juan les Pins?" Chevalier asked.

Paul told him that he had been at the Cannes Film Festival and was here now for a few days' rest.

"I'm giving concerts in the summer circuit," Chevalier said. "Here in Juan I am playing the Orpheum. It's not the best house—but you probably know how it is with me. I am not very popular in France. And I cannot go to America because Washington will not give me a visa. They put a black mark on my name because I signed the Stockholm Peace Appeal. I am not political and never have been. It was just plain stupid to sign that paper! But how could I have known it was connected with the Communists?"

Chevalier had been in trouble for a long time. At the end of the Second World War, the Maquis accused him of collaborating with the Nazis because he had visited a French prison camp in Germany. He had gone there to entertain French troops, but the mere act of visiting Germany during the war made him suspect. Although the Maquis finally acquitted him, the publicity had hurt his career.

"You've known me for a long time, Paul," Chevalier said sadly. "I have lived through three wars. I have never belonged to a party, to a movement. I am an entertainer—not a man of politics."

"How could I be of help, Maurice?"

Chevalier shrugged expressively. "In Hollywood they wanted me for a picture. But Washington said no. No visa. No work permit for Chevalier. It is a great injustice. I want to clear my name. If you can help me do that, I would be forever grateful."

Paul told Chevalier that he would do everything in his power to exonerate him and get him back to Hollywood. "Come to think of it, Maurice, there might be a great part for you in Billy Wilder's next film. You know the book *Ariane*. The part of the French detective would be ideal for you."

"It is a big part?" He immediately perked up.

"The biggest—next to Gary Cooper and Audrey Hepburn, who are already signed. Billy is looking high and wide for a French actor."

"I would give the *recette* of my mother's *bouillabaisse* to Billy Wilder if I could play in his film. I like him. And you know how I love America."

"Do you have an agent, Maurice?"

"Not in the States."

"Would you permit me to represent you?"

"It would be my pleasure."

They shook hands.

When Paul called Wilder in Hollywood, the director responded enthusiastically. Certainly Maurice Chevalier would be perfect casting for the part in *Love in the Afternoon*.

Wilder and Paul then worked to clear Chevalier with the State Department. Soon afterwards Chevalier got his visa—and returned to Hollywood.

On an early visit to Paul's office, he inspected the gallery of clients' photographs displayed around the walls. "I too will present you with a picture," he said magnanimously to Paul, "to add to your collection."

The photograph arrived that afternoon and was given a prominent place. It was only the first of many photos Paul received from his French client. Every Christmas a new one arrived, carefully wrapped—showing the never-aging face of the eternal performer smiling broadly into the camera.

Ten years to the day after they had met on the beach of Juan les Pins, Paul happened to be in Paris. To commemorate the occasion, Chevalier invited his American agent and some mutual friends to a luncheon at Maxim's. At the end of the meal, Chevalier disappeared. He returned with a huge, beautifully wrapped package. First he lifted his glass and gave an eloquent toast extolling Paul Kohner. Then he presented him with the gift.

For a fleeting moment, Paul had visions of a Picasso or a Utrillo painting.

It was, however, merely a new photograph of Maurice Chevalier, larger than life, doffing his straw hat and twirling the inevitable cane.

41

Gregory Ratoff

WHEN PAUL HEARD that Gregory Ratoff lay dying in Switzerland, he called him.

"Paul, my frand," Ratoff said, his rich bass now reduced to a rasp, "I know why you are calling. You have heard I am dying. Well, let me tell you, my palsie, I am still fighting. It's a tough fight—but I have hope. I have the grrreatest doctors money can buy and I am by nature an optimist. Now let me ask you a question for your information: How is my darrrling Lupita? Give her a kiss from me."

Next day he was dead.

In passing, Ratoff garnered no more than a few lines in the trade papers. Yet this White Russian émigré—actor, director, producer, "Hollywood character"—had been a man of unusual magnetism. His vocabulary bristled with such stock Hollywood hyperboles as "stupendous," "terrific," "supercolossal"—or simply his own unique "sansetional."

One day in 1934 he called me in London. "Your brother is telling me you are a sansetional writer," Ratoff said over the phone. "Of course we have to discount that it is your brother. So tell me, my frand—are you a sansetional writer?"

At the time Ratoff was just an actor, but he had higher ambitions. He wanted to become a director—and had acquired the motion picture rights to *Job*, a modern Biblical allegory by the Austrian writer Joseph Roth.

We made a luncheon date at the country club in Elstree, close to the B.I.P. studios, where Ratoff was playing the lead in a small-budget film.

He made his entrance dressed as a lion tamer. The staid clientele of the club stared in amazement at the enormous, ruddy, barrel-chested man with a huge red mustachio, who came in cracking his whip. He strode up and threw his arms around me. It was quite a performance.

"Now, my frand—tell me about yourself," he said, ordering a sumptuous meal.

I gave him a résumé of my professional work.

"Now we don't have to talk about that any more, my frand. I can see you are an honest man. So I will be honest with you too, for your information. *Job* will be one of the grrreatest pictures ever made. I will direct it, and I will also play the lead. Now as for the screenplay, I have hired one of the most sansetional writers in America—Ossip Dymov. He is coming to London in two weeks, and you will work with him. A vonderful combination. And you can write your brother that he has made me a happy man."

Somewhat to my surprise, he did call when Dymov arrived and asked me to meet them at the Dorchester Hotel. He had a contract ready for me to sign. He even made a down payment.

Ossip Dymov and I worked harmoniously for a few months on the script of *Job*. When it was finished, Ratoff invited us to his suite and had us read it to him. He became violently emotional. From time to time he broke into tears. When we finished, he embraced us—and paid us. And then he was off to America.

Half a year later, he wrote that he had sold our script to Zanuck, that he had indeed directed the film, and that the preview in Hollywood had been absolutely supercolossal.

"You realize, of course," the letter continued, "that I had to make some minor changes in the script. But never mind—your name is big up there on the screen. And when you come to Hollywood, your fortune is made."

Minor changes? The novel's protagonist Mendel Singer, a *schamus* in a Russian *stedtl*, had become Walter Terlinden, a bellringer in a Swiss mountain village. His son, who in the book turned out to be a world-famous violinist, was changed in the film into a stunt flier. Every trace of the original Jewish milieu was gone. And the title of the picture was no longer *Job*, but *Sins of Man*.

Ratoff was gifted with genius—mainly, the genius for boasting. He spoke of himself as the *grrreatest* actor alive. And, later, the *grrreatest* living director. Of course when he hired you to work for him, he went around telling everyone that you were absolutely the most sansetional writer in the whole world. Thus he transformed you into a genius, too.

In the fabled time of the Forties, Gregory Ratoff was a fixture at the Zanucks' home. Darryl Zanuck loved Ratoff, who was his court jester and personal friend. And as long as Zanuck ran Fox, Ratoff directed and produced for the studio.

Paul was fond of Ratoff but found him difficult as a client. He always demanded immediate attention from his agent.

Once he barreled his way into the office just as Paul and two lawyers were discussing a major deal.

"I must see you right away!" Ratoff shouted. "It is a matter of the grrreatest importance."

Paul excused himself and ushered Ratoff into an adjoining room. "Can't it wait, Gregory?"

"Not a second, my palsie," Ratoff went on. "This is the most important deal you will ever negotiate for me."

"What is it?" Paul asked impatiently.

Ratoff laid a heavy hand on his shoulder and fixed him with a grave stare. "You know, of course, Lady Eleanor Smith?"

"No—what about her?"

"You mean to tell me that you don't know Lady Smith? And I thought you were an educated man."

"Please, Gregory. I can't let those people wait any longer. What about the woman?"

"What about her? She is just about the most supercolossal writer in England, my palsie. That's all."

"So what?"

"So I just finished reading a book by her. It is called *Ballerina*. It is *fan-tas-tic!* You must buy it for me. At a price, of course."

"But can't that wait?" Paul said in exasperation.

"I am amazed at you, my frand," Ratoff said sadly. He reached into his coat pocket and extracted a book. "Here. You must read it right away and then you must get in touch with this woman and buy an option. It is the chance of a lifetime. If I lose it, I kill myself."

Paul took a quick look at the copyright date. "My God, Gregory," he cried. "That book was published ten years ago. And now it cannot wait another day?"

"Well—" Ratoff said, suddenly reasonable. "Maybe another day. But not longer."

Next day Paul got in touch with the book's publisher. The rights were still available and an option deal was worked out. Then he called Ratoff to brief him on the negotiation and to ask him to come to the office and sign an agreement.

"Impossible, my palsie. Not today."

"But you were in such a hurry! And now you can't drop by the office?"

"If you are my frand, Paul, you get in your car and drive to my house. I am leaving in half an hour for Santa Barbara. Come with me and we can discuss the deal on the way."

"Why Santa Barbara?"

"I am on a diet, my frand," Ratoff said. "My doctor says if I don't lose fifty pounds I will drop dead tomorrow."

"That still doesn't explain Santa Barbara."

"Well, there is a sanitarium up in the hills where they feed you the most sansetional diet. The food is nothing to rave about, you understand, but the doctor—he is a Hungarian—guarantees I will lose fifty pounds in four weeks if I eat his vegetables."

"And you can't get that stuff here?"

"Please, my frand—you're making me very nervous. Call your darrrling wife, tell her we're going to Santa Barbara and will be back tonight."

Paul, curious because he also was overweight, acceded.

They set out from Ratoff's house in a hurry. "You understand I must be in the dining room at seven the *latest*. They close at seven-thirty. So you will excuse my fast driving."

Approaching Ventura, Ratoff slowed down. "I am hongry," he said. "How about a cup of coffee, my palsie?"

They stopped at a coffee shop. "I know this place," Ratoff said as they went inside. "Grrreatest apple pie in the world."

They sat down at the counter. A pretty waitress greeted Ratoff.

"Now, my darrrling—tell me, how is the apple pie today?"

"Just fresh from the kitchen."

"Okay, my beautiful, my sweetheart," Ratoff said and patted the girl's hand. "You bring me a nice hot slice of that apple pie and a cup of coffee. Full to the top. And for my frand here the same. And by the way—this man is the grrreatest talent agent in Hollywood. If you are nice to him, he will discover you. Right, Paul?"

The girl brought the pie and coffee.

"Gregory," Paul said, "I thought you were on a diet. The reason we're making this trip is so you can have dinner at Santa Barbara."

"Ah—but it's only five-thirty. Still plenty of time for dinner. How do you like that pie, my frand—have you ever eaten such a fantastic pie in all your life?"

A truck driver now sat down next to Ratoff and ordered a bowl of chili. As the man crumbled soda crackers into the steaming bowl, Ratoff watched him closely.

"How is that chili?" he asked the trucker.

"Not bad."

Ratoff deliberated for a few seconds, then called the waitress. "Darrr-ling, give me a bowl of that sansetional chili. And another cup of coffee. Full to the top!"

Half an hour later they were speeding along. "Take it easy, Gregory," Paul urged.

"They are closing the dining room on me," Ratoff almost wailed. "I must be there before seven-thirty."

With just about five minutes to spare, they came to a crunching stop in the driveway of the sanitarium. Ratoff jumped out of the car and raced to the dining room. Paul followed him.

The table was set for Ratoff. Waiting for him were a dish of granola, a plate of raw carrots, celery, nuts and raisins, and a bowl of green salad. He wolfed it all down.

"Now we go to this sansetional restaurant," he said to Paul. "And you will have *your* dinner. I will keep you company, and we will discuss the contract."

At the restaurant Paul ordered a steak and a baked potato.

"You bring this man here the finest steak you have in your kitchen," Ratoff said. "He is writing for *Holiday* magazine, and if he likes your steak he will give you a big boost!" He winked at Paul.

While they were waiting, they talked about the terms of the deal—which, of course, proved unacceptable to Ratoff.

"We will do a little more finagling, my palsie," Ratoff said. "After all, no one wanted that book for ten years. And who has ever heard of that Eleanor Smith lady, right?"

The steak was served. Ratoff avidly watched Paul eat. "How is the steak?"

"First class."

"How many calories does a steak like that have?"

"Plenty."

"It makes me very nervous, my palsie."

"Why don't you go for a little walk instead of torturing yourself?" Paul suggested. "It won't take me long to finish."

"Smart idea," Ratoff said and left the table.

He came back in five minutes. "My frand," he said, "I have just made a sansetional decision."

"What is it, Gregory?"

"I will have a steak like yours—and to hell with that Hungarian phony at the sanitarium!"

42

Hemingway

IN THE EARLY Fifties Paul was promoting an independent producer-director "package" deal for his friends William Wyler, John Huston, Billy Wilder. Huston had expressed interest in filming a Hemingway short story, which gave Paul the idea of having the three directors do a Hemingway story apiece. Then the three short films could be released as a single feature.

Huston was particularly enthusiastic, so a meeting was arranged with Hemingway, who at the time was staying at a small French seaside resort.

Paul and John Huston took the train together from Paris. On the way, Paul gave thought to his long association with Huston. He realized that he was beholden to him not just for friendship and a perennially thriving business connection, but also because Huston had often given him a good excuse to travel off to some faraway spot in the world, to visit him while he was filming on location. And whenever and wherever they got together, they had a glorious time. Egypt, Spain, Ireland, Scotland, France, Mexico, Italy, parts of the United States: Paul saw places and people and did things that added to the rich variety of experiences in his life.

They were met at the station at St. Jean-de-Luz by Peter Viertel, a writer friend of both Hemingway and Huston. He took them to the small hotel where "Papa" Hemingway and "Miss Mary" had taken up residence.

Paul had eaten something that didn't agree with him. He excused himself and went to his room. A while later Mary Hemingway knocked at the door. She brought some pills which, she said, always helped Papa. Touched by her solicitude, Paul took the medicine.

Next morning he felt better. When he came to the breakfast room, he found the Hemingways, Huston and Viertel waiting for him. Hemingway and his wife had recently returned from Africa, where they had had a near-fatal airplane accident. Hemingway still sported some broken ribs but otherwise seemed in good shape.

Eventually they got around to talking about Paul's project. Huston liked "Cat in the Rain." Hemingway thought it didn't have enough substance to sustain a motion picture.

"We could do a damn good half-hour film of that story," Huston protested. "Couldn't we, Peter?" Viertel agreed.

Paul had reread all the Hemingway stories which he considered possibilities, and he now began to discuss them with Hemingway. The writer listened attentively. Then he suggested a walk through the town.

It was a fine day. The sky was blue. A flock of seagulls flew overhead. Hemingway stopped, looked up and pointed an imaginary rifle at them. "Can you handle a rifle?" he asked Paul.

The only shooting he had ever done was in a shooting gallery, Paul confessed.

"A great sport and pastime," Hemingway said. "You should take it up."

He was in high spirits. He spoke about his African safari, about the accident, about his work in progress. Once he stopped, pulled a silver flask out of his pocket, unscrewed the top and took a swig.

As they passed a bookstore on the marketplace, Paul asked Hemingway whether he would inscribe a couple of books for him—one for Lupita and one for Susan—if he could buy them there.

They went inside. Hemingway, in pidgin French, first inquired whether the store had anything by Mickey Spillane. The clerk shook his head. Never heard of him. "How about Faulkner? You know Faulkner?" The clerk shook his head apologetically. There was a pause and then Hemingway asked: "Any books by a writer called Hemingway?"

The clerk perked up. "Ah—'Emingway, *bien sur*—monsieur." And he brought out a collection of short stories in the Scribner edition.

Hemingway was pleased. He insisted on paying for the two copies himself before he signed them.

Later they ate lunch in a bistro. Hemingway ordered champagne. A rapport of sorts had sprung up between the writer and Paul, expressed in the easy resonance of their voices, in their eyes. Hemingway spoke enthusiastically about Peter Viertel and said that he would be his choice for the screenwriter on the project.

When Paul tried to pick up the check, as was his custom, he found out that Hemingway had already paid.

Now Hemingway wanted to have some pictures taken. Paul had brought his camera along. Huston took shots of Hemingway with his arm around Paul, looking benevolent, paternal, happy.

Hemingway accompanied them to the station. Warmth radiated from him as he said goodbye to Paul. "You must visit us in Cuba," he called out as the train started. "And make it soon!"

"You certainly hit it off with the Old Man," Huston said. "He hardly talked to *me*."

The next evening, in Paris, Huston got a call from Viertel.

"Hemingway sure went for Paul," Huston said to him. "Is he always that chummy with agents?"

Viertel laughed. "You'll get a kick out of this, John. When we walked out of the station, Papa said, 'This fellow Kohner—what is his part in the set-up?' I was surprised he didn't know. You should have seen his face when I told him that Paul was the agent. 'Agent? Christ!' he said. 'And I thought he was the *money-man*.' "

43

Lana

OR DECADES NOW a corps of leather-skinned ladies in huge sunglasses have set up card tables on Sunset Boulevard close to the main entrance to Bel Air. There they hawk maps to movie stars' residences—or what is left of them. Thousands of tourists in cars prowl the leafy, winding roads of the vast parklike estate to gaze at the homes of once-famous film personalities.

Stone Canyon Road, where Paul's home is situated, is relatively free from tourist gapers and doorbell ringers. A Spanish hacienda with sycamore trees and a swimming pool is no object of special attention. There are too many of them. Yet Paul's place is lovely. His bedroom windows look out onto a broad expanse of lawn and lush vegetation. And—as befits the region's name—the air is heady with the scent of gardenias, honeysuckle and orange blossoms.

One sleeps well in Bel Air. It comes "with the territory," almost as if guaranteed in the title deed. So sound is Paul's usual sleep that once, when a mudslide descended close to his house and almost crashed into his bedroom, he slept through the whole disaster.

Paul was snoring peacefully when the phone on his bedside table rang one April night in 1958. Lupita answered the call.

Lana Turner. Frantic, she wanted Paul to come over right away. An emergency. Then she hung up.

Lupita stood for a moment, undecided. It was two in the morning. They had come home late. Paul had been very tired. Yet Lana was one of his star clients.

She shook him gently. "Sorry, darling, but there was a call from Lana. I have no idea what happened—but she sounded hysterical."

Paul moaned. Half-asleep, he dialed her number. The phone was busy. He waited, dialed again. The phone had gone dead.

He sighed and swung his feet out of bed. "Well, I'd better go over," he said.

As he was dressing, he thought over his history with Lana. He had already had a full share of her hysterics in the many years he represented her. What was it now?

Then around forty, Lana was one of the few remaining superstars of the "Golden Age" of Hollywood.

Paul was fond of Lana, and Lana trusted him. Changing agents for her was as simple and frequent as changing husbands (seven, all told). But Paul had staying power. He remained her manager and confidant longer than any of the other middlemen she had employed in her long career.

And Paul was responsible for the change in her "image." When the script of *Peyton Place* landed on his desk, he sent it to Lana. Having read it, she asked him what part he had in mind for her. The teen-age daughter?

"The mother," Paul said. In his opinion, and in Hollywood parlance, the part was "tailormade" for her.

Lana was stunned. Did he really mean she should play a *mother?* Why not? Paul asked. She hung up on him.

Yet after thinking it over, she accepted—though friends and family had tried to dissuade her. Maybe something in the mother's character had struck a chord in her. After all, didn't she have her own troubled and confused teen-age daughter to contend with? In some ways the fictional girl in the script seemed the counterpart of Cheryl.

Cheryl Crane was Lana's only child, from her second marriage to Steve Crane. Born to Hollywood purple, raised in ever-changing homes, hotels, private schools, Cheryl never knew emotional security or found her own identity. A plain, unhappy girl, she constantly had to cope with comparisons to her "glamorous" mother, the Hollywood movie star.

Perhaps, Paul thought as he drove along the deserted Sunset Boulevard, Lana was having trouble again with Cheryl. Only a while ago she had run away from a Catholic boarding school and had been picked up in downtown skid row. The poor child had probably gone off on another "trip." And poor Lana, thought Paul—trying to keep his eyes open.

Then a far more chilling thought crossed his mind. There might be more trouble with Johnny Stompanato. Suddenly he was wide awake.

Stompanato was one of the many clever, good-looking men with no visible talent or means of support who moved in certain Hollywood circles and attached themselves to lonely, vain, bored women—entertaining them, escorting them, using them. Most of them were quickly discarded, replaced and forgotten.

But not so Stampanato. His hold on Lana was solid. He had been around her for quite some time. Lately he had proudly displayed a gold locket around his neck, containing Lana's picture and a strand of her blond hair. He made sure that everyone read the engraving on it: "For Johnny—My Love—My Life."

How foolish, Paul had thought. And how pathetic. Especially now. For he knew what only Lana's closest friends knew: that the romance had turned sour. She had tried desperately to rid herself of the former bodyguard and ex-Marine, but she lacked the strength and determination to succeed. For Stompanato liked all the glitter surrounding Lana. He liked that locket around his neck. And he did not give up easily. When Lana went to London on an assignment, hoping to put distance between them, he had followed her and had taken a suite at her hotel.

Lana had become frightened not only for career but for her very life. More than once, she had told Paul, Stompanato had choked her into insensibility. He had also threatened to disfigure her face if she tried to oust him.

My God, Paul realized now with a shudder, the call probably *was* over Stompanato!

He drove past the Beverly Hills Hotel, then turned south on Bedford Drive. A siren shrieked. He quickly moved to the curb and let an ambulance pass. It came to a halt in front of the Spanish mansion a few hundred feet away. Lana's house.

A dozen or so vehicles were already there. Fire engines. Police cars. Automobiles.

Paul jumped out and dashed towards the entrance. A couple of plainclothesmen blocked his way. He told them he had been summoned, that he was Lana Turner's agent. Asked for identification, he searched for his wallet, realized he had left it at home. One man went inside to clear him while his partner stood guard. Paul asked him what had happened. The man shrugged. Paul waited a few tense minutes before the other man reappeared. Okay, he could go in.

Just as Paul was about to enter, two white-frocked young men came out with a stretcher. Paul stood rigid for a moment. Horrified, he looked at the covered body—and then went inside.

A few men stood around in the living room. He knew most of them. There were Glenn Rose, Lana's press agent; Dr. McDonald, her physician; Anderson, the chief of the Beverly Hills police department; and a short, stocky man with a high nasal voice whom Paul had once met socially— Jerry Geisler, Hollywood's most publicized criminal lawyer.

Geisler's presence in the room confirmed Paul's fear that something hideous and irrevocable had taken place.

Paul moved close to the circle of men who were deliberating what to do and how to do it and what to say to whom. Since he still didn't know what had happened, he beckoned Glenn Rose aside. The two went into the bar adjoining the living room, where Rose poured them brandies. Then he told Paul the story.

It was Friday, April 4th. Good Friday. Violent arguments between the lovers had started in the house in the late afternoon. Nothing unusual— except that Cheryl, home for the Easter holidays, witnessed the altercation. Cheryl was fourteen but looked twenty. A tall, robust, steely, no-nonsense girl from whom it was impossible to keep secrets.

Around seven, Stompanato had left the house in a fury, but Lana knew that he would come back. She confessed to her daughter that she felt in deadly fear of him. In his rage he might carry out his threat to disfigure her face—and that would mean the end of her screen career.

"Don't be a coward, Mother," Cheryl urged her. "Lock all the doors. Keep him out!"

He returned after an hour. No one had locked him out after all. The arguments continued, shifted from the kitchen to the living room, then from the bar to the second floor.

Lana's bedroom, all pink and satin, was next to Cheryl's. Cheryl was watching television, but the noise of the lovers' quarrel drowned out the sounds of the program. The fight became a marathon brawl.

Cheryl heard her mother plead with Stompanato to leave her alone. Then Stompanato ridiculing her and threatening bodily harm.

Cheryl had heard enough. She opened the door of her room, leaving the television on, ran downstairs to the kitchen, grabbed a butcher knife lying on the drainboard and returned upstairs.

The voices in her mother's bedroom were continuing loud and ugly. Accusations, obscenities. Suddenly the door flew open. Lana stood there, yelling at Stompanato to get out. Cheryl saw him wielding a metal clothes hanger, ready to whip it across her mother's face.

"You don't have to take that, Mother," Cheryl said—and rammed the knife into Stompanato's cashmere sweater.

Various attempts to resuscitate him failed.

"Should I go up and see her?" Paul asked.

"You might try," Rose said. "She's under sedation. Her mother is with her. And the doctor."

Apprehensively, Paul went upstairs. The bedroom door stood ajar. Lana, looking waxen, lay on her pink satin bedcover, while Mrs. Turner held her hand. The doctor was packing up his satchel.

Paul tiptoed to the bed.

"Paul is here," her mother whispered.

Lana looked up. When she saw Paul, she began to sob uncontollably. He sat on the edge of the bed. Taking her in his arms, he cuddled her as if she were his own child.

"Oh, Paul," she cried. "It's all over. I'll never get a job again. I'm through!"

She wasn't "through," of course. The excessive publicity created by the Stompanato murder made Lana Turner once more a famous name. Millions of people around the world avidly consumed all the lurid details of the affair. Reporters of every major publication were assigned to dredge up whatever information they could find. Somebody discovered a bundle of love letters and put them up for sale. The price was paid, and a few of the letters appeared in facsimile in newspapers from Lisbon to Singapore.

Curiously, Lana's letters—with their vapid, girlishly romantic outpourings—restored the early image of Lana Turner. The high-school dropout discovered in a revealing sweater at a Hollywood soda fountain counter. The sweet, rosy-cheeked girlfriend of Andy Hardy.

Offers now poured in. Not just parts in cheap exploitation scripts written on the quick, but also good dramatic roles. Paul screened them and selected a few he thought worthy of Lana's talents.

The part she eventually accepted was the lead in *Imitation of Life*. She played—in Hollywood press-release lingo of the day—"the ambitious stage actress who sacrifices the man she loves and the bringing up of her daughter for her career."

The picture, directed by Douglas Sirk, became one of the all-time big moneymakers manufactured by the Hollywood dream factory.

44

My Brother—My Agent

IKE MOST PEOPLE around Hollywood, I too needed an agent. What was more natural than for me to turn to my brother Paul? He had brought me to America to begin with, through some clever stringpulling. I long believed that he was the best possible agent for me. For twenty-five years neither occasional failures nor disappointments could knock that conviction out of my head. Especially since he saw to it that I was perennially employed.

Paul was aware that my strongest talent was for inventing stories. I could also put them down on paper so that they read well. And since I could also *tell* them well later, he set up appointments at studios during which I could sell those stories by narrating them.

He sold most of the stories I invented and got good prices for them. Not always the best price, but perhaps that was because he didn't want to take risks with his brother's livelihood. "Take it," he would usually advise when an offer came along, "they might get cold feet after lunch." Yet to another client he often said: "Sit tight. We can do better." Or he might make a counteroffer—and then get more.

My first story—the one he submitted to Pasternak for Durbin— provides a good example. Paul asked, and got, thirty thousand dollars for the Bercovici story when it wasn't even on paper. (And, by the way, it was never filmed.) But he got only fifteen hundred for my story, *Mad about Music*, which was made into one of Durbin's most successful films and earned me an Oscar nomination.

After he had sold a few of my stories, though, he became a bit more

151

enterprising. I had written a story he thought was just right for John Garfield. He talked to Garfield and arranged for me to see him. I went to his house. The star—highstrung, mercurial—at first refused to listen. Couldn't he get the whole thing in writing? I didn't let on that I had it all on paper—some fifty-odd pages. I insisted on narration. Narration time: fifty minutes. I had clocked it already. Okay, Garfield said edgily, go ahead. Fifty minutes later, he grabbed the telephone and called Warner Brothers. When he asked them to take my story, they hesitated. So he called RKO and promised to star in the picture if they would buy it. Since Garfield's name guaranteed success, Paul was now in a good bargaining position for me. *Gallant Weekend* was a war story, but it was never made. By the time the screenplay was finished, the war had ended.

At the beginning of the war, I visited our soldier-brother Walter in boot camp somewhere near Cheyenne, Wyoming. He showed me around the barracks. Suddenly we heard some lovely, warm music and found in a dimly lit corner a G.I. playing on a concertina. We sat down to listen. He sang American folk songs—beautifully, softly. Obviously touched by our response, he showed us his instrument. It had a small, scratched silver plate on it which read, in ornamental script, "Jonathan Smith." He said it had belonged to his great-grandfather.

All the way home on that slow, wartime train the concertina and its sound haunted me. How would it be to tell the story of America through its folk music, centering around the life of an old instrument—a concertina? From the station I rushed to Paul's office to tell him my idea for a script. He quickly saw the possibilities.

"There is only one man in town who would be right to collaborate with you," he said, doubtless starting to juggle high figures in the back of his head. "Unfortunately he is very busy right now. But if you could get him to agree to work with you, I could get you a fortune."

Paul called his friend John Huston. Huston was working on two scripts already. He was also in uniform and liable to be recalled for duty at any moment. But he did make time to listen to my idea one afternoon, and as Paul had correctly sensed, it caught fire with him. He dismissed his secretaries, ordered a bottle of Scotch and some sandwiches—and we started talking story. The session ended at four A.M. By that time we had a complete outline.

There were only four pages, barely a thousand words—but they were the most expensive words I had ever helped to write. *Concertina* was bought immediately—but never made. She still rests somewhere on the shelves of Columbia Picture's archives. And when Huston later tried to buy her back, the price was so exorbitant he abandoned the idea.

My brother Paul did good things elsewhere for me too. He even kept his eye on Broadway.

"This would make an amusing stage play," he said when I told him my idea for a story of the problems arising with three teen-age girls when their divorced mother marries again. "Why not try it?"

A fine challenge. But I doubted that I could write dialogue for Broadway. Enter a new collaborator. Albert Mannheimer—many years my junior, witty, brilliant—grew excited when I told him the outline. We set to work.

When the play was finally on paper a year later, Paul suggested giving it to a New York agent who dealt exclusively with the Broadway scene. The Broadway "expert" had no faith in the play and turned it down. My spirits were low—but not Paul's. He had read the play and liked it.

"*One* agent's opinion means nothing," he said. "Anyway, it may take some time to find a Broadway producer. Even then you won't get any money at first except a small option. But I think I can sell the script as a movie."

Encouraged, my collaborator and I decided to forget our theatrical ambitions and see whether Paul could generate some interest in a film production.

Luck often plays a significant, sometimes even absurd, part in dividing success from failure. I don't want to diminish the special effort Paul expended to sell our play. But luck certainly played a decisive role in his selling *The Birds and the Bees* a few days after we turned the manuscript over to him.

At MGM they happened to be looking for a story that would display the talents of three of their starlets. The comedy we had written fitted the studio's need perfectly. More luck came our way. Since the play had been submitted simultaneously to other studios, we got other offers, which strengthened Paul's bargaining hand. So we received a handsome sum of money for our play, which was turned into a successful musical called *Three Daring Daughters*. Furthermore, the comedy was subsequently purchased for stage production and had a modest run on Broadway.

One March day in 1950, while in a snowbound cabin up in the skiing country of Ketchum, Idaho, I got a telegram from Paul:

HOW DOES APRIL IN PARIS SOUND TO YOU?

I was on the phone right away. "When do I leave?"

"If you want to, next week."

But when he told me of the assignment, I was jolted. A script for Laurel and Hardy.

"Wait till you hear the idea," Paul said. He proceeded to tell me the plot of *Atoll K.* A highly sophisticated idea by a French writer, it was the story of a couple of stowaways shipwrecked on an atoll in the Pacific. According to international law, an unclaimed island belongs to the first person who sets foot on it. Thus Atoll K. is Laurel and Hardy's possession. Since the tiny paradise turns out to contain a rich deposit of uranium, the nations of the world—who had barred the homeless bums from crossing their borders—now frantically compete in wooing them. Refusing all offers made to surrender ownership, they lead a Robinson Crusoe-like existence—until one day Atoll K., as atolls sometimes do, slowly sinks below the ocean's surface and disappears.

The project sounded intriguing, especially since I was assured that I would be given free range and also that the comedians wanted to try out a new style.

Laurel and Hardy hadn't made a film for five years. The vagaries of fortune had dealt harshly with these two past-masters of the art of silent comedy. Without visible means of support for some years, they were considered passé. While Stan Laurel, a North Country Englishman, had made provisions for the lean years, his partner Oliver Hardy practically lived on the dole. Once in a while he got an insignificant part in a Western. Alone or together, when they walked down Sunset Boulevard now, not one head turned. They were forgotten men. In America.

But in Europe their script read differently. If they sauntered down the Champs Elysees or the Via Veneto, people cheered them from the sidewalk cafes and matrons rushed up to kiss their hands.

Paul was well aware of this. He had set up the "American part" of the *Atoll K.* deal. The picture was to be made in three versions—English, French and Italian. The French government would provide the main share of the financing.

Trouble started right away. I was joined by another American writer, and soon two French and three Italian colleagues jumped into the writing pool. Collaboration became impossible. Aside from the language problem, there were national differences in philosophical matters—and, worse, in working habits. The French hated the sunlight and could only work at night. My collaborator and I preferred the morning hours. The Italians preferred not to work at all. Thus we finally agreed that each team should write its own version of the screenplay.

After a half-year of this unholy entente, the comedians arrived in Paris. When presented with three scripts of *Atoll K.*, they were stumped. What was this all about? What had the many writers been doing for months? And, anyway, where were all their tried-and-true routines? The banana peel that landed them on their behinds? The piano they moved across a narrow suspension bridge and the gorilla that met them midway? Where in God's name was the familiar and unbeatable "Laurel & Hardy" formula?

Smack into the wastebasket went thousands of typed pages. A Hollywood gag writer of the silent days was dispatched to Paris. An old pal of the comedians, he knew what they wanted—needed. Almost overnight he assembled and rehashed all of their old comfortable clichés. The formula had worked ninety-nine times—so why shouldn't it work with the hundredth?

It didn't. The international hotchpotch that emerged to the tune of three million dollars was terrible to behold. Everyone blamed everyone else for the disaster.

It's a moot question now whether the comedians would have had a more fitting last curtain by accepting one of the three scripts we had written—preferably mine, of course.

Be that as it may, I can thank my brother for a lovely Paris spring—and summer and autumn—at a time when the American dollar was still the world's most respected currency. I could sit next to Sartre and de Beauvoir at the Café des Flores. And no skyscrapers spoiled the haunting memories I relived in the Dôme on Montparnasse—which resulted later in my book of Parisian memoirs, *Kiki of Montparnasse*.

And Paris wasn't the only faraway sack my brother's magic scissors opened up for me in the postwar years, giving me access to new adventures. He sent me off on an assignment in Mexico City, set a deal in New York, and even arranged for an eighteen-month contract in the divided city of Berlin before the East put up the Wall.

Around Christmastime in 1956, when I was "between assignments," I wrote a story about a girl and a surfboard out in Malibu. I had watched my fifteen-year-old daughter Kathy trying to master the difficult sport of surfing and had listened to her colorful accounts of the small group of surf-bums who had built a Quonset hut on the beach.

I called the new story *Gidget*—the nickname my daughter had acquired among the surfers, a portmanteau word for "girl-midget." I finished it in three weeks, a fact which I viewed with suspicion. I mistrusted the ease with which I had written it. For some reason I had always believed that the more agony a writing chore exacted, the better the final product was likely to be.

Writing in a style and language altogether new to me, I had no yardstick by which to measure whether I had brought it off or not. One way to find out if the story was marketable, of course, was to get Paul to read it. He had always shown good judgment in evaluating my work, and though he tended to overlook my shortcomings and emphasize my strong points, his verdicts were generally sound.

And as a rule, his response was quick. But not this time. After waiting for a couple of days, I drove to his office. Clearly he was hedging. He had read *Gidget*, but, well—

"I am sorry, Fritz. I can see that a lot of work went into it, but somehow I couldn't warm up to it. Maybe you should try to sell it as a book. Get a literary agent."

I followed his advice. The agent, a young man fresh from New York, called me immediately after he read it to say that he would be quite willing to take on the property.

Within the week, he had sold *Gidget* both as a book and a film.

My brother, as always, generously praised my success. As for me, I had lost my agent—and the agent, for once, had lost his ten percent. But he was happy that I had finally achieved full independence.

45

Keeping Afloat

T ROUBLES CAME TO Paul starting in the Fifties—troubles intricately connected with the painful changes overtaking Hollywood. The traditional studio operations declined with the rising costs of producing films and with the emergence of new production methods. Television, the most addictive popular entertainment since the Lumière brothers invented the movie projector, completely changed the nature of audiences and movies. The dependable star system collapsed. And the so-called "runaway productions" removed much of the production activities from Hollywood. Filmmaking was spread all over the globe.

For both producer and agent making a living in Hollywood became like playing Russian roulette every new day. The Paul Kohner Agency, which represented many foreign directors and actors, suffered more from the evolution and recession in the film industry than did the larger agencies with more diversified interests, since the import of European talent greatly decreased.

By "packaging" films, the big agencies broke dependency on the studios and set the pattern for a new type of production, in which they made the stars they represented partners in the enterprise. They also packed in as many other clients as possible into the film packages. Agencies now became the primary shapers of the whole motion picture industry—or what was left of it. They acquired a power that previously seemed inconceivable in agents.

And what happened with independent operators like Paul? The tentacular conglomerates such as MCA and William Morris started raiding their much smaller competitors by stealing important clients. Or they offered to buy them out, thereby acquiring star clients, sometimes by giving the independent agent a long-term contract to work for them as an employee. The job served as bait. They rarely had any use for him. Young agents were on hand—a new breed trained in the law, who were also as conversant with tax write-offs as with guiding their clients' careers, and acutely alert to the potentials in television. Formerly a contract with a studio consisted of a letter memorandum. Now it read like an international peace treaty.

Another factor leading to the downfall of the independent agent was the diversification of talent agency functions. The huge combines estab-

156

lished specialized departments for actors, directors, writers, producers, television presentations, musical groups, recording artists, night-club acts. This widespread approach required a large staff and entailed a big overhead for operating expenses.

The Paul Kohner Agency could not keep pace with all this. The agency's finances began to falter.

Paul had made money all his life, whether employed or on his own. Money was a commodity he didn't worry about. It was simply there.

Until the day his bookkeeper informed him that it wasn't there. Where had it gone? Well, into routine business expenses. Mostly minor items.

Like the telephone. Paul loves the instrument. He treats it almost as if it were a beloved. It is a device that suits his personality. He enjoys its usefulness, its readiness—the ease with which a conversation can be begun and ended. Except that he never seems to terminate a call unless the party at the other end is ready to hang up.

Calling—almost daily—Rome, Stockholm, Paris, London, Tokyo, Buenos Aires, Tel-Aviv can be expensive. Some months his telephone bill ran into five figures.

Then traveling. Paul traveled a great deal whether there were deals to transact or just clients to visit on foreign location. Wherever he went, he went first class, in style, as he had promised himself long ago in his youth. Far-flung expensive hotels of the world were his second homes. At the Hassler in Rome it had to be not the best room—but the best *rooms*.

Eating could run up sizable bills too. Not only because he frequented three-star restaurants exclusively, but also he never ate alone. Everywhere he was surrounded by clients and friends—and people who were neither but hoped to be. It was so easy just to charge it, to "write it all off" as a legitimate business expense.

And there were other things that could be "written off." Like gifts for V.I.P. clients. An original Degas drawing. A pre-Columbian sculpture. A Sèvres tea set.

Add to these ever-mounting costs the weekly office payroll—and finally there was little left to subtract from. By the early Sixties Paul awakened every morning depressed by his inability to stop the downhill slide of his once-thriving business.

Facing now the possibility of eventual bankruptcy, Paul called an emergency meeting. Expenses had to be cut. But where? Let one secretary go? Send out only a hundred Christmas gifts to clients instead of three hundred? Cut down on telephone calls?

No, retrenching was not the solution. Paul would have to try a whole succession of magical tricks. He must lure some new clients into the office. Arrange "packages." Sell a big property. Multiply and expand his agency's departments. Be inventive, creative. Maybe acquire a much younger partner.

By redoubling his efforts, maybe the foundering ship could be kept afloat.

46

Apple of His Eye

U SUALLY WHEN PAUL returned from a European jaunt he was especially buoyant. Not this time.

I went over to see him at his house on a Sunday, the day after he got back. I saw at once that something had gone wrong. He looked rumpled, tired.

We walked down Stone Canyon Road, which we sometimes liked to do. He didn't talk.

Finally I asked: "What happened?"

"Terrible trip," he said. "Absolutely terrible. One disaster after another."

I didn't probe further. I knew he would talk when he was ready.

There were several "For Sale" signs out in the Bel Air canyon. A sign of the times. We walked into an empty "Open House," looked around, went out into the backyard. Paul wandered aimlessly about. He wasn't interested in anything. We sat down on a garden bench. Then he started talking.

At first there seemed to be nothing specific bothering him. Just an accumulation of small annoyances. A picture scheduled for one of his director clients cancelled and the producer refusing to settle. Another client walking out on a film in the middle of shooting. Lawsuits, threats, loss of commission. Fellini: a mercurial man, he changed his mind about coming to Hollywood to direct an American picture. On the flight from Rome to Stockholm Paul had felt sick. Gall bladder? It worried him. Then in Stockholm, Ingmar Bergman was working on his island retreat and couldn't be reached.

"Did you see Pancho?" I asked.

"Oh, Pancho. Sure, I saw him." And for a moment his face lit up with fatherly pride.

Pancho had been working for quite a while now in Europe as a production manager. Efficient, dependable, knowledgeable and naturally charming, the son had inherited most of the appealing traits of his father.

"Everyone loves Pancho," my brother said. "If he weren't my son, I'd say he was just about the nicest boy I've ever met. He is on location somewhere in the south of Spain, but he flew to Rome just to have dinner with me."

He drew some pictures in the sand with his shillelagh. Eventually he

158

said: "Remember our Old Man when he tried to communicate with us? Well, talking with a son isn't easy. It wasn't easy for Papa either. Whenever he asked me to go for a walk with him, I got very excited. I always knew he had something important on his mind. But as we walked along, he never could get around to what he really wanted to say to me. I never understood it at all. But now I do. When you finally have the same problems, you begin to understand your own father."

There was a pause. "How's Pancho doing?" I asked.

"Oh, yes, Pancho. Great. He'll have it easy in life. A 'favorite of the gods'—isn't that what your Greeks said? Yet he's not really happy with what he's doing right now, so it seemed like a good time to bring up what I wanted to talk about. I told him that things didn't look too rosy for the agency at the moment. But I also told him that I am by no means pessimistic about the future."

He gave me a searching look. "You probably know what I suggested to him?"

"Not really."

"Well, I said that I'm obviously not getting any younger. And that though I'm proud of the way I've built the business up, I know I now need a young, vigorous man around to help me. Sure, Walter is a damn good agent, but he's not so young any more either. Now, Pancho—with his connections, his know-how, his way with people—a natural, don't you think? Eventually he could take over, run the whole show."

"So what did he say?"

Paul shook his head. "He had a simple answer," he said. "No."

The hurt was right there on his face and in his voice. "The moment he said it I realized how right he was," Paul continued. "You know why? I remembered how it was when I was young—and what I would have said if Papa had asked me to give up my own career and take over the family business. I had turned to Pancho at a time of weakness, and he must have felt it, because he said: 'All you need is a good, long vacation, Pop. You don't really want to throw in the towel, do you? You know you'd be the most miserable person in the world if you weren't working.'"

My brother smiled. A tired smile.

"I guess he was right," he went on. "That is, I'd like to think so. But I'm not sleeping very soundly lately. Imagine that—*me* having difficulties sleeping! I've even had to take sleeping pills."

We got up. "That'll pass now that you're at home. You'll be sleeping fine again away from trains and planes, hotel rooms, eating out all the time."

I was trying to make him feel better—all the while knowing I was offering him only a placebo.

47

Turning Point

MOST OF HIS life Paul has been blessed with a come-what-may-I-don't-give-a-damn kind of sleep. Sitting, reclining, even standing up, he could sleep.

I envied him for it. "How do you do it?" I once asked him.

"Training," he said. "Discipline. When I go to bed—even if something awful has happened or some terrible problem is facing me next day—I tell myself: There is nothing, absolutely nothing I can do during the next eight hours. To function in the morning I *have* to sleep."

His sound sleep explains to me his extraordinary energy, his capacity to work sixteen hours at a stretch, as if he were more than one man.

All that changed now. Pills appeared. Pills in the morning to dull anxiety. Pills at noon to get through the day. Pills in the evening to summon sleep.

And it showed. Often he had a vacuous stare. Listening to clients and their problems, he smiled. Not his usual confident smile, but a put-on grin which indicated he wasn't really listening.

Some people, when troubles come, somehow can stay above them. He couldn't—not now, anyway. Friends told him to get hold of himself. Not to show that he was worrying: bad for business. To look at things in the proper perspective. Maybe going away for a while would help.

Away? Where to?

At first there was the customary yearly lull in the industry. March. But this season the lull didn't seem to end for Paul. It extended into summer. Into fall. Into winter.

And all the time he brooded. Brooding, though, he still went through the motions. Forced himself to make the daily phone calls. To go on the rounds of the studios.

Even more acutely than before, he noticed the changes that had taken place in Hollywood. Gone were the bosses he used to deal with—Mayer, Cohn, Zanuck, the Warners, the Laemmles. Even though they had their quirks and power manias, they nevertheless had been passionately devoted to the business of making movies. Here and there were men who had worked upwards from the ranks—even a few former agents who had moved into executive positions. But increasingly he met new faces behind polished desks in polished offices. "How do you spell your name?" They were cool, button-down organization men who had been sent out to the Coast by the big Eastern concerns. People who were neophytes to the film business were running the studios nowadays via computers, with an icy logic divorced from the risks and intuitions of the past, which had made filmmaking unpredictable and fascinating.

"Maybe," Paul said to me one day, "I should chuck the whole thing. Just turn the agency over to other people. Sell the house and move to Cuernavaca. Our new place down there is delightful. I could live the lazy life in the sun. After all, I've done my job."

He searched my face for a reaction. "Okay," he said when I didn't answer, "I can also sell out."

He must have had that thought in the back of his mind for a while. Now that he approached it realistically, it seemed the best solution.

How does an agent sell out? And what does he sell? First of all, he sells his "inventory": his clients. Paul still had a number of highly desirable talents under contract—actors, directors, writers, composers. Then there were "deferments": revenues coming into the office from royalties spread out through the years for tax reasons. And of course there was his name too, which had been around for a long while and carried valuable prestige.

Big combines usually offer a lump sum for the buy-out and take-over of a small, independent agency. The agent may get a contract that runs for a few years. Although the salary is impressive, the agent's name gradually loses its special identity, blending with the title of the vast, impersonal new outfit: like "General Artists" or "Creative Artists Management" or "Music Corporation of America."

Once he let it be known that he was looking around for a buyer, Paul began to receive enticing offers. Each one would have guaranteed him a substantial lifelong income. Yes, all those high figures sounded quite attractive to a tired man. So for a while, periodically, there were deceptive resurgences of his characteristic ebullience, replacing the ubiquitous gloom.

Lawyers appeared. Meetings were held and books inspected. People he had never seen before whacked him on the back and told him how great, how absolutely great, it would be to have him join their agencies.

Big manipulators from the East came to town. They had to be shown a "good time." Lupita dutifully entertained them at small dinner parties. She was charming, helpful.

Eventually the decision narrowed down to the one company that really wanted *him*, not just the clients of the Paul Kohner Agency. More lawyers now. Flights to New York. New lawyers. Contracts drawn up. Sixty, eighty, hundred-page documents. Drafts going back and forth.

And then, even though negotiations were supposed to be strictly confidential, the news of the impending merger leaked out. His employees—the people working for him, with him, for years, some for as long as the agency had existed—worried. It would be painful for them to go elsewhere. And they couldn't imagine being anywhere else or working for anyone but Paul.

As the date approached for the closing of the deal, Paul began to have second thoughts. How much of the pot of gold could he actually take home? There were ways to get around the high tax payments—or so the lawyers had assured him. But it still seemed vague.

Maybe, he thought, he should take time to read the legal document he was supposed to sign. One night he stayed up till two in the morning going through more than a hundred pages of the "merger script." Yes, the legal minds had taken care of the tax problem. He could keep quite a portion of the money.

But then he came upon a clause in small print—one that he had overlooked before, or if not overlooked had dismissed from his mind as negligible. But it now seemed unacceptable. That clause stated that he could never again operate an agency under his own name—and that after the termination of his three-year contract he couldn't take back any of his clients.

He realized with a start that he was selling more than his business. He would be selling his very identity. Of what use would his life be after that?

The mere thought that he was giving up the rights to his name was intolerable. After a sleepless night he called his lawyer. That clause, he told him, had to be eliminated. The lawyer said he would attempt to re-negotiate that point.

More waiting. More pills.

One afternoon the lawyer called to say that a compromise was in the offing. Paul seemed relieved. He walked up Sunset Boulevard to the black glass-and-steel building that housed the company he was about to join. He had so far refrained from taking a look at his new quarters—maybe unconsciously hoping that the deal would never materialize. For it would mean giving up his own small office building.

The new quarters were located on the eighth floor of the antiseptic skyscraper. There were the usual thick wall-to-wall carpeting, the fluorescent lights, the long row of anonymous plastic offices. Immediately he was aware of the great contrast between where he had worked for years and where he would soon be moving.

He was given a grand tour by one of the company's vice-presidents, an elder-statesman in the agency business. The executive took Paul into each office on the floor to introduce him around. It was close to six. All the agents were on their telephones. They briefly interrupted their calls to shake Paul's hand. He noticed that they all wore dark suits and dark ties.

"And where will I work?" he asked.

"Right down here," his escort said, leading the way to the very end of the corridor.

He opened the door to an empty cubicle. It was the size of all the other rooms—about fourteen by fourteen feet.

"Is that the one you've picked for me?"

"That's the way they build these goddam cells," the vice-president said, sensitive to the dismay in Paul's voice.

"May I see the president's office?"

The president was in New York, so Paul was shown his office too. It was twice the size of the other rooms—but still starkly depressing in its cold uniformity.

"What does your own office look like?" Paul asked.

"It's next door here." His room was small like the rest. On the desk stood a framed photo of his family. "After all, it's just a place to dictate letters and make phone calls," he said with an apologetic grin. "Most of the day we're out in the field. You know how it is with agents, Paul. Always on the move."

Paul sat down. "Well, we have a problem here," he said. "You see, I'm very seldom in the field. Most of *my* day I spend in the office. Clients come in to see me. Producers too. Friends. I wouldn't feel right in a place like this."

The vice-president coughed. "Maybe we could knock out a wall and give you two offices. Of course it would have to get an okay from the home office in New York."

"I see," Paul said and got up, suddenly feeling oddly elated. He thanked his colleague for his courtesy and left. He could hardly wait till he got back to his own building.

Out on the boulevard he took a deep, joyful breath. In a wild surge of renewed energy he almost ran the few hundred feet to his own place. And there he summoned the heads of his "family" of co-workers. His convivial brother Walter, second in command, and dapper Carl Forest—both in charge of the television department. High-spirited and wise Ilse Lahn, who directed the literary department. And the steadfast, indispensable Irene Heymann.

"I know you've all been under the same tension I have," he said. "But you can relax now. I am not selling out. We're going on."

And then he called his lawyer.

A heightened sense of being his own man again sustained Paul throughout that evening, when he went home and told Lupita about his decision to forgo the merger. Nothing had really changed—except that he felt free. And once more miracles were invited to make an appearance, as they had often done before.

The first announced itself a few days later via Paul's miracle machine, the telephone. His old friend William Wyler asked whether they could meet for lunch.

Although a close friendship had existed between the two men ever since they roomed together in New York, they had walked different ways during their years in Hollywood. Willy, who early won renown as a great director with a world-wide reputation for high artistry, had entrusted his representation to another agent—a powerful competitor of Paul's. If this rankled Paul, he didn't let on—for, in his style, he never mentioned it. But a certain barrier—perhaps strictly of professionalism—had arisen to separate them. Aware of it, each had retreated behind it.

They met now at one of those green-lawned country clubs abounding around Hollywood. When they were through the hors d'oeuvres and the usual amenities, Willy fixed Paul with a quizzical grin. Haltingly, he said: "My agency contract with MCA is coming to an end, Paul, and I'm not going to renew it. I wonder whether you would consider taking over my representation."

Not easily ruffled, Paul put down his fork and stared incredulously at Willy. In the strange alchemy of timing, was this a miracle he had hoped for? Or was it an act of fealty toward an old friend that had prompted Wyler to come to his aid at this crucial turning point in his career? Either way, or both ways, it was most welcome.

"I won't be a difficult client to sell," Willy said with a sly chuckle. "Actually, I probably should have gone with you long ago. But you know how it is. One makes certain decisions and commitments—and mistakes. I'm sure you could have done as well for me as MCA. Anyway, here I am. But I hope it isn't too late—"

"I am delighted," Paul said. And for once it was an understatement.

To put William Wyler on his client list now made a new triumph for Paul that gave a decided boost to his morale and the prospect of increased income.

The news traveled fast and helped his rehabilitation. The concomitant glow on Paul's face didn't come from some happiness pill—but from his reactivating his dedication to full-time and full-fledged agenting, in his own personal style.

48

Lucky with the Vikings

PAUL'S SECRETARY IS quite accustomed to handling phone calls from celebrities and faraway places. But one morning some time ago a call came in that catapulted her right out of her swivel chair.

Irene Heymann charged into Paul's office. "Mr. Kohner—the White House!"

Calmly Paul peered over his hornrimmed glasses. He smiled. "You mean Walter again?" An unsurpassed voice and personality mimic, our younger brother is not averse to tweaking Big Brother's nose now and then.

"No, no!" Irene hollered. "This is no joke. It really is the White House—I swear."

Coolly Paul picked up the receiver. "Yes—?"

"Is this Mr. Kohner speaking?"

"It is."

"This is Dr. Kissinger's secretary," a male voice said. "Dr. Kissinger would like to talk to you. Just a moment."

"Okay," Paul said pleasantly, curious as to how this new practical joke of Walter's would go.

There was a short pause, some more clicking. Then a guttural voice came over the wire. "Mr. Kohner?"

"*Jawohl, Herr Doktor,*" Paul said with an exaggerated Prussian inflection, still playing along with the gag. "*Was kann ich für Sie tun?*"

"I prefer to speak in English," said the voice on the other end. "I understand you are the agent of Miss Liv Ullmann."

"Yes, I am," Paul said—not quite so sure of the game any more.

"I am a great admirer of your client. She is a very fine actress—and a very beautiful woman."

"She is," Paul agreed. Was this indeed Henry Kissinger?

"I have no assignment to offer your client," the man went on. "But do you think she would consider being my date at the John Ford Testimonial Dinner?"

Paul did some swift thinking. "I don't know, Dr. Kissinger," he said cautiously. "I cannot speak for Miss Ullmann. Maybe you would like to call her personally and ask."

"Fine. I will do that if you let me have her phone number."

Paul gave Henry the K. the unlisted number.

"Many thanks," said Dr. Kissinger. "By the way, I would like to present her that night to the President and First Lady."

The agent in Paul began to function one thousand percent. For his star client to be escorted by the President's chief foreign affairs adviser to a dinner attended by Hollywood's elite would be a supreme publicity coup that neither money nor enterprise could possibly arrange on their own.

Then Paul's face clouded. "I'm afraid there's a problem, though," he said. "I have just checked the date of the banquet here. Miss Ullmann has to leave for Oslo on that particular day."

"She *has* to—why?"

"A stage commitment. She's appearing in an Ibsen play there. She has already changed the opening date twice because of work obligations here. I've had to pull quite a few strings to make that possible, so I don't dare ask for another postponement. The performance is sold out weeks in advance."

Pause. "And nothing can be done?"

"Well, I really don't see how."

"You leave it up to me then, Mr. Kohner," Kissinger said amiably.

After some banter, Kissinger expressed his wish to meet Paul at the dinner honoring Ford and then terminated the call.

Obviously some very sensitive diplomatic negotiations were carried out, for the State Theatre in Oslo once more changed the date of the play's opening.

Miss Ullmann accompanied Henry Kissinger to the banquet, where he introduced her to the nation's chief executive and his wife. And at midnight a police escort whisked her off to the airport. Liv arrived in Oslo the following evening—just in time for her first rehearsal.

On one of his many Scandinavian forays Paul met Liv Ullmann—whose first name means "life" in Norwegian—through his old friend and client Max von Sydow. At that time she was primarily a stage actress in Norway. She had given some fine portrayals in plays, had appeared on television and had just finished her first film, *Persona*, for Ingmar Bergman.

Delighted to hear her speak a surprisingly fluent English (she had lived in Canada with her family during the war years), Paul charmed her into signing a representation agreement. Immediately he found a "four star" assignment for her: the female lead in *Man's Fate*, based on the book by Malraux, which was being prepared by Fred Zinnemann for MGM release. Drawing two hundred dollars per week, Liv Ullmann waited two years for the production to start. On the first day of shooting, the project was called off.

But in the meantime Liv Ullmann's face had become well known to Bergman aficionados throughout the world. First came *Persona* and *Shame*, made at the start of the love relationship between the young actress and the Swedish director, four times married and in his late forties.

166

By the time Bergman's *Cries and Whispers* was released in the United States, insiders in the film business knew that an incandescent new superstar would soon burst onto movie screens everywhere. Suddenly everyone wanted to have Ullmann. The offers poured into Paul's office, creating a clamor of bidding he had never experienced before with his other top clients. Liv's amazing range and versatility as an actress— combining the vibrant and sensitive, innocence and worldly wisdom, candor and guile, the ethereal and the sensual—enabled her to take on a wide variety of roles in such films as *Lost Horizons, Forty Carats, Zandy's Bride, The Abdication,* Jan Troell's *The Emigrants* and its sequel *The New Land.* The problem for Paul has never been in getting leading and lucrative parts for her. It comes in obtaining the *right* roles for her—and here a good agent's best skills must operate in tandem with a client's developing script judgment, to avoid casting errors and overextended efforts.

"An ordinary, extraordinary woman" was how *Time* headlined its cover story on Liv Ullmann in 1972. "Whatever she does," says Max von Sydow, "she does with a simplicity, a directness that gives great presence to her roles." Coming from the awesome acting partner in some of her films, this is high praise indeed—especially considering the megalomania often besetting the fraternity of actors.

Liv Ullmann somehow still finds time between a busy schedule of film assignments to appear at her beloved State Theatre in Oslo, to bring up her daughter Linn, to read serious literature and to pursue her own writing.

"Writing," she once confided to me, "is my true passion." This woman who gets men to dream, women to empathize and audiences to cheer carries paper and pen at all times in her handbag. She jots down notes constantly—on the film set between "takes," on plane trips around the world, at night before she retires.

Whatever Liv has to say is said simply and touchingly. Under a photo showing her and Ingmar Bergman and Paul in Rome, she wrote: "Here we are in Rome. We both—I mean Ingmar and me—look a little clumsy. But we are 'out in the world' for the first time—and having five wonderful weeks in Roma—visiting the Church of St. Peter every day. Paul looks a little embarrassed, because we really do not look too elegant. Only happy! So Paul is embarrassed—and happy too. The year is 1968—and spring."

At that time Liv and Ingmar were living together. At first Bergman was like God to her: "I admired him so much, and I was scared to death of him. When he spoke I blushed." Their five-year liaison produced their daughter Linn and significant changes in both of them. Liv seemed to instill a warming, humanizing effect on both Ingmar and his films. And in turn his powerful influence on her artistry was incalculable. Bergman helped Ullmann gain confidence in her own intuitive instincts as an actress. From him she learned the value of an economy in expression: "how little you can do rather than how much." He widened her vistas, increased her intellectual sophistication. And he encouraged her to assert herself, by his own example, both in her creative and her personal lives. ("He is not afraid

167

to do what he wants to do," she says.) When the two finally parted pathways, she was able to see that "We were both strong and so much alike we canceled each other out." Since then, a friendly and fruitful working association has been possible, resulting in such remarkable films as *Scenes from a Marriage* and *Face to Face.*

After being Paul's client for some years, Liv Ullmann sent him a photo containing the inscription: "To Paul—My father—My brother—My friend—With my love ..."

The framed photograph occupies a solitary spot on Paul's cluttered desk. Could any agent ask for a finer testimonial?

Altogether, Paul has been lucky with the Vikings. Somehow Hollywood managers never really bothered with the Scandinavians. But Paul did. He introduced the brilliant actor Max von Sydow to American and world audiences and brought to Hollywood the exquisite Ingrid Thulin, the romantically exciting Bibi Andersson and the talented new director Jan Troell. And the list goes on—with names like Christine Schollin, Per Oscarson, Nilgo Sjorman, Bo Widerberg. And there is also the Swedish Sven Nykvist, one of the world's master cinematographers, whose beautiful craftsmanship is usually at the service of Ingmar Bergman.

Then there is Ingmar Bergman himself.

If it is possible for a man of advanced age to have a hero, then for Paul that hero is Ingmar Bergman. Paul worships the "Big Swede." Something in Bergman's films fascinated him, touched him, spoke to him long before the two ever met.

The director was virtually unknown outside of Sweden for years. America became infected with Bergmania late in the Fifties after *The Seventh Seal* was released. To Paul, however, Bergman was no sudden, surprise discovery, for he had encountered the genius in him long before, at various European film festivals. He made it almost his life's work to "stalk" the shy director on his homeground. Paul pursued him year after year, persistently, obdurately—as votary first, as agent second.

From the moment he was introduced to Bergman, Paul felt thoroughly at ease with him. Yet Bergman was Janus-like, a person with two very different faces. If infuriated, he could tear phones off the walls, then in the next moment change into a sweet, considerate bourgeois. In those days he was called "The Icebergman"—someone who often confessed that he couldn't feel because he had a heart of ice.

Paul came to know this side of the director when, after years of courting him, he approached Bergman with an offer to do a film in Hollywood.

"I have spent fifteen years forging my instrument," Bergman replied, "and now I have become part of it. All the legs of the millipede are working at last. Why should I leave? Why should I go to America?" And then, "Was that what was on your mind all the time?"

For once Paul had no repartee.

Nothing changed in their relationship, though, so Paul continued his pilgrimages to the Swedish capital. Gradually a genuine friendship and trust developed between the two men, which both now nurture and treasure.

This reciprocity in their relationship was demonstrated when Paul paid a visit to Stockholm during the "dark period" of his professional life. Bergman is finely attuned to the doubts and sorrows that lick at other people's souls. He quickly perceived that this time his American agent had no "deals" on his mind.

Bergman took Paul for a long walk around the city. Then they stopped at the Thiel Museum, a place where people can commune in solitude.

"I see that you are troubled, Paul," Bergman said. "And I know that it is not easy for you to talk about it. Remember, though, that I am your friend—and that I have gone through many terrors of my own but always come out stronger and better afterwards. Life has meaning. You must believe that, hold on to that—although we may never know precisely what that meaning is. I have learned that what really matters is just being alive, each day."

Paul is a man with strong emotions that he cannot readily or easily reveal to others. As he started talking now to Bergman, the words came tumbling out. He bared his problems and touched upon his inability to make compromises.

"When I was younger I was convinced that compromise in art and life is the worst thing a human being can do," Bergman commented. "I think differently now. We all have to make compromises. We couldn't live or work otherwise. I thought I could be above it. For instance, I frowned on television. Yet now I will do work for television—in my own way. And I could never see myself working in America. I still cannot. But working *for* America—I might do that. One day I may even come to America, to California. Would that please you, Paul?"

Paul was greatly moved by Bergman's helpful advice. The offer to work for American producers was a breakthrough in their relations: genuine evidence of Bergman's caring. But to suggest the possibility of someday coming to America: Paul had to regard that as a touching yet apparitional gesture of a friend. Yet was it?

49

Has Success Spoiled Charles Bronson?

PAUL SCAMPERED TOWARD Charles Bronson as if pulled by a magnet. For years the actor had been typecast in tough-guy parts. And all the while Paul, watching him from afar, was fascinated by what Bronson could do with his face. Didn't anyone else see it?

To Paul it seemed as if some sculptor lived within Bronson, subtly altering those strong yet malleable features—large nose, wide mouth, heavy-lidded eyes, bushy eyebrows, square jaw—when scene and mood required. Then there was his muscular body with its undeniably compelling "animal magnetism" in motion. Nothing pretty about Bronson, to be sure. But a lot that was taut, forceful, masculine—handsome in a rugged way rarely seen in Hollywood's heroes.

Bronson's time would come, Paul felt—and *told* him so at that stage in the actor's career when he was mainly relegated to "Spaghetti Westerns." On a European jaunt, Paul lunched with Bronson. And in his hyperbolic style he urged, "Put your career in my hands, Charlie, and you'll be the hottest thing on the screen in a while."

Looking at him dubiously, Bronson still said okay. He probably felt instinctively that Paul might give him better representation than the huge MCA had done.

"You won't regret it," Paul promised.

"I hope I won't," Charlie said.

"And someday—" Paul continued, carried away by the rich vocabulary of the Hollywood Dream—"we're going to get a million dollars for you."

"You might," Bronson said abstractedly, as if thinking now of something else. Then he added, matter-of-factly, "And on that day you'll get a Rolls-Royce from me."

The luncheon ended on that cheerful and easily forgettable note. A few days later Charles Bronson—formerly Charles Buchinsky, the one-time coal miner from Pennsylvania—set his name on the agency contract.

Paul's great personal interest in his new client's potential took the forms of clever bargaining, selecting the right roles for him and steering him away from the wrong ones, searching for exciting scripts in which he would take the active, leading role. By skillful maneuvering on Paul's part and a lot of dedicated hard work, and traveling, on Bronson's, an offbeat superstar was being created.

There were luck and good timing in it too. In Europe moviegoers took

170

to Bronson's characterizations, responding to his manly and weathered physiognomy, which lent itself to a variety of roles and nationalities. After he appeared in the highly successful French film *Adieu, L'Ami* in 1968, a Bronson boom swiftly developed. New movies and old which featured him played side by side along the Champs Elysees. And the cult even spread to Asia and Latin America.

By 1972, with *The Valachi Papers*, the Bronson brouhaha hit America at last like a sonic boom. The movie grossed more for Columbia that year than all the rest. And Charles Bronson received the Golden Globe Award as the "World's Film Favorite," based on polls taken throughout the world.

Offers—even pleas—for Bronson's services deluge the Paul Kohner office almost daily. Producers know by now that they must pay the top price for Bronson, but they know that his name above a movie title on the marquee is worth the expenditure. By now he has made about sixty feature films.

Just what is the attraction of this actor?

As an actor Bronson is a man of action more than words. There is something basic and palpable and refreshingly direct in his performances. Delicate or ambivalent thoughts and feelings may be underplayed, understated. Actions and reactions are powerful, exciting, identifiable—never murky. Whether portraying a rootless drifter, a dispossessed maverick, an angry redskin, a grim mafioso or a hired killer, Bronson invariably gives an authentic performance. Anger, lust, weariness, love, cynicism, even humor erupt in him. We do not question what he feels or why, for he has shown us physically how it is with each character.

Bronson's personal life rather reflects his bent for the primary and direct style. He is a wholehearted family man. His marriage to the British film actress Jill Ireland in the early Sixties has given him a firm home base. It brought together their five children from previous marriages and then added a daughter of their own, Zuleika. Husband and wife have made about a dozen movies together. They *like* to work conjointly but will take on other projects too.

One morning as Paul walked out of his home, he found a chauffeur at his door, who handed him a golden key and pointed to a large silver-grey Rolls-Royce parked at the curb.

"Mr. Bronson would like you to try it out," the man explained. "He said you could also have the same model in black."

At first Paul didn't connect. Bronson? Ah, he had just put through a million-dollar deal for Charlie. But long ago he had put the actor's casual remark far in the back of his mind. He learned long ago that few of his "eternally grateful" clients ever honored promises to him, sensible or wild. Paul's disappointment with their forgetfulness or ingratitude was not materialistic—but human. He had come to expect nothing more than the customary ten percent from his efforts. Thanks-yous were welcome too of course, but sometimes even they were sparse.

171

But a Rolls-Royce? Paul stared at the shiny, sleek, impressive machine. Excitedly, he called Lupita out. They both inspected the gift. Everything about it, inside and out, looked first class.

Paul stepped into the car, sitting next to the chauffeur. "Let's go," he said.

As they cruised swiftly and smoothly along Sunset Boulevard, Paul at first lost himself in the vehicle's unbelievable luxuriousness. The present was truly astounding.

What was the cost of such a car? Why, it must be close to forty thousand dollars. Then a disturbing thought hit Paul. A gift like this didn't come free. From the giver, yes. But the Internal Revenue Service had a different attitude. This car was taxable. Highly so. Making a rough calculation, Paul figured that he would have to pay close to twenty thousand dollars to Uncle Sam just to keep the Rolls.

When they arrived at the office, Paul sadly dispatched the chauffeur. For there were limits, after all, to traveling in first class style.

Then he phoned Charlie Bronson. "You're an extremely generous man, Charlie," he said. "But I'm afraid I can't accept your gift."

He explained the tax problem—which hadn't occurred to Bronson. Immediately the actor offered to pay the tax too, but Paul refused to let him. Graciously, Bronson took back the car.

As for Paul, he was left with something far better than expensive equipage. He had a steadfast and grateful client who kept a promise uttered rather recklessly a decade before over a restaurant table in Spain.

Neither success nor wealth have managed to spoil Charles Bronson.

50

Visitor from Sweden

PAUL SAT NERVOUSLY in the chauffeur-driven limousine. It was an October day, and he and Lupita were heading for the Los Angeles International Airport.

Lupita patted his hand reassuringly. "Everything will be just fine, Papa."

"I have a hunch he won't be on that plane," said Paul.

"Ridiculous."

"Why ridiculous?"

"He would have wired—or called."

"Ingmar? You know how he is. Remember when I expected him in Cannes, but he turned back right in the Stockholm airport? Never let me know." He was brooding, scowling, in anticipation.

"Not this time, Papa. He'll come."

"I pray you're right," Paul said. And he reached into his coat pocket, first to extract his glasses and then to remove a crumpled cable. He studied it now as he had studied it, disbelievingly, at least a dozen times before.

ARRIVING SUNDAY OCTOBER 26 AT 4:35 PM SAS FLIGHT 933
LEAVING FRIDAY OCTOBER 31 LOVE INGMAR

"Very mysterious," Paul mumbled.

For it was all most strange and sudden. Was Ingmar Bergman really coming to Hollywood? This shy, secluded man disliked air travel perhaps as much as crowds and publicity. Even short distances from his home-base at Stockholm or his island retreat at Faro in the Baltic, he traversed by ship or train. So his impulsive decision to fly for thirteen hours to visit the American film center for the first time puzzled Paul. But he had learned from years of experience that his director friend and client was an unpredictable and sometimes contradictory person.

The limousine pulled up at the SAS terminal. The chauffeur opened the door, and Paul and Lupita stepped out. Lupita was carrying a bunch of long-stemmed red roses.

They checked on the arrival time at the desk and were told that Flight 933 had just landed. As they hurried down the brightly lit, white-tiled corridor toward the gate, Lupita suddenly stopped.

173

"Look!" she cried, pointing.

And there he came. Ingmar Bergman, his arm linked with his wife Ingrid's. He was casually dressed in a beige sport jacket. As soon as he saw the Kohners, his face brightened.

The red roses got crushed as everyone hugged everyone.

"How was the trip?" Paul wanted to know.

"I am very tired, Paul, that's all," Bergman replied. "The trip was hard on me. Yet I got through it all right, I guess. But I have not slept for two whole nights—the one before leaving, and now the one on the plane."

"You should sleep well tonight," Paul promised. "I've picked a very quiet place for you."

"Excellent," said Bergman. "I trust your judgment."

As they went along, Paul put his arm around the director while Lupita walked with Ingrid. They waited a while for the luggage to come down the chute to them. Then they proceeded to the limousine, still waiting at the curb.

Just as Paul was helping the Bergmans into the car, the chauffeur of another limousine parked behind them approached him.

"Is that gentleman Mr. Bergman?" he asked deferentially.

"Yes," Paul said. "Why?"

The uniformed chauffeur gestured toward his car. "Miss Ann-Margret would very much like to greet him."

Ingmar looked at Paul and shrugged. "Thank you," he said politely to the man, "but—"

And then he turned to Paul. "Who is Ann-Margret?"

"The actress. She's Swedish," he added.

"Oh—?"

"You might just say hello to her," Paul suggested gently.

"All right. If you say so," Bergman said. He got out of the car and walked over to the other limousine. When Ann-Margret stepped out, they embraced—Hollywood-style. There was a brief exchange of words in Swedish. Then they laughed, shook hands and parted.

Bergman came back. "Thanks for telling me, Paul," he said. "A very beautiful woman."

They drove off.

Paul needed to take his cues from Ingmar, so he waited.

"We will not talk business, Paul," Bergman said after a while. "Not on our first day here, anyway," he added with a sly grin. And then, "I hope you have not made any public announcement of my arrival?"

"Of course not," said Paul.

They arrived at the Bel Air Hotel, where Paul often places his V.I.P. clients. It is a quiet hostelry providing the privacy that Bergman needed. And it is situated within walking distance of the Kohner home. To Paul it seemed to have the ideal location and ambience for the Bergmans.

Ingmar and Ingrid acted very pleased as they inspected their hotel suite. Flowers were everywhere—living room, kitchen, two bedrooms. Paul had attended to every detail. He had stuffed the small refrigerator with all the delicacies he knew the Swedish director liked. Cold cuts, Knaecke bread, yogurt in many flavors. In the pantry there was even a case of the Swedish mineral water Ramloesa—the only water Bergman drank. And of course many sweets, which he enjoyed. A special stereophonic unit had also been provided, with cassettes of Bergman's favorite composers—Mozart, Beethoven, Bach.

Settling down, they opened a bottle of champagne to celebrate the event. Paul raised his glass in a toast—and soon afterwards departed. The strain of Ingmar's two sleepless nights was showing.

Early the next morning Paul was awakened by a gentle tap on his shoulder. Lupita told him that she hated to rouse him, but of course he would have to know. Mrs. Bergman had just called and said that they were packing.

"Dammit!" Paul exploded, jumping out of bed.

"Ingmar couldn't sleep at all. Not a wink."

"Jesus," Paul moaned.

He dressed in a hurry, and in a short while was at the Bergmans' suite at the Bel Air Hotel.

Ingmar looked miserable. He had gone to bed early, he said, but something was wrong with the air-conditioner. It wouldn't stop working, and he didn't know how to regulate it, and they practically froze. There were noises outside. People. Animals. Cars. The mattress was squeaking too.

"This is the third night of no sleep, Paul. I am simply desperate. You must arrange for me to fly back in the afternoon."

"I'm going to get you another hotel, Ingmar," Paul proposed soothingly yet firmly. "A fine, quieter place where you'll sleep well. Then you'll feel much better. You've come a very long way. Don't turn around yet. Stay for a while. Try to rest and relax."

Since this plan seemed to mollify Bergman, Paul swung quickly into action. He called the Beverly Hills Hotel, the Beverly Hilton, the Beverly Wilshire. All were booked to capacity. But being a Beverly Wilshire stockholder, he had a certain pull. He knew that a special suite was always reserved for emergencies. And this was truly an emergency. Paul explained it, told them to hold the suite for him. He'd be over in just a few minutes.

He drove Ingmar to the hotel. The suite, ideally located on the top floor of the annex, was absolutely soundproofed. Paul even tested the mattress by throwing himself down upon the bed and bouncing. Not a squeak. Not a lump.

"I like it here," Ingmar declared. "It feels good to me, Paul." His mood had switched from gloom to near euphoria. "I know I can sleep here," he added, as if convincing himself of an inalterable fact.

"Everything is going to be great!" Paul assured him. He left at once to collect Mrs. Bergman and their luggage.

Business is seldom absent from Paul's mind. So after giving Bergman a twenty-four hour respite, he dropped by the suite to cautiously probe whether his client would feel like meeting some of the people in the movie industry.

Bergman so far had made only one picture for an American production company. Although *The Touch* was a fascinating film, it did not make money. But since then, both *Cries and Whispers* and *Scenes from a Marriage* had been artistic and commercial successes in America. Paul was sure that every major studio would want to finance a new Bergman film.

Ingmar, who had slept that night for ten straight hours, was now in a more receptive mood for socializing—and possibly deal-making.

"Fine, Paul. Arrange anything you think will not be too much of a—*hassle*. Is that the word?"

"That's the word, all right."

And his agent swiftly shifted into high gear. Within an hour Paul had lined up for that day a studio visit, a luncheon with some prominent directors and producers and an intimate dinner at his own home.

Hollywood is rather like a small town. Big and interesting news gets around fast. During the past few years Bergman had become well-known not only to "art-house" moviegoers, but also to the film industry's workers.

When they arrived at Universal, a reception committee awaited Bergman at the studio's entrance gate. Paul introduced the Swedish filmmaker to the big brass: Lew Wasserman, the studio head, the executives—and also Walter Mirisch, the president of the Academy of Motion Picture Arts and Sciences.

During all the back-slapping and hand-pumping, onlookers flocked around to discover who was at the hub of this wheel of admirers.

"Would you like to take our studio tour, Mr. Bergman?" Lew Wasserman asked.

Bergman looked questioningly at Paul.

"I think Ingmar would enjoy it," said Paul.

So Ingmar Bergman, like any other tourist, took the studio tour in an open bus, with Paul and Mirisch acting as guides.

Bergman seemed entranced throughout. He watched a "staged" brawl on the Western set and admired the pop-up plastic head of an awesome shark that had been used in the production of *Jaws*.

"Imagine—" he said as he surveyed an open "set" of a street with magnificent fronts and no backs— "one day our civilization will disappear. Thousands of years from now archeologists will go on a dig and find these house fronts. And they'll think *this* is the way we lived." Everyone laughed.

When they came into the studio commissary for lunch, a group of filmmakers, summoned in a hurry, greeted Bergman. During the luncheon around a large, horseshoe-shaped table, the director's American colleagues rose, one by one, to offer brief toasts.

"Do you want to know how we feel about having you here, Mr.

Bergman?" Billy Wilder asked. "We feel like the personnel in a backwoods hospital when Dr. Christiaan Barnard is making a call."

Bergman graciously thanked everybody, giving compliments that were sincere and honest, designed to make people feel good.

Seeing how ebullient his client was acting during his first direct contact with the Hollywood world, Paul stole away from the table to phone Warner Brothers. He got through to Ted Ashley, the studio's production head. Telling him about Bergman's visit, Paul asked whether he would like to meet the director. "Bring him over, Paul," said Ashley. "I'll be delighted."

They drove over to Warners at Burbank, just a few miles away from Universal. There the figurative "red carpet" had been rolled out for the visitor from Sweden. After the meeting with Ashley and his staff, Paul took Bergman onto the lot itself, where his producer son Pancho was shooting a picture starring Charles Bronson.

Paul worried over how the sometimes irascible Bronson would react to the group's intrusion on the set. As they tiptoed in, Bronson was sitting in a bullet-ridden car in a garage. The cameras were about to roll. But when Charlie Bronson spotted Ingmar Bergman, he jumped up, interrupted the "take" and opened his arms wide in a gesture of welcome. Bergman at once responded in kind, and the two went into a firm embrace.

Paul's face lit up with delight. Then Bergman hailed Pancho, whom he had already met before, in Sweden. Bergman insisted that his presence be disregarded while the work continued. He took a chair.

Bronson went back into the battered automobile, and the scene was shot. Bergman watched, fascinated—looking like a kid who had never been inside a film studio till now.

As he looked around, his eyes took in the multitude of workers encircling the set. "How many people work here on the set?" he whispered to Paul.

"Sixty to seventy."

"Incredible," Bergman murmured. "When I need a large crew, we have fourteen. At the most."

"This is Hollywood, Ingmar," Paul said.

Late that afternoon Paul brought the Bergmans over to his house in Bel Air. They entered the driveway, where a sign at the entrance, imported from France, said RUE PAUL KOHNER. The proud proprietor led them into his rambling, bungalow-style hacienda furnished with European furniture and walls lined with books or serving as galleries for an impressive collection of paintings—Mexican art particularly, with Diego Rivera's portrait of Susan and Pancho Kohner as children the standout. It was colorful, neat, homey.

"It is so much like you and Lupi," Ingmar commented approvingly.

Paul then took them sauntering around the grounds, where huge old trees were interspersed with green lawns and flowerbeds of chrysanthemum varieties in bright bloom. They saw the swimming pool and summerhouse up on the hillside—and the large orchard of fruit trees, where Paul also grows his delectable *fraises des bois.*

"Beautiful, Paul, beautiful!" Ingmar exclaimed, beaming.

Knowing that Bergman disliked a larger crowd than eight around a dining table, Paul had purposely kept the evening affair intimate. The small group of guests that night included William Wyler and his wife Talli, Pancho and the French actress Jeanne Moreau.

Raising his wine glass, Bergman toasted the lady of the house—the hostess of this perfect evening.

"Well," said Paul later on that night, before he dozed off, "I think we got the show on the road."

"It looks like it," Lupita agreed. "You were just wonderful, Papa."

Paul got up early the next morning. Bergman had expressed interest in visiting the clinic of Dr. Arthur Janov, the well-known psychiatrist-author of *The Primal Scream.* Paul had difficulty in persuading Janov to make time to see Bergman, but he finally succeeded in arranging an appointment for the next day.

Thinking about it, Paul wasn't really surprised about Bergman's urgent request to talk with Janov. The therapy that the doctor proposed, administered and taught others to give involved carrying the patient back to his or her early childhood, there to relive traumas that had been repressed and "forgotten" in the conscious mind. Experiencing anew the pain, terror, fury, anxiety of these long-ago events, the patient may shout, weep, strike out or scream. Repeatedly having a "Primal" ultimately helps to reintegrate the split pieces of the self and lead toward becoming the ideal "Primal" person. To Paul, the whole Janovian therapy process actually sounded very much like a Bergman film. Perhaps the two men were working in strangely parallel ways—one in giving psychotherapy, the other by creating art.

Paul then contacted the writer Erica Jong in Malibu, since Ingmar had wanted to discuss her new book. She invited them to come to her home that very morning. Afterwards, Paul managed to fit a visit to the J. Paul Getty Museum into the forthcoming day's itinerary.

By now, of course, all three phones on his bedside table were in operation. While he was on one phone, the two others would keep ringing insistently until he would ask the callers to hold on. This was business as usual. Wherever Paul is, phones ring automatically.

Predictably, Irene Heymann phoned up to read him a long list of people who had tried to reach him the day before—all on urgent matters.

"Tell them something, like I'm sick," Paul said. "I really haven't got a minute's time to return their calls today."

"They'd never believe me, Mr. Kohner. You know that." And then she asserted in her authoritative tone: "You'd better come in, Mr. Kohner. You simply *must* take care of some of these things immediately."

"All right, all right," Paul assented. A command from Irene is not to be ignored. He phoned the Bergmans and heard that Ingmar had slept well again. He decided not to drive with Ingmar to Malibu, to see Miss Jong, but to go instead to his office and attend to essential business.

Later on in the day, the Bergmans dropped by Paul's office, where they snacked on soft-boiled eggs, yogurt and tea prepared by Miss Heymann. Afterwards, sitting out in Paul's patio and basking in the late-afternoon sunshine, Bergman looked pleasurably around him. The large potted plants gave a country air to this bit of the city.

"It's good here too," he said. "It's like your home, Paul." Then his eyes riveted on the tall modern office building just to the west of Paul's place. "How could anybody ever work for long in a structure like that without going mad?" he asked.

"Many people somehow manage to," Paul replied.

"But could you?"

"I almost tried it out once a few years ago," Paul answered—smiling now at this recollection.

"You were wise to stay here," Bergman told him. "You must always stay here. I cannot possibly imagine you anywhere else. This place is *you*."

Ingmar Bergman had asked to see the Mexican film classic *Santa*, that nation's first "talking picture," in which the eighteen-year-old Lupita Tovar had starred. Ever since that appearance, Lupita had enjoyed great fame south of the border, where she was known as the "Sweetheart of Mexico."

The screening took place that evening in Pancho's beach home at Playa del Rey. A forty-five-year-old print, shown many times over, cannot possibly do justice to any motion picture. Yet the artless beauty of the young Lupita remained clear and undiminished. And despite technical flaws and sundry shortcomings to be expected in an old film, Ingmar Bergman was obviously moved.

The last day of the Swedish director's stay in California Paul had set aside for some wheeling and dealing. The studios were actively seeking him out, asking whether Bergman would consider discussing working arrangements with them. Because his client had come on a quasi-incognito visit, Paul found it appropriate to arrange several informal business sessions rather than high-level, high-pressure meetings.

During one of them, Bergman told producer Dino de Laurentiis the basic plan of the filmscript he was currently working on, which he called *The Serpent's Egg*. It made a radical departure from the director's usual themes. The story, set in Berlin at the time of the ruinous inflation and increasing racial violence, when the "eggs" of the impending Nazi regime were already laid and incubating, was a stark and forceful narrative. De Laurentiis, visibly impressed, virtually asked Paul to write his own "ticket" for Bergman to do the film for him. Bergman emphasized that he wanted to shoot it right on location in Germany with his "family" of actors and technicians.

The next morning went equally well. At Universal Paul was offered "carte blanche" for Bergman. Any story the director wished to do, any price he wanted to set for the production and his own services—within reasonable limits, to be sure—would be acceptable to them.

Bergman was happy. Paul was happy. This was what a healthy association of agent and client is supposed to achieve.

Bergman was invited to speak that afternoon to the students of the prestigious American Film Institute. In the morning the students had attended a showing of Bergman's new work, a transposition onto film of Mozart's opera *The Magic Flute*. It had been a rare experience for the budding filmmakers, Bergman was told when he arrived.

The reception for the Swedish director took place in the Greystone mansion's theatre. The big auditorium was packed. Good spirits prevailed throughout Bergman's ensuing talk, which eventually evolved into a bull session on the art of the cinema. Bergman took off his jacket, feeling thoroughly at home among the young, enthusiastic Americans. His responses were relaxed and expressive. He seemed to be just another student at the Institute. And when he got up to go, everyone in the hall sprang to his feet to salute him. The tumultuous applause and cheering followed him out the door.

"That was a wonderful experience, Paul," Bergman said on their way back to the hotel. "I am so glad I came. I had such a different picture of Hollywood. Now I can even see myself working here someday."

Next morning Paul and Lupita drove the Bergmans to the airport.

Paul felt an enormous glow of accomplishment and pride. Because he had respected his profession and perfected his talents for it, he was not a lowly salesman and "flesh-peddler," a scorned "ten-percenter" after all. He had become a trusted companion to the most revered creative filmmaker of the century. So much so, in fact, that he had managed to bring him and Hollywood together at last.

51

A Day in Cannes

THE CANNES FILM Festival is the supermarket of the international motion picture industry, attracting more producers, distributors, exporters, importers, exhibitors, journalists—and agents—than all other festivals put together. During a fortnight in May the town in the south of France provides a microcosm of the world of the cinema. Creative and merchandising talents in filmmaking from every corner of the globe show up to be seen and publicized or to initiate deals.

Cannes also has another function: it serves as the convenient locus for an annual colloquy in which a multitude of key film people gather for intense sessions of inspecting, discussing, debating and dissecting their mutual craft, as well as assaying its current progress and problems.

Every year close to a thousand new films are shown at Cannes. And some ten thousand people—all of whose business involves movies— converge on the pebbled shores of the Mediterranean. Among them always is Paul.

Since he has never missed a festival in all the years of its postwar existence, Paul has become something of a fixture at Cannes. At the Carlton, where the same suite awaits him year after year, he is inevitably known as "Mr. Phoner."

It seems weird, almost lunatic to me to go to a sun-drenched resort and commit oneself to sit so much in darkness. And it doesn't make good sense to me either to have for two weeks no better activities than rushing frenetically from one auditorium to another, from one congested, indoor cocktail party to another and then on to a crowded restaurant. But because I wanted to complete my learning process about the talent agent at work, I had to know what an agent actually *does* on a "normal" day in Cannes, besides viewing the new film products. So I decided to follow my brother around for a full day—as unobtrusively as I could.

Paul and Lupita made the yearly pilgrimage this time on the *S. S. Michelangelo*, from New York. I had come by automobile, driving through the Provence. On a Monday morning I walked to the pier in Cannes to meet their boat.

Paul was in high spirits, primed for the heavy schedule ahead. The transatlantic crossing had been pleasant and restful. For a whole week, cut off from the world except for an occasional radiotelephone call, he mainly lounged on deck chairs and looked into the blue. The cuisine was excellent: much to his chagrin, he had gained five pounds.

Their luggage was piled into a car sent by *King Kong* producer Dino de Laurentiis. They drove up the main boulevard, the Croisette, where the great Côte d'Azur hostelries are lined up. The Miramar. The Majestic. The Carlton. Of course the newer hotels are just as deluxe as the Carlton. But the Carlton is the traditional hub of the action, the place where it all happens.

The Kohners rammed their way through the throng of people outside and inside the hotel. It was noon: the time when human traffic can be thickest. Sooner or later everyone must pass through this lobby—everyone who is someone, or was, or would like to be.

It took Paul a while to get the desk clerk's attention. When the clerk recognized him, he greeted him theatrically, assuring him that his arrival had been most eagerly expected and that his usual suite had been readied for him. With his face wreathed in pleasant anticipation of the size of his eventual tip, he emphasized his extraordinary maneuvers in safeguarding that particular suite for my brother.

Paul thanked him and turned around, bumping into a spidery-looking man wearing dark glasses and olive pants.

"Paul!" the man exclaimed, throwing his arms around him. "Great to see you, old man! When did you get in? How long will you be around? We've got to have lunch together. What's your room number?"

Paul, looking puzzled, gave his room number.

"I'll call you, first thing tomorrow," the man said and was gone.

Paul shrugged. "Never saw him before in my life." They moved toward the elevator. A bunch of people emerged—among them a stocky, amiable-appearing man. His face lit up when he saw Paul, and he held out his arms.

Luggi Waldleitner, a Munich-based German producer, took an iron grip on Paul's arm, attempting to corner him. He had some terribly important matter to discuss—immediately. After Paul sent Lupita ahead to their suite, they looked for a relatively quiet spot but couldn't find one.

"Let's go up to my room," Waldleitner suggested.

The elevator door opened again, spewing out more people. By the time the two men got in, the cage was packed. Conversations went on noisily in four languages.

"Paul!" someone pressed into a corner called out.

"Marcel!" They waved at each other over the cluster of heads. When the elevator stopped on the seventh floor, Paul, Waldleitner and Marcel all stepped out. Then Marcel Hellman—an English producer with a jolly, industrious face and big hornrimmed glasses—embraced Paul.

"I have a table at one-thirty in the dining room," Marcel said. "Can you and Lupi make it? Where is she?"

She had gone up to their suite, Paul told him. They would try to join him for lunch.

Waldleitner again grasped Paul's arm and propelled him into his room. They settled down in a couple of chairs out on the balcony overlooking the Mediterranean.

"Tell me what you're up to, Luggi," Paul said.

Waldleitner spoke enthusiastically about his next two films, both to be written by the highly talented writer Manfred Purtzer, who had been working with him for a long while. He wanted to enlist Paul's aid in procuring an American partner for co-production. And he welcomed his ideas about casting.

"What are the stories?" Paul asked.

"Hans Habe's new novel *Palazzo*," said Waldleitner.

"Excellent!" Paul exclaimed. And he immediately suggested Katharine Hepburn for the leading role of the Italian *principessa* dwelling in a decaying Venice slowly and symbolically submerging below sea level.

Waldleitner liked that possibility. "The other film," he went on, "will be based on *Elixir of the Devil*."

This project too intrigued Paul, who had always liked E. T. A. Hoffmann's famous, haunting novel. "How about our new client Peter O'Toole?" was his immediate reaction.

"Our budget, I'm afraid, won't be big enough to accommodate such an important star," Waldleitner said. "But would you be willing to help me get American financing and to line up casts for the pictures?"

"No problem," Paul replied. "I'll be glad to." His friend beamed. Then Paul checked his watch. "I have to go now, Luggi. But see you later—"

Arriving at his suite on the ninth floor, he found Lupita standing in the middle of the room, talking on the telephone.

"Yes, I'll tell him.... Yes, of course he'll call back." She hung up in mock exasperation. "It's been ringing constantly. I haven't even been able to change my clothes."

On the table were a pile of unopened mail and a beautiful flower arrangement. "From George Marton," she said, giving him the card. "He wants us to have lunch with them at the Felix." Marton, a prominent literary agent, had recently turned to playwriting.

"We've got to beg out," Paul said. "I've already made a luncheon date with Marcel."

"Maybe you can have a drink with George first," Lupita suggested, "and then meet Marcel for lunch."

The phone rang. It was Elaine Heilbronn, an attorney who worked in the Paris office of the Beverly Hills law firm of Leon Kaplan. She had to leave for Paris at three; for hours she had been trying to get Paul on the phone. He had to sign some papers for a deal with French producer Robert Dorfman.

"Let's have coffee at two-thirty," Paul said.

Elaine Heilbronn warned him that this was cutting things a bit close but agreed to be at the Carlton bar.

Paul hung up. "I'd better leave now," he told Lupita. "I'm running over to the Majestic to see Huston before luncheon."

Lupita, who wanted to take a bath now, said she'd come down to the lobby by one-thirty.

"*Please* answer the phone," Paul pleaded.

"All right," she said wearily. "But when I'm in the bathroom I can't very well keep rushing out here."

"A phone's in there too," Paul said. "I arranged for it when I made the reservation." And he handed her an extra pad and pencil.

"Oh—*great,*" said Lupita.

Now the Carlton lobby was even more thickly populated than before. Paul fought his way to the exit door, then crossed the boulevard. At the hotel's private beach, photographers swarmed around a starlet who had shed her bikini top. Some of the *paparazzi* brandished cameras over their heads and blindly snapped away.

On the short walk to the Majestic Paul stopped every few feet to greet acquaintances. Rudi Joseph, curator of the Munich Film Museum. Peter Riethof, an international dubbing expert. Bosley Crowther, former film critic of the *New York Times*, now a special consultant to Columbia Pictures. Paul made cocktail dates at the Carlton with each of them. ("How can you keep all your engagements straight?" I asked him, noting he had not written anything down. He laughed. "I don't have to. They'll all be there anyway. It's easier this way.")

He spotted a beautiful woman coming toward him. It was his client Jeanne Moreau, whom he greeted with a well-executed Continental hand-kiss.

Next Paul ran into a small, Neapolitan-eyed man who unleashed a flood of Italian.

"You're too fast for me, Sergio," Paul said. "Talk English."

And Sergio Leone, a director famous for doing early "Spaghetti Westerns," switched into a quick but rough brand of English. He was eager to get Bronson to do another picture for him. Paul made a date for the next day.

He had only walked two hundred feet—and it was almost one o'clock. ("Any moment the streets will be empty," Paul predicted to me. "Everyone drops everything for lunch and siesta.") The international gypsies in jeans were beginning to pack up their sidewalk displays of brass and silver jewelry, leather work and watercolors.

When Paul finally got to the Majestic, he went up to Huston's suite.

"Well—Paul!" said Huston with genuine warmth in his deep voice, putting his arms around him. Lean as ever, his thick hair now grown grey, he was still in his pyjamas. He invited Paul to sit down. "Some breakfast?" Paul declined.

"The advance notices on *The Man Who Would Be King* are really something," Huston said, pointing to a stack of papers on the table. "Have you read them?"

Paul told him that he had a cable aboard ship from Ernie Anderson telling him that it looked as if the Kipling film was going to be a big hit.

Huston flopped down on the couch, lit a cigarette, drew deeply on it and smiled broadly at Paul.

"It's wonderful, John," Paul said. "Just what we needed right now." And he told Huston that before he left the Coast, he had discussed him with Ted Ashley at Warner Brothers for an important assignment. "Ted thought the figures were too high, but I told him just to wait for *King* to come out!"

Huston was pleased. "Sure you don't want a drink? How about some champagne?"

Paul checked his wristwatch. It was one-thirty. He got up to go. "I've got a lunch date at the Carlton. Lupi's waiting."

The streets were deserted now. Even though the Carlton was only a short walk from the Majestic, Paul took a taxi. He asked the driver to stop at the Felix. The restaurant was filled to overflowing. The *maitre-d'* blocked the entrance.

"I'm looking for Mr. Marton," Paul said.

"Ah—Monsieur Marton!—this way!"

Seated at a round table were George and Hilda Marton, Steven Pallos, a British producer of Hungarian extraction, George's stepson Peter Stone, the play- and screen-writer, and Marta Andras, an attractive, volatile Hungarian who ran Marton's Paris office. Paul greeted everyone by shaking the men's hands and kissing the ladies'. He had dropped by, he said, to make his apologies. He had a previous luncheon engagement with Marcel Hellman. Couldn't they all meet later at the Carlton bar for cocktails? Indeed, they could.

Paul weaved his way out of the restaurant. Someone yelled out his name. A paunchy, hawk-nosed man with sad, moist eyes gestured him over. It was Sam Spiegel, producer of *The Bridge on the River Kwai, Lawrence of Arabia* and *Nicholas and Alexandra*. He was currently preparing a production of Fitzgerald's novel *The Last Tycoon*.

"Sit down, Paul, relax," Spiegel said. "How is my darling Lupi?"

As he talked to Paul, his eyes roamed restlessly around the room. He waved at someone just leaving the restaurant.

Paul told him that he was already late for a date at the Carlton.

"Let's have lunch at the boat tomorrow," Spiegel suggested. The "boat" was his yacht *Mahlanee*, anchored in the Cannes harbor. Spiegel mentioned the pier number.

By the time Paul got to the Carlton dining room, it was past two. The air was thick with the aroma of food and tobacco smoke. Marcel presided at a round table in the middle of the plush Victorian room. Lupita chided Paul for being late.

Paul ordered *canard truffe*. A waiter, who looked like Belmondo playing a waiter, served wine. "You have any *fraises des bois?*" Paul asked. The waiter nodded suavely. Of course they did. Paul made certain that at least two orders would be put aside for him. "We grow them at home in our garden," he told the waiter, "but they're not as good as they are here in France. I'd make a special trip to France just for the *fraises*." The waiter offered a perfunctory smile.

Marcel Hellman wore a navy blue silk suit and a polkadot tie. Not everybody seemed to know everyone else. Next to Hellman—stately, happy with everything around her—sat Mrs. Hellman. Then there were Elaine Heilbronn, the attorney Paul was supposed to be meeting momentarily at the bar, a nondescript man who had come from the States with a hardcore porno film, and Thomas Quinn Curtis, the movie critic for the Paris *Herald Tribune*.

When the waiter placed the *canard truffe* on the table, Paul eagerly cut into it. Suddenly at the next table there was a flurry of getting up and going. Somebody whacked Paul on the back and he jumped up, almost upsetting the table.

"Dino!"

Dino de Laurentiis threw his arms around Paul. The Italian producer, looking more Roman than Marcus Aurelius, exuded delight in seeing Paul—for he had urgent, most urgent, business to discuss with him. Would he and his Signora join him that evening for dinner at the Ambassadeurs? The Russian delegation to Cannes was throwing a highly capitalistic-style caviar and vodka and champagne party there. But now he had to dash over to the Palais, where the new French entry *Les Valseuses* with Jeanne Moreau was being shown. Waving generously at everyone, he rushed out in a barely constrained frenzy.

Elaine Heilbronn now moved in, reminding Paul that she soon had to leave and shoving some legal papers next to his *canard*. He put on his reading glasses and leafed through them. "They look okay to me—I'll trust you," he said, signing them. Miss Heilbronn said goodbye and departed. Presently the waiter placed a double order of *fraises des bois* topped with whipped cream in front of Paul.

The porno producer from New York invited everybody to come to a private projection room he had rented and see his latest *chef-d'oeuvre*, which he'd be showing a half-hour from now.

"The ladies are invited too?" Mrs. Hellman asked, raising her eyebrows.

"Of course!" he cried. "We're particularly interested in the reaction of the ladies."

Renting one of the dozen or so projection rooms in Cannes to show films privately has become routine procedure for producers who cannot book a movie house. Some of these filmmakers are dedicated idealists who have made low-budget pictures. They come to Cannes, rent a projection room, take out an advertisement in the festival paper, tape announcements to lamp-posts and house walls, sneak leaflets under hotel-room doors and hand tickets out freely. What they want is an audience. They wish to be seen and, hopefully, appreciated. If a prospective buyer wanders in, he is welcomed—but rarely pressured.

Although the porno film was not exactly the work of a cinematic idealist, it certainly filled the projection room. When Paul and his party arrived, not a seat was empty. The exultant producer brought in some folding chairs.

Five minutes was all Lupita could tolerate of the unabashed skinflick, which had started right off with an orgy. Her departure went unnoticed. Reluctantly, Paul followed her out.

"Wasn't it just nauseating?" Lupita asked.

"Of course," Paul agreed—gallantly.

They strolled along the Croisette towards the Carlton. It was close to four. The weather was lovely. Traffic both in the street and on the sidewalks was dense. Policemen in bright blue pants and red tabs waved their white batons frantically—ignored by everybody.

Paul stopped to watch a young painter on the beach side of the promenade. He faced the ocean, but what he put on his canvas was not blue sea or white yachts or swarms of seagulls—the typical Riviera subjects for generations. He was painting a still-life, a bouquet of flowers. Roses, daisies, purple irises, lilies of the valley—one could almost smell them. He worked with a palette knife. Within ten minutes the canvas was finished.

"Isn't he good, Mamacita?" Paul asked. Lupita agreed. "How much does that one cost?" he then asked the artist.

"A hundred francs."

That was twenty dollars. Paul bought it. "Don't forget to sign," he said. The painter looked surprised—but put in "Lechaire." "If your name were Léger, you'd get a thousand times the money," said Paul.

"*Sans blague,*" the painter agreed with a lopsided grin.

Since the canvas was wet, Paul held it carefully as they moved along. "He's got something, that fellow," he said to Lupita. "How about ordering a dozen for Christmas gifts?"

"Must you always buy everything by the dozen?"

"It saves me time and money."

They turned back. Already Lechaire had a new bouquet half finished—in the same technique but with different flowers.

"How long would it take for you to paint a dozen canvases for me?" Paul asked.

"I can deliver them to you in the morning," Lechaire said nonchalantly. Paul gave him his card with his hotel room number written on it—plus an advance on payment.

Back at the Carlton, he quickly scanned the numerous telephone messages.

"No phoning now, Papa," Lupita said, taking the slips away from him. "You've got to rest."

"I will. But I have to return Fellini's call." He dialed a number. Fellini wasn't in, so he left a message. Then he placed the new painting on the mantelpiece and stood for a while admiring it. At last he followed Lupita into the bedroom. She had taken the phone off the hook and was already asleep. He tiptoed to the main door and hung a "Do Not Disturb" sign on the outside knob.

He got up around six, while Lupita was still sleeping, and left a note telling her where he had gone.

In the hotel bar and out on the adjoining sea-front terrace, hundreds of people crowded together, trying to make themselves heard and understood. The common theme was film. Stars gave interviews. Producers haggled with distributors. Heavy-lidded men stood in grave conversation with other heavy-lidded men.

As Paul pushed his way through the mob, people waved at him from all corners of the room. He table-hopped, arranging more dates for later in the evening and for the next day. Then he spotted Federico Fellini out on the terrace and made a beeline for him, receiving the accustomed Italianate exuberant greeting and embrace.

Fellini's new film *Amarcord* was being shown at the festival. The director told Paul that he had reserved seats for him at the premiere that night. He hoped he would be able to go.

"I wouldn't miss it," said Paul.

And now "Paul Kohner" was paged over the din. A pageboy led the way to a phone booth. The operator had three parties on the line: in Hollywood, New York and Munich. Paul took them in order of distance.

First came independent producer John Foreman, who was so excited about the response to the rough-cut of *The Man Who Would Be King* that he wanted to get Paul to consider letting him have John Huston direct two more pictures for him. "Let's talk it over later," Paul said. "Everybody's going to be after John now."

Then the operator put through the New York caller—Paul's astute associate, urbane Robby Lantz, who told him that Joseph Papp was eager to sign Liv Ullmann for an Ibsen play at Lincoln Center. The usual amenities about family, health and the weather terminated the conversation.

The final call came from Aurel Bischoff in Munich. Paul, who had branched out into selling European-made films to American distributors, could tell Bischoff that he had found a buyer for a picture Bischoff was representing. Well-pleased, the German producer said he planned to fly to Cannes. Paul told him he'd be staying a week and then would move on to Rome. "I'll be arriving on the weekend," Bischoff said. "I want you to read my new project. It's absolutely *wunderbar! Fantastisch!*"

When Paul returned to his suite, the phone was ringing insistently. Lupita, in the bathroom, paid it no heed. Paul took it. Leon Kaplan was calling from Beverly Hills to tell him about a meeting with an important tax-shelter group based in Munich and Vienna. Paul promised to look into the matter right away. Instantly he placed a call to Felix Guggenheim in Los Angeles.

Sometime in the early Fifties Paul had shrewdly availed himself of the services of Dr. Guggenheim, who had a reputation for having a brilliant legal mind. Years before he had run the Deutsche Buchgemeinschaft (the German equivalent to the Book-of-the-Month Club). As a refugee in southern California during the wartime, he had published German exile literature by prominent writers. Not only was he an adviser and stimulator for authors, but he had become an expert on international copyrights and a master-negotiator between contesting parties. Paid a retainer to serve as legal counsel and financial adviser in the Kohner Agency's transactions with Europe, Guggenheim often accompanied Paul on forays abroad. In Hollywood circles he has been referred to as "Kohner's Kissinger."

Paul now alerted Guggenheim to the possibility of utilizing the tax-shelter group—and since he trusted the lawyer's knowledge and judgment concerning money matters, turned the whole issue over to his investigation.

He began to look through a batch of mail that had just arrived from California. Lupita appeared in the doorway, wearing a gossamer blue dinner gown embroidered with silver. She reminded him to get ready for dinner and for the Fellini film afterwards at the Festival Palace. It took him about fifteen minutes to shower, shave and change.

Eight o'clock! The lobby was teeming with people. On his way out, Paul ran into a solidly-built man with jet-black hair being followed by a porter with a luggage trolley. Another Italian producer—and another emotional exchange of salutations. Roberto Haggiag kissed Lupita and told her in three languages how absolutely devastatingly delighted he was to see her. They made an appointment for breakfast the next morning.

Since there were no taxis around, Paul and Lupita walked. The Ambassadeurs was so jammed that hundreds of would-be patrons were being turned away. Paul spotted Bosley Crowther in the waiting line. They conferred and decided to give up the siege and go to the nearby Voile au Vent, a reliable bistro with excellent sea food. Situated at the Old Port, it gave diners a view of battered fishing boats and beautifully appointed yachts jostling democratically for anchorage.

Crowther too planned to see *Amarcord*, so after dinner they all took the ten-minute stroll to the Festival Palace. As might be expected, the place was packed. The air was stifling, for the theatre had been in constant use since early morning. During the film showing, Paul, overcome by fatigue, fell asleep. The applause at the end awakened him. Bravos thundered.

"We've got to congratulate him," Paul said, wide awake now. They found the usual mob scene out in the lobby, but Paul managed to get to Fellini and shake his hand amid such superlatives as *magnifico! fantastico! capolavoro!*

Among the well-wishers was Dino de Laurentiis, who was disappointed to have missed Paul at the Ambassadeurs. He now asked him to join the Italian contingent for supper. So they had more food—lamb cooked in herbs—and champagne at the L'Avventura, a heavy-beamed restaurant with strolling musicians playing Italian songs.

Past midnight Paul gave Lupita the familiar sign. Whispering apologies to de Laurentiis, he discreetly followed his wife to the door.

The lobby of the Carlton offered a rare sight. It was empty of people. The enormous Persian carpets, however, were strewn with the day's debris: papers, pamphlets, phone messages, invitations, publicity releases, ticket stubs. Paul picked up a copy of the *Herald Tribune* at the desk, and they went upstairs.

Half-circles of fatigue showed under his eyes as he undressed for bed. "Why don't you tell the operator not to disturb us?" Lupita suggested.

"*Now?*" Paul said. "It's one o'clock. No one calls now." He has an aversion to cutting off the communication line with the outside world.

Lupita turned off her light, but Paul read the paper for five minutes. Then he too switched off his light. The phone started ringing. Paul looked at Lupita. She was asleep. He took the receiver up and said, sotto voce, "Hold it." He quickly got up and went into the living room, where he picked up the extension.

The operator had a transatlantic call. "Okay," Paul said wearily, "put it through."

It was Irene Heymann calling from his Hollywood office.

"What is this?" Paul said edgily. "I was fast asleep. It's past one."

"I know what time it is," Irene said, "and I'm sorry, Mr. Kohner. But it was the only way I could be sure to get through to you." Then she rattled off a whole list of important office business going on. As she talked, Paul occasionally emitted some sleepy monosyllabic comments, trying hard to pay attention.

After he had hung up, Paul stood up. Undecided, he looked at the phone. He was awake again. He checked his wristwatch and did some figuring, then called the operator and asked for a New York connection. As he waited, he sauntered over to the fireplace and inspected his brand-new Lechaire.

A while later the phone rang. He quickly lifted the receiver. "Hello, baby," he said. "Are you just having dinner?"

His daughter Susan told him that John was in Florida on business and Chris and "P.J."—for Paul John or Paul Junior—were watching a TV show.

"How are the boys?"

"Wonderful," Susan said. "Can you hold on a few seconds? I want to get Paul. He's got something to tell you."

Paul junior came to the phone, quite excited. "Guess what, Grandpa—they picked me for the lead in the new school play!"

"How come? You already had the lead in the last one."

Pause. Then, on a note of barely suppressed pride: "Why, Grandpa? Well, after all, I'm the only professional in the class."

Both of them chuckled. A propensity for show business had passed on to the fourth generation.

After some more family talk with Susan, he hung up.

It was two in the morning. He walked out onto the balcony. The sea was moonlit and quiet. In the distance the lights on some yachts tried to outblink the stars. He could hear the footsteps of people walking home on the promenade below—intrepid but exhausted film buffs.

Paul tiptoed back to the bedroom, carefully closed the door and slipped into bed. Before he dozed off, he felt in the dark for the phone next to him.

Just to make sure it was there.

Index

C

D

E

F

G

H

194

198